FROM RUSSIA · to · THE WEST

FROM RUSSIA · to · THE WEST

The Musical Memoirs

and Reminiscences of

Nathan Milstein

BY

NATHAN MILSTEIN

AND

SOLOMON VOLKOV

TRANSLATED FROM THE RUSSIAN BY ANTONINA W. BOUIS

A Donald Hutter Book
HENRY HOLT AND COMPANY   NEW YORK

Published by Henry Holt and Company, Inc.,
115 West 18th Street, New York, New York 10011.
Published in Canada by Fitzhenry & Whiteside Limited,
195 Allstate Parkway, Markham, Ontario L3R 4T8.

Library of Congress Cataloging-in-Publication Data
Milstein, Nathan, 1903–
From Russia to the West : the musical memoirs and reminiscences of
Nathan Milstein / by Nathan Milstein and Solomon Volkov.—1st ed.
p. cm.
"A Donald Hutter book."
ISBN 0-8050-0974-4
1. Milstein, Nathan, 1903– . 2. Violinists—United States—
Biography. I. Volkov, Solomon. II. Title.
ML418.M4A3 1990
787.2′092—dc20   89-27157
[B]   CIP
                        MN
Henry Holt books are available at special discounts
for bulk purchases for sales promotions, premiums,
fund-raising, or educational use. Special editions
or book excerpts can also be created to specification.
For details contact:
Special Sales Director
Henry Holt and Company, Inc.
115 West 18th Street
New York, New York 10011

FIRST EDITION

Book Design by Claire M. Naylon

Recognizing the importance of preserving the written word,
Henry Holt and Co., Inc., prints all of its first editions
on acid-free paper.∞

Printed in the United States of America
1 3 5 7 9 10 8 6 4 2

All photographs, except where otherwise credited, are
from the personal collection of Nathan Milstein.

Contents

Contents

Photographs follow pages 90 and 218.

1. Childhood
in Odessa

I was born in Odessa, a beautiful and gay city on the Black Sea, in the south of the Russian empire. I grew up a hellion. I would run outside, shout, fight with other kids, then save myself by running home. It wasn't very brave or risky on my part, but Mother worried about me anyway. A neighbor in our building, Mrs. Roisman, gave advice: "You have to keep Nathan busy! Let him take music lessons!"

Mrs. Roisman's advice had ulterior motives: I picked on her son. My favorite pastime was to come up behind him, hit him on the head, and run away. My blows didn't keep Josef Roisman from becoming a marvelous violinist. Many years later, in New York, I attended the concerts of the famous Budapest Quartet. Roisman was first violin. I didn't ask him for passes, even though he was a child-

1

hood friend. I paid full price for the tickets and enjoyed the Haydn quartets. Still, Roisman ducked his head every time he saw me. As a joke, of course.

My older sister, Sara, already played piano. That must be why my parents decided to make a violinist out of me. One fine day (this must have been in 1911; I was still seven years old), Mama announced, "We're going to a concert today. The wunderkind Jascha Heifetz is playing."

I didn't want to go. But I didn't dare argue. I was afraid of ending up in the corner. (That's how my parents punished me: they didn't hit me, but made me stand in the corner. I might have to stand many hours. My parents would leave the house, and then my youngest brother, Miron, would bring me something to eat in the corner.)

Jascha Heifetz's concert was at the old Turkish fortress, in the open air. I remember the ornate Moslem arches and the embrasures for the cannons. It was summer and very hot. People sat at tables, eating and drinking. There were lamps on the tables. Flies swarmed all around, fighting for a spot on the lamps. A captivating sight. The flies were so numerous that even without buzzing they made noise!

Little Heifetz came out. I think he played concertos by Mendelssohn and Paganini; I can't swear to my accuracy. In fact, I have no memories of Jascha's playing, and I'm not about to make them up now. To be honest, I paid more attention to the flies than to the performance. But I do remember how Jascha looked: a real angel! A curly-haired blond in a sailor suit, short pants, and knee socks. He was so beautiful! How that cherub turned into such a less than handsome man, I'll never know. . . .

What ultimately made the greatest impression on me came when Jascha finished playing. Immediately he was surrounded by imposing Russian policemen. I thought they were arresting him. Actually, the police were there to protect Heifetz from his frenzied fans. Odessa is a southern city. The audiences there are temperamental and express their delight raucously. (As in Mediterranean countries like Spain and Italy, where to this day policemen sit in the halls during concerts, sometimes right onstage.)

Mama and Papa, like the rest of the audience, were delighted by little Jascha's playing. As I said, it made no impression on me. After the concert I went home and slept soundly. I didn't know then that my fate was sealed and I was going to become a violinist.

We were a large family; there were seven children—two sisters and five brothers. The first six came along at two-year intervals: Sara, David, Lazar, Nathan, Nahum, and Miron. Then came Dorotea, the second sister, five years after Miron.

I was born on the last day of 1903. Twenty-two years later, when my friend of the same age, pianist Vladimir ("Volodya") Horowitz and I were preparing to leave Russia for the West, we both had to be a year younger. Otherwise we would not have been allowed abroad: the military were drafting our year. That is why many reference works give 1904 for both Horowitz and myself, but it's not so.

My father's name was Miron and my mother's, Maria; but of course we called them Mama and Papa. We all loved Mama a lot. If she had an argument with our father, we always took her side. Everyone in her family had dark hair. Father's family were blonds, with a reddish tint. That's about all I know of my parents' families.

In Odessa we first rented a medium-size apartment in a large building at 12 Ovchinnikovsky Alley. Later we moved to Tiraspolskaya Street, not far from the Passage Hotel. Papa was a representative of the large import firm Gourland and Co. He bought wool fabric, for suits, from Scotland (Glasgow and Edinburgh) and from Poland (Lodz and Częstochowa). I remember the fabric delivered to our courtyard in large trucks. The bolts were tossed into the cellars. Then the cellars were shut with iron bars.

Our family was quite assimilated. At home we spoke Russian, so I never learned Yiddish, much less Hebrew. Not many Jews lived in our neighborhood. Of the fifty-odd families in our building, only a few were Jewish.

But one of the residents was the eventually famous Zionist "revisionist" Vladimir Jabotinsky, a young man who already looked important. He resembled a doctor, with his opulent glasses in gold frames. When Jabotinsky appeared in our courtyard, we children stopped playing and chanted, "Four-eyes! Four-eyes!" Jabotinsky would get angry and try to catch us, but in vain. No one could catch us!

Papa did not attend temple and did not permit me to go either. He was afraid that I would get religious. But I liked the Odessa synagogue—the choir was excellent, the cantor was good, and an assiduous, hardworking musician (whom I later met in Vienna) played the harmonium.

Nor did Papa attend the Russian Orthodox Church. He was a Tolstoyan, a follower of the moral teaching of the writer Leo Tolstoy. So being a Tolstoyan impressed me as good and honorable, until one time the police came to see us. I discovered that the tsarist regime persecuted Tolstoyans, considering them dissidents, practically revolutionaries. The Orthodox Church had excommunicated the writer for his "heretical" religious views, and throughout all of Russia priests denounced Tolstoy during the Orthodox mass.

We celebrated Orthodox Christmas: we set up and decorated a tree. When the needles fell and messed up the apartment, we swept up and took the tree away. We kids enjoyed Christmas, even though our presents weren't grand: sometimes children's long stockings, sometimes picture books.

The infamous pogroms that ran through the south of Russia at that time missed us. They hit the Jewish neighborhoods, on Moldavanka. But still, a cross was glued to our window. The landlady ordered the superintendent to glue on the crosses. If the "black hundreds," as the thugs were called, should come, let them see that Orthodox Christians lived in her house.

Mama did not attend church or temple either. But she prayed according to Jewish tradition—once a week, on Friday, at home. She covered her head with a black veil that was both exotic and erotic. I liked the ritual. I also liked sweets and fruits being placed on the table: chocolate and oranges. Each orange was divided into quarters.

Oranges were rare in Odessa. They came from Turkey, and I thought they tasted divine. Now, when I can eat all the oranges I want, they seem sour. . . .

Mama prayed silently while we sat at the table and watched. It was a solemn moment, but we all felt joyous and happy. Sometimes Papa did not even come home for Mama's ritual. He said, "A ritual is nonsense, it doesn't matter. What matters is what you feel."

Mama and Papa must have lived in harmony: otherwise they would not have had seven children. But Mama was head of the house. Women are better at running families because they make many decisions instinctively. That's a real talent, like a talent for music.

Mama was very beautiful. She looked like a Jewish Sophia Loren. We just didn't like her always making us wash our hands, ears, and necks. She had a strong will.

I did not go to school, but I was better educated than my peers who attended the *Gymnasium* daily. We had a governess at first and then a tutor. The governess's name was Mlle Kisser, and she taught us French and German. Many years later, after a concert I played with the conductor Ernest Ansermet in Switzerland, a woman came up to me and asked, "Do you recognize me?" (Like all touring musicians, I would never admit not knowing someone. I would tell polite lies, like, "I seem to recall, but I'm not sure. . . .") She told me she had been my governess in Odessa. Only then did I realize why both the French and the Germans had so much trouble understanding my speech: I had learned both languages from a Swiss!

My brother David studied at a very good commercial school. He wore a handsome uniform, and I envied him. I also envied his love affairs. He was an elegant and social man and went regularly to the skating rink, where he flirted with beautiful girls, and I was jealous.

I did not want to study violin. Mama made the decision for me. I realized she was serious when she handed me a small violin and found me a teacher, a student from Odessa Conservatory.

The appearance of this student in our apartment had a big effect on my sister Sara, the pianist. In short order they became friends and played together constantly. But I didn't like the teacher at all. He probably wasn't a good musician, but what I really hated was the way he hit me on the head whenever I made mistakes—even though I tried so hard.

I decided to get rid of him. Every time he hit me, I cried extra loudly. I knew that Mama wouldn't tolerate child abuse. And I was right: the student was fired.

After another consultation with Mrs. Roisman, I was taken to see the famous professor Pyotr Stolyarsky, who had his own school in Odessa. We went to his apartment on Preobrazhensky Street. The professor knew that my father could afford to pay for the lessons, so he was extremely pleasant. "The boy has such wonderful hands, wonderful fingers! Just made for the violin!" That was pure baloney. He simply did not want to lose a potential pupil.

There were other good violin teachers in Odessa—like the Czech Franz Stupka and Max Fiedelmann—but a huge myth had been created about Stolyarsky that lives to this day. I am always asked about Stolyarsky. I reply that his reputation was exaggerated, and that much of it was the result of successful public relations. Whether I was so critical of Stolyarsky when a boy, I'm not sure, but I can definitely say that he never awed me.

I found Stolyarsky funny. He was a short, blond man, already going gray, who looked like a typical teacher. Whenever I came, there he was, eating—with just his two front teeth, like a bunny. At the time I was sure he did it on purpose, to make us children laugh, but eventually I realized that the professor was missing most of his teeth.

The pupils took lessons at Stolyarsky's apartment. Every day, ten to fifteen little kids came to him. The professor had four rooms, and musical squeaks and noises came from each of them.

Often Stolyarsky brought us together and we would play in unison. I remember doing Tchaikovsky's "Sérénade Mélancolique." Some cellists from the conservatory joined us and we sounded incredibly beautiful. Stolyarsky selected pieces for his pupils that could be played in unison—not only because it was easier for him to control the horde but because it was good for us: by playing together we learned from each other. We would glance around to see who was doing what and who was better.

Stolyarsky was not a particularly profound musician, but he did know the violin. Yet I don't remember his ever spending time on basic technique. We all played exercises by Sevčik and Schradieck, études by Kreutzer. I didn't yet like the violin; in fact, I couldn't imagine that any normal child could enjoy practicing an instrument, unless he was a "freak." And I was an utterly normal child.

I liked playing soccer then. But since Mama did not allow me to play soccer, I had to go to Stolyarsky's instead. At least it was fun at his school: we kids shouted, played with each other, fought, and jumped around like mad.

Stolyarsky lived in a building with a steep marble staircase. One time I was leaving with a classmate, Edgar Ortenberg, who later played in the Budapest Quartet. Stolyarsky had rewarded us for a good lesson with tickets to *I Pagliacci* at the Odessa opera, and Ortenberg was so happy with the honor, he bounced around on the stairs and banged against my shoulder. I fell down the stairs and cracked my left temple. Blood was pouring down my face, but I kept smiling. Dr. Auslender sewed up the gash.

I got to see *I Pagliacci* at a later performance, with Caruso. He was short, fat, and sang deafeningly loudly.

At that time, at the turn of the century, Odessa was a rather important cultural center. Of course it was no Moscow or Petersburg, but Odessites loved music dearly, and so we had a marvelous opera theater. The handsome building with small columns of pink and green was world-famous for its divine acoustics.

They said that the Odessa opera house resembled the Vienna opera house, but when I found myself in Vienna I discovered that our opera house was actually a copy of the Burgtheater. But no matter: the architects of the building in Odessa were still Austrian.

The most popular composers in Odessa were Italian (Rossini, Verdi, Puccini) and French (Bizet and Massenet). Among more modern works I remember an interesting production of Wolf-Ferrari's *The Jewels of the Madonna*. Battistini and Titta Ruffo appeared in Odessa. Caruso came regularly.

My peers all went to the movies. One of the theaters in Odessa was called Ostrovsky's Illusion. A good name, because that's what they sold inside! But I went to the movies rarely. However, Mama often took me to concerts.

Even before the First World War I had heard Jan Kubelik,

Bronislaw Huberman, and Jaroslav Kocián. A brilliant Czech violinist, Kocián actually lived in Odessa for a few years. Eugène Ysaÿe
came almost every year.

I remember Ysaÿe playing at a huge skating rink that could hold
four thousand people. And he was still sold out! We boys would get
into Ysaÿe concerts this way: some of us would make a scene, dis-
tracting the police, while the others would sneak in without tickets.

After his program, Ysaÿe came out without his violin, wearing
an open fur coat, like a big bear. He took out a pocket watch and
put his cheek on folded hands, to show that it was late and time for
him to go to bed. He probably went off to an Odessa nightclub
instead.

Ysaÿe and Kubelik were great performers, of course, but I wasn't
very interested in them then. But the Odessa music lovers went wild
over any visiting celebrity. Swarthy and handsome, Kubelik drove
the audience crazy, especially the women, as he played one fiend-
ishly difficult piece after another. The local ladies threw diamond
rings down at the stage, I saw it myself! They would close the curtain immediately afterward . . . and a servant probably picked up
the rings. Then the curtains opened again and Kubelik would continue the concert as if nothing had happened.

There were several very good dramatic theaters in town. Among
the celebrated actors were Elena Polevitskaya and Stepan Kuznetsov. Kuznetsov was brilliant as Khlestakov in Gogol's *Inspector General* and in the popular farce *Charlie's Aunt*. And I still remember his
reading of Maxim Gorky's *Adder and Falcon*. "He who is born to
crawl cannot fly!" Kuznetsov exclaimed bathetically, to the accompaniment of music by Borodin. That was the now forgotten art of
"melodeclamation" in all its glory. Call it Russian kitsch, I don't
care—I loved it! Because it is true: "He who is born to crawl cannot
fly!" There were other marvelous lines, about it being worth your
life to know the joy of flying even once. That's true too! If you've
flown just once, that's enough, you're a genius. After that, it doesn't
matter. . . .

Odessa was a cosmopolitan city, planned and built by the French.
The most famous of its planners was Duc de Richelieu (not to be

confused with the cardinal). Grateful Odessites erected a monument to the duke. Odessa also had boulevards de France and de Paris, a Richelieu Street and a Richelieu High School. There were many wealthy French homes, in addition to large Italian and Greek colonies.

Rich Italians and Greeks—like Mr. Anatra, one of the first aviation manufacturers, and Mr. Duvarzhobulu, in the export-import business (chocolate and Turkish delight)—donated money to the Odessa city opera, directed by Mr. Nikitin, and so it was natural that works by Italian composers predominated—along with French ones, of course.

It's interesting to recall that in prerevolutionary Russia foreign companies manufactured many excellent products. The French sold Sioux, the favorite chocolate of the tsar's daughters . . . as I learned when I appeared in Petersburg in 1916 at a concert organized by the Russian Red Cross: one of the grand duchesses gave me a Sioux chocolate—God, it was delicious!

The perfumes in Russia were also marvelous—Raleigh, Brocard—just as good as those in France. Russians traditionally think that foreign goods are of better quality, but when I got to France in 1926 they spoke approvingly of Russian perfumes and colognes.

Russian engineers and technicians were skilled professionals who were highly regarded in Europe. The famous ships *Normandie* and *Ile de France* were built from blueprints made by Russian émigrés.

Many foreign ships came to the Odessa port. Once I saw a bunch of kids at the beach. What's up? It turned out they had surrounded a Negro sailor from an American ship. The black man was cheerful and dressed flashily, in a red vest and green socks. He laughed and danced a jig. This was an incredible event. We had never seen a Negro before; we thought they lived only in Africa. And here was an American Negro!

Every summer my big brother David and I went to the Kochubeyev estuary and would spend several days at a time at a rented dacha. The dacha was not very attractive and we were afraid of the big rats. We went sunbathing at the Austrian beach. David liked to swim, but I didn't. In fact, I never did learn. We also went out sailing, until we almost drowned in a storm. I remember we were listing so hard our sail was practically scooping up water. I was very frightened, and you could never get me into a sailboat again.

I often ran away from home to play soccer in the city park. In Odessa everyone was crazy about soccer then; foreign teams came from Turkey and Greece. I had a strong offense and was even allowed to play center forward. I ran until I was out of breath. That's how my parents knew I was playing soccer instead of practicing the violin . . . and I was regularly punished: I had to stand in the corner.

Another thing everyone was crazy about was flying. One of the most popular Odessites of the time was both a soccer player and an aviator, Sergei Utochkin. And I, young Milstein, could boast that I played a violin made by Utochkin's brother! The violin was a nightmare. You could flick off its varnish with a fingernail. Or, if you wanted to, you could use your nail to dig a deep furrow in it.

Meanwhile, our house was filled with music. My youngest brother, Miron, took up the cello. And I was his teacher! Somehow I had mastered the instrument. Miron eventually became an excellent cellist; he was concertmaster at the Odessa opera. And I still play the cello.

Gradually the violin began to interest me in earnest. I didn't like the other youngsters playing better than I, so I started making an effort. It came easily, because I was a bright boy and learned fast. I have kept that ability to this day.

Once in 1915 Professor Stolyarsky called us at home. I answered the phone. (In order to reach that old-fashioned telephone, I had to stand on a chair; I fell and almost cracked my head again.) Through the crackle and hiss I heard my teacher's voice. "Do you play Glazunov's concerto?"

I lied. "No."

Actually, I did play the Glazunov concerto; I liked it—it was difficult and interesting, and as I said I was a quick study then; one, two, and the piece was already in my fingers!—but I didn't tell Stolyarsky about it because he always grumbled, "Why do you play what you like and not what's good for you?" And so I lied about the Glazunov concerto. I was afraid Stolyarsky would yell at me.

But he didn't believe me anyway and said, "All right, get your mother."

Stolyarsky explained to Mama that there was going to be an anniversary concert in Odessa honoring Glazunov's fiftieth birthday. Alexander Konstantinovich Glazunov himself would come from Petersburg to conduct, and the famous pianist Geshelin-Chernetskaya (wife of Dr. Auslender, who had sewn up the gash on my temple) was to have played his piano concerto. It was her warhorse. But she had become indisposed and the organizers of the concert were searching for a replacement.

Glazunov's violin concerto is a fresh, attractive work, brilliantly orchestrated (although the Rondo is a bit heavy). At the rehearsal I played something at the beginning of the concerto in my own way. Obviously I was a brazen boy—the presence of the composer did not intimidate me. Glazunov looked down at me through his pince-nez and murmured, "Don't you like the way I wrote it?" I played it his way then, but when the rehearsal was over Glazunov turned to me and said, "Play it any way you want!" Because he saw that my version was better.

A wise and calm man, Glazunov. He was not afraid that his authority would somehow be undermined. Unfortunately, his conducting was listless and amateurish. But that didn't affect the success of the evening: Glazunov's reputation in Odessa as a great composer and director of the Petersburg Conservatory was enormous. Everyone was interested and flattered to see him in the flesh, and I was proud to share the stage with the maître.

At Stolyarsky's school the examination concerts, given every half year, were important events. The pupils tried to outdo each other. I must have been progressing well, because one day—this was 1916—Stolyarsky announced that he would show me to Leopold Semyonovich Auer, the famous professor at the Petersburg Conservatory.

All the boys at Stolyarsky's school practically prayed by saying "Auer, Auer!" He was our god. And Auer was in Odessa to perform! He was accompanied by the Greek pianist Irina Eneri. I remember that she played marvelously. But Auer, who played sitting down, squeaked. (I don't understand why he played sitting down;

he wasn't all that old then, around seventy.) The program was Beethoven's *Spring* Sonata and a violin sonata by Petersburg composer Leonid Nikolayev. (Volodya Horowitz and I played the Nikolayev later. It has a good, singing beginning, but then Nikolayev didn't know what to do with it, and it gets terribly boring. We met the composer eventually in Petrograd. Nikolayev, an incredibly refined, even effeminate, gentleman, was a respected pianist and a professor at the conservatory. The best Petersburg pianists studied with him: Maria Yudina, Vladimir Sofronitsky, and young Dmitri Shostakovich.)

And so, Stolyarsky told me that he had talked with Auer; the Petersburg professor was willing to listen to me after his second concert. Mama and I went to the Londonskaya Hotel, a grand building where Auer was staying. We waited a long time and then were invited into his suite.

Auer seemed exquisitely elegant to me. He was wearing beautiful soft slippers. He asked me, "What do you play, boy? Do you play Bach?" I replied that I played the G Minor Partita for solo violin. That was all of Bach we were familiar with in Odessa then. We knew about the existence of the famous Chaconne, but no one dared play it because it was so demanding and difficult to master.

I started the Presto from the partita. I must have taken it too fast, because Auer started clicking his fingers trying to slow me down. So I couldn't go as fast as I wanted to. And I didn't like that: if you play for the famous Auer, then you should show off everything you can do!

Auer must have liked me anyway, because when I was done he gave me two gold five-ruble pieces. That was big money! (Later, in Petersburg, I learned that getting any money from Auer was an incredible reward: the professor's stinginess was legendary.)

Mama and I got silver change for the gold coins. I came home proud, my pockets weighed down with silver. I jingled my loot for greater effect.

2. Petersburg

After long family discussion it was decided that I had to go study with Auer in Petersburg. I went with Mama. First we stayed in the Abelsons' house at 28 Mokhovaya Street. The three Abelson brothers were wealthy financiers. One of them was even chairman of the stock exchange committee. His wife was from Odessa and was the sister of the engineer Vurdgaft, a friend of my father's.

We spent several months at the Abelsons'. One of the brothers had a son whom I liked to tease. He was afraid of me. I tried to explain that I was joking, but he would just whine, "I don't understa-a-and jokes!"

The Abelsons lived well. They gave balls and receptions regularly, and their guests were big shots—like Protopopov, minister of the interior, and Purishkevich, deputy of the state duma, the Rus-

13

sian parliament. The guests sang and shouted and tossed their glasses at the ceiling. This made it hard for Mama and me to sleep. Years later, I met all three Abelsons in Paris. They were rich there, too, but not as they had been in Petersburg.

At their house in Petersburg I met young Sergei Prokofiev, pianist and avant-garde composer, who made a strange, even frightening impression on me, mainly because of his unusual lips. They were swollen, almost bursting with blood, and had flecks of foam in the corners. I was always afraid when Prokofiev picked up some sharp eating utensil: what if he pricked his lip by accident? Blood would come gushing out!

Prokofiev was touchy, clumsy, and ugly, with the colorless eyes typical of blonds. But his energy compensated for his clumsiness. You could see he was a young genius. The difference in our ages did not allow us to become friends then.

We met again in the U.S.A., in Hollywood, before World War Two. We were staying at the same hotel. Prokofiev was already planning his permanent return to the Soviet Union and was negotiating doing some film music, but as far as I know nothing came of it. We had breakfast every day for two weeks, spending an hour and a half to two hours over the meal, talking about everything under the sun.

Prokofiev polished off his bacon and eggs greedily. He ate carelessly, grease dripping down his chin, so engrossed in conversation that he didn't notice.

For such an organized and punctual person in music making and business, Prokofiev was sloppy and careless in everyday things. Everything he touched became a mess.

I like Prokofiev's music a lot, but I think he did his best work in his youth: the *Classical* Symphony, the First Violin Concerto, the first piano concertos and sonatas. After he returned to the Soviet Union, he did not write anything of significance. I cannot say with certainty that this creative tragedy was the result solely of the repressive Stalinist regime. Perhaps Prokofiev would have faded in any case, even if he had stayed in the West. But I still feel that adverse political circumstances stifled his enormous gift.

Prokofiev did not understand much about politics. He also lacked George Balanchine's scruples. Balanchine understood early on that he could not work in a totalitarian state and left for the West. Prokofiev, judging from our conversations in Hollywood, did not give this much thought. And he paid for it dearly.

My first lesson with Professor Auer at the Petersburg Conservatory was marked by an incident. Auer gave lessons twice a week: on Wednesdays and Saturdays. Mama and I went to see him on Wednesday. I played Ernst's concerto. There were many other pupils in class; that was Auer's teaching method. I remember Miron Poliakin and Toscha Seidel. When I finished playing, Auer turned to them and exclaimed, "How do you like the Black Sea technique?" That was a nice turn of phrase, "Black Sea technique."

And what a coincidence: a reporter from the popular Petersburg newspaper *Birzhevye vedomosti* (the Russian *Wall Street Journal* of the day) happened to be wandering around the conservatory in search of a good story. Auer's pupils must have told him a few things. The reporter rushed off to his office.

Mother and I, suspecting nothing, returned from the conservatory to the Abelsons' house and went to bed. They were having a big ball, as usual. Suddenly, at four in the morning, Mrs. Abelson woke us. There was big article about me in *Birzhevye vedomosti*!

The reporter had spun it out of whole cloth, typically. Mama and I were described as "refugees from Odessa." (We weren't refugees at all, but that gave the story color.) Furthermore, the reporter wrote that famous Professor Auer had almost fainted with delight when he heard me play. Then, supposedly, he had said that after Milstein he couldn't and wouldn't listen to anyone else that day.

Auer hadn't fainted, of course. True, no one played after me, but only because it was late, seven o'clock, and the professor was in a rush to get home to dinner.

The article in *Birzhevye vedomosti* created an unwanted sensation. Soon Mama was informed that the director of the conservatory,

Alexander Glazunov himself, wanted to see us. We showed up in his office, and Glazunov started off on a tangent. He ran on about the great musicians who had taught and were teaching at the Petersburg Conservatory, that it was an institution with glorious and noble traditions, that those traditions had to be respected.

Heavyset and flabby, Glazunov spoke slowly and softly, yet Mama could not understand his point. Then Glazunov brought up the article in *Birzhevye vedomosti*, and it became clear that he suspected Mama of planting the story! Glazunov was trying to explain that behaving that way was unethical, it was not done. Of course, Mama had had nothing to do with that unfortunate article.

Clearly uncomfortable from the start of the discussion, when Glazunov saw that he had accused a respectable woman unjustly, he was completely embarrassed. In order to get out of a sticky situation and smooth over the injury (Mama was insulted!), he offered to get me into the opera *Boris Godunov* at the Imperial Maryinsky Theater. The legendary bass Feodor Chaliapin was singing Tsar Boris, and Glazunov was conducting.

To hear Chaliapin as Boris! What an incredibly generous offer, especially since it was to be a command performance. Emperor Nicholas II and the diplomatic corps were going to attend. No tickets were available, but Glazunov promised to get me into the orchestra pit.

It turned out to be one of the most memorable events of my life. I couldn't find the administration door at first, it was to the side of the main entrance. I was afraid of being late, but when I was finally led into the orchestra pit and was seated, and it was time to start, it turned out everyone was waiting for the tsar. Nicholas, who was coming from his military headquarters in the city of Mogilev—this was at the height of World War One—was forty-five minutes late. So the performance began an hour and a half late, at half past ten, and I had lots of time to look around.

Brilliant officers and beautifully dressed ladies—oh, those hats, jewels, and long gloves!—sat in the boxes. The diplomats of the tiniest country looked like kings! I thought that when our emperor came out, he would be dressed even more fabulously and would look even more impressive. But when Nicholas appeared (I was sitting right opposite the royal box, on the left) I saw a small, modestly dressed man, without pomp or galloons or medals. Only the St. George Cross gleamed on his chest.

They started playing anthems—first the Russian, then those of our wartime allies. Everyone stood up. The tsar stood, twirling his reddish mustache with a melancholy air. I devoured him with my eyes.

Then came the opera, the first time I'd seen *Boris Godunov*. Chaliapin's singing astonished me. But even more astonishing . . . He suddenly fell to his knees! He hadn't stumbled; no, it was a flamboyant theatrical touch: Chaliapin, tsar on the stage, on his knees before the real tsar. The audience gasped and buzzed. Everyone had been electrified to begin with, and Chaliapin's unexpected gesture added to the tension. But Chaliapin continued as if nothing had happened. Then it became increasingly clear that he was dissatisfied with Glazunov's conducting, that the phlegmatic composer was holding back the temperamental singer. At last Chaliapin couldn't stand it anymore, came stage front, bent over, and in his marvelously deep voice roared at Glazunov, "Sasha, hurry it up!"

After seeing *Boris* with Chaliapin, I had chills for ten days. They thought I had caught a bad cold and kept taking my temperature—but I had no fever. I was quivering with excitement. I had overdosed on high art.

As a student of the conservatory, I had the right to live in the capital as an exception to the quotas that applied to Jews. And since I was a minor, Mama had the right to stay in Petersburg with me. But she still worried that the police would come and ask for our documents and that there would be problems. Mama turned to Professor Auer for help.

Auer called Glazunov, who invited us once again to see him in his office. He was very kind. He offered me candy from a beautiful box and right then and there asked his secretary to call Prince Volkonsky, a deputy minister of the interior. "Listen, I have a talented boy here, a student of Auer's. You know, I've told you—yes, yes, Milstein, with his mother. So please take care of things so that they're not bothered."

And everything was done instantly! When we arrived home in a carriage (we always took a carriage), the superintendent and a policeman in white gloves were waiting for us! Mama got scared when she saw them, but the policeman had no intention of arresting us. On the contrary, he saluted Mama solemnly. Glazunov's call to Prince Volkonsky had done its work.

In Petersburg we lived in an enormous house on Gorokhovaya Street. We got up early, at seven. We had breakfast: bread and butter, and tea. Following the example of the rich Abelsons we also had cheese. Then Mama sent me to the store for groceries. After that, I would go to my music stand and practice the violin.

Mama would sew, embroider, or write long letters home to Odessa with detailed instructions for all contingencies: the sofa leg was broken, be careful with it; put one chair here and another there. Such worries! And all those mornings I was practicing, maybe four or five hours.

At last Mama would say, "Go eat." Sometimes there was steak for lunch. Other days I went to the conservatory and dropped by the canteen, where Glazunov's portrait hung. They had excellent borsch and bitki (small meatballs in sour-cream sauce) with kasha. I love those dishes to this day.

Almost every day Mama took me to the famous Filippov Bakery. That was a magical place! Glamorously dressed ladies and gentlemen, the cream of society, drove up in carriages. They came for the world's best pirozhki. Filippov's enormous salesmen, in aprons and white cuffs, used special forks to pick up the steaming pastries stuffed with meat and other fillings, which they wrapped in special waxed paper to keep the grease off ladies' dainty hands. Filippov's was a Petersburg institution. When you walked in, you had a sense of incredible wealth and well-being, even though there might be beggars just around the corner.

I have never had pirozhki like that anywhere else! Whenever I go to a Russian restaurant in the West, I always order pirozhki, but they're not the same. They're like mere memories of dishes Mama cooked when I was a child—you can't repeat the taste or aroma. . . .

Mama and I often went for walks in a small park not far from our house. I would wear a navy coat lined with beaver and with a beaver collar, and a leather hat that covered the back of my neck and my ears. When it snowed, the white birches in the park took on various hues—yellow, pink, green. And the snow was iridescent, like pearls: pinkish white, light blue and green.

I noticed things like that because even then I was interested in painting and went to the famous Hermitage museum. I never took art lessons. But back in Odessa I had begun drawing on my own. We had a large white room there with two black grand pianos, made by Becker and by Schroeder, which were considered the best in Russia. Lithographs hung on the walls, portraits of Bach, Mozart, and Schubert. I began copying the lithographs. Bach and Mozart in their wigs were easy enough, but making a successful likeness of Schubert was a much harder task. I remember being troubled trying to get the shadow of Schubert's glasses just right.

I never did learn to draw professionally, but I feel that I have good artistic instincts. That's why I work in watercolors. In that area, as in all others, you must have courage. When you work in watercolor a lot, you get used to it, get into the rhythm of doing it. But then, if you stop for a while, you don't know how to start again. Many of my friends have landscapes done by me, *echt* Milsteins.

Once, in New York, the Metropolitan Museum of Art held a benefit exhibit of paintings by musicians. I remember that Schoenberg, Lotte Lehmann, and Gershwin took part. I exhibited a watercolor depicting Petersburg in May, when the snow is melting, with the white birches I remembered from childhood. The picture sold for five hundred dollars.

In Petersburg my favorite amusement was taking a sleigh ride along Nevsky Prospect. The horses' hooves beat on the wooden street paving. The panorama was unforgettable: the long, elegant prospect, marvelous buildings, palaces, churches; in the distance, the golden spire of the Admiralty. The store windows filled with fashions, furs, and Flemishlike still lifes of fresh fruits and vegetables. The window displays of Eliseyev's store and the Passage, particularly brilliant. Lively crowds, the gentlemen in top hats, the ladies in small veils. Nevsky Prospect, whose praises were sung by Gogol—the main street of the Russian empire, and for me the main street of the world.

The bearded coachmen, sitting above us on their boxes, were imposing figures. In their large caftans with quilted lining they resembled monuments. I was so intrigued by these pompous coachmen that I made special trips to watch them drink tea in the saloons on Staro-Nevsky. They spent hours that way, sipping tea from saucers, emptying samovar after samovar. The saloons were so full of steam that when the door opened the steam rushed out onto the street with a sound like a barreling locomotive's warning whistle.

In Petersburg I began reading—Pushkin, Gogol, Krylov's fables, Chekhov's stories. Like all boys, I thrilled to cheap detective series. For a few kopecks you could buy a bright book that recounted the adventures of the famous detectives Nick Carter and Nat Pinkerton. Greedily I devoured Sienkiewicz's novel *Quo Vadis?*.

(Only later did I come to appreciate Leo Tolstoy: he was engrossing, epic, and decorative. But Dostoyevsky, so popular in the West, never really appealed to me. I preferred Leonid Andreyev, the Russian Oscar Wilde.)

There was something magical about Petersburg. Even now, tourists in Leningrad are captivated by the city. It's not the Soviet architecture that they like, however, but the palaces built by the Russian tsars. The Soviets didn't build anything outstanding in Leningrad except perhaps for the metro. But I recall prerevolutionary Petersburg: the golden Admiralty spire, the Maryinsky and Alexandrinsky theaters, St. Isaac's Cathedral. (I didn't like the Kazansky Cathedral as much; it is an unsuccessful imitation of San Pietro.)

And the marvelous Mikhailovsky Theater! In my London house I have an old French engraving depicting the square in front of the Mikhailovsky Theater (before the revolution they did plays in French): winter, bonfires in the snow, people warming themselves . . . a typical Petersburg picture.

And that special Petersburg smell! The air! Where did that magic come from? Was it because the city is on water? Stockholm is a maritime city, too, yet it lacks that charm. As does Mexico City, which like Petersburg is on a swamp. (I played at a theater there once, and when I returned ten years later I had to go down to the dressing room as if to a cellar: a part of the theater had sunk into the friable land on which it was built.) No city on earth is like Petersburg. . . .

In Petersburg I became especially close to my mother. I loved being alone with her. I felt that anyone else present was taking from me this special experience of being only with Mama. Sometimes it was so cold in Petersburg that I could not fall asleep. Mama suggested that I could come to her bed if I was cold, so I did just that. In the beginning it was unusual, but eventually I got used to it, because it was so warm and cozy, and I didn't want to be by myself and lonesome.

We used to talk about the future, and Mama would tell me that an artist has to be as pure as possible. The most important thing was to aim at the highest quality in what you did and not think about what you'd get for it.

In Odessa, I was often asked to play in a concert (an Auer pupil meant "quality"), but Mama told me not to appear when the ambiance was not dignified enough. This advice from my mother left me with an uncompromising attitude. Later in my career even my wife was not always in accord with my mother's indoctrination, the effects of which last up to this day.

Probably my mother's influence was due to her own wonderful purity and hypnotizing personality. To my regret, when I left Russia in 1925, I did it without seeing my mother. I can't forget that. There wasn't time for me to go to Odessa, where Mama lived at the time, because I could not abandon certain artistic obligations.

When I came to Petersburg, Auer freed me from mandatory attendance at classes in general subjects. He also freed me from orchestral playing, which made Mama happy: it meant that I was being groomed for a solo career. I was only required to participate in chamber ensembles.

A handsome student named Petrovsky came to our house to help me study math, literature, and geography. I was supposed to take exams in these subjects at the conservatory every trimester. I was a good student, so I remember my disappointment when I once showed up for exams and Lavrov, the gray-haired inspector of the conservatory, announced, "Come back next trimester!" I had worked so hard—and in vain!

When I was with Stolyarsky my main pleasure and goal had been to play as fast as possible. I only began truly liking the violin after I played for Auer. It was a very important turning point. Auer was considered a great teacher, and that affected my vanity. Stolyarsky almost never made any comments to his pupils, they just ran through their works. And he never picked up a violin at all. Auer stopped his students—especially good ones, like Heifetz, Poliakin, and me—quite often, even though he almost never demonstrated. (When Auer did demonstrate a passage, it wasn't so impressive, because the professor, who had played marvelously once, was already past his prime.)

They used to tell this story about Auer. He was playing a sonata with Anton Rubinstein, who was an extrovert, very temperamental. Auer didn't have a big temper or a big sound, and he pleaded, "Anton Grigorievich, you're playing so loud I can't hear myself!" To which Rubinstein replied, "Lucky you!"

In general, I think the role of the teacher in developing talent is exaggerated. Talent develops on its own, in a natural way. Gradually an understanding of the limits of expression unfolds. Here a lot depends on temperament. If temperament carries you away, if there is no analysis or control, the technique, the dynamics, and the interpretation will be exaggerated, crude.

I remember asking Auer, "How should I study?" Auer replied, "With your head, not your hands!" Then it seemed a meaningless answer. With time, of course, I understood what Auer meant: trust your fingers less than your head; think about the conception and approach to a work, and don't just hammer away foolishly and endlessly at the virtuosic passages. It seems rather simple and obvious, but real comprehension of that truism comes only with age.

Auer liked to recall great violinists of the past. He told us in particular about how marvelous Henryk Wieniawski had been. A young lady from Finland was playing the Brahms concerto in Auer's class and kept playing off pitch. Auer stopped her. "What's wrong with your intonation?" The lady began justifying herself by saying she had fat fingers. He struck his forehead and said, "You're fat here, in the head! Wieniawski had fingers as thick as a fist, and that didn't keep him from playing cleanly!"

In class, the pupils sat along a wall, in a line, like Arabs before a dance. When the professor approached, the pupils jumped up so that he would notice them and pick them to play for him. One of the pupils, a black boy, we called "Black Beethoven," because he looked so much like that composer (except that he was tall). I remember one time he jumped up as Auer approached and the professor demanded, "What are you doing here?"

"I'm your pupil!"

It turned out that the last time he had played for Auer was three years earlier.

Interestingly, we almost never played Bach in Auer's class. Bach was not at all popular in Russia then. In Odessa at Stolyarsky's, we had studied the Allegro Assai from Sonata no. 3 for solo violin and played it all together—Josef Roisman, Misha Fainget ("Kreisler in miniature"), David Oistrakh, Edgar Ortenberg, and I. It was something of a musical *kolkhoz* (a collective farm), but it was of good quality. That allegro has to be played in controlled tempo, but we little Russians shot it out very fast, without problems, like a *perpetuum mobile*. And since we played all together, Stolyarsky didn't have to work with each of us individually.

For Auer I played the Fugue from Bach's First Sonata for solo violin, also very fast. The professor demanded that I stress the theme. Now that demand seems wrong to me: after all, it's only the theme, only the material. You can't build a Bach fugue that way. But at that time, no one understood this.

Auer wasn't interested in listening to Bach. He didn't know what to say, and so he said practically nothing. Of course, pieces like Dvořák's "Humoresque" and "Méditation" from Massenet's *Thaïs* were another thing entirely. In those works Auer was delighted to show us everything he knew. Obviously, you can't compare

Dvořák with Bach, but still, "Humoresque" is a flashy piece, well written. And I consider Massenet's opus a masterpiece, a lucky find.

I was drawn to Bach instinctively, on my own. I tried to learn as much of his music as possible. I even tried to go through *The Well-Tempered Clavier* on the violin. Interestingly, one of the ways I opened up to Bach was through my interest in Max Reger's polyphonic music. After Reger, who was a fashionable composer in avant-garde Russian musical circles for a while, I understood a lot more about Bach's works. That happens sometimes. Modern music helps open your eyes to the old masters.

Bach's sonatas and partitas for solo violin give the performer an opportunity to bask in the most glamorous light. For a long time this was hardly obvious. I remember an incident some time ago in New York. Three great conductors were at my house for lunch: Dmitri Mitropoulos, George Szell, and Charles Munch.

After lunch, Munch said, "Milstein, do you know when we met?"

"Wasn't it in 1934 in Athens?"

"No, much earlier! I was concertmaster of the Gewandhaus orchestra in Leipzig when you played the Tchaikovsky concerto with us under the baton of Bruno Walter. And for an encore you played Bach's G Minor Sonata, remember? It turned out to be the big hit of the program! The newspapers wrote, 'Milstein played Tchaikovsky well, but he had even greater success with the Bach.' "

It was true, and it had come about accidentally. When I finished the Tchaikovsky, Bruno Walter suggested, "Why don't you play Bach for an encore?" Conductors are always jealous of a soloist's success, and Walter thought that I would play the Adagio and put the audience to sleep.

I did start with the Adagio from the G Minor Sonata, but then moved on to the Fugue. It was hard to stop. At the Siciliana, I thought, What am I doing? But there could be no retreat, and I finished the sonata. (I was inspired, among everything else, by the Gewandhaus hall, so significant in the fate of Bach's music: it was here that Mendelssohn resurrected many of Bach's compositions for the audience.)

My favorite musical work is Bach's Chaconne. In my youth,

while I admired it, I didn't place it at the apex of musical literature. But in recent years, I feel so much when I play that music. I am so much at one with it that I sometimes improvise fingering right on-stage.

At different times Auer's pupils included Jascha Heifetz, Mischa Elman, Efrem Zimbalist, Miron Poliakin, Toscha Seidel, and Cecilia Hansen. And I can tell you that Auer liked Poliakin more than Heifetz. Yet it was Heifetz who became world-famous. This doesn't mean that the old professor was deaf and blind, it's just that he preferred Poliakin's nervous impressionist style to Heifetz's grand manner of playing.

In my time Heifetz rarely came to class with Auer. He was already touring, and he had even appeared abroad, in Scandinavia. But I was present a few times at his lessons: he and Auer worked mainly on small pieces, one time on Elgar's concerto, rather new in those days; Kreisler had premiered it only in 1910.

Once I witnessed this scene: Jascha came into the classroom where Auer worked and was followed by his father, who as usual was carrying Jascha's violin. There was an enormous mirror in the classroom, and Auer, even though he had his back to the door, could see them come in. But he continued working as if they weren't there, maintaining his professorial dignity.

The Heifetzes waited in the doorway quite a while for Auer to greet them and ask them to sit down, but Auer persisted in ignoring them. Finally the Heifetzes gave up waiting for his greeting and quietly sat down. In their place I would have left!

I remember Miron Poliakin playing in class, gracefully performing Tchaikovsky's Waltz-Scherzo. Poliakin was a marvelous violinist, though not very consistent. Ideally, an artist should always play above a certain level.

Not all of Auer's students were first-rate talents. Many had come to him for prestige, in order to have an easier time getting a job with an orchestra, and they made money by playing between shows in the movie theaters. Auer often blew up at them, but his wrath died down at the sight of one of our accompanists, a Scandinavian blonde with luxurious curves. Often when she sat at the piano, he would bend over the keys for a better view of her cleavage.

Auer could be most unpleasant when angry. I remember playing Beethoven's concerto in his class. For some reason, Auer wasn't happy with me. He shouted and jabbed his finger at my head so hard, I thought he would make a hole.

Another time he flew into a frenzy when Jascha Heifetz was playing Jenö Hubay's "Zéphyr." We all could see that Auer was spoiling for a fight. Heifetz could feel it, too. He tried to avoid a catastrophe, but in vain. There were two pianos in the classroom, and suddenly Auer banged his fists on both keyboards: bang! bang! He had turned red and was shouting wildly. I remember being surprised: why had he made such a scene? Now I understand his tactics better. It's important for the teacher to be unpredictable and potentially explosive. Then the pupil tries harder to avert a scene and subsequent punishment. In the final analysis, this instinct for survival improves the quality of playing.

I played for Auer frequently, almost at every lesson, so sometimes when I jumped up with the rest as he approached, Auer would have me sit down. But he would make me play for him later anyway!

Whenever Auer missed lessons at the conservatory because of illness, he invariably sent for me so that I would come to his house to play. The professor lived at 28 Angliisky Prospect, not far from Teatralnaya Square, where the conservatory was. At his house I sometimes had to wait a long time for the professor to be free. I remember one time when Auer was eating fish. I waited patiently, almost an hour, as he dealt with the fish very methodically, sucking every bone.

I was a diligent student, and Auer appreciated my hard work and attention to advice. I've mentioned how he gave me two gold five-ruble coins after hearing me play in Odessa. In Petersburg he presented me with a bow! (I later learned that the bow was very cheap, but for the notoriously miserly Auer it was an amazing gesture.)

Recalling those days, I can say once again that I truly came to love the violin in Petersburg. I liked going to the conservatory, and

I liked the atmosphere of competition in Auer's class—talented children playing the violin, one better than the next, inspiring me to try harder.

In my memories, the conservatory and Petersburg are inextricably entwined. That must be why the time spent in that magical city seems like the best time of my life. Returning home from the conservatory and going to bed (Mama and I went to bed around eight or nine in the evening), I would recall with pleasure my lessons with Auer, the conversation at the conservatory, and the whole lovely day. And the next day promised to be just as beautiful.

3. Revolution and the Beginning of My Career

Life in Petersburg in those days was strange, fantastic, almost miragelike. Terrible events were taking place, with fateful consequences for the future of the Russian empire and the world as a whole. Living in the center of Petersburg, twelve years old, I found it hard to avoid these events.

Once, in December 1916, I left our house on Gorokhovaya Street to take a walk in the direction of the Moika River. Marvelous palaces of Russian aristocrats lined the embankment. A crowd was gathered in front of one palace, which had belonged to Prince Felix Yousoupov. The people were agitated and spoke in low voices, glancing around. They were clearly afraid of the police, of which there were many in the crowd.

I came closer. I heard: "Rasputin," "murder," "serves him

right, the bastard." Some people were leaning over the parapet to look down at the frozen river.

The water below was not fully shackled by ice. I saw an open spot and in it some pinkish swirls. People insisted that it was the blood of Grigori Rasputin, the infamous "mad monk" who had come to the capital from Siberia and held the tsaritsa in his sway.

Many people in Petersburg then considered Rasputin the cause of all the troubles that had befallen Russia. He was hated by the people and by the aristocracy alike. But the tsaritsa was implacable in her support of Rasputin, whom she called "Holy Father": he had a miraculous way of stopping the bleeding of her son, Tsarevich Alexei, who suffered from hemophilia.

So Prince Yousoupov, with Grand Duke Dmitri, Duma Deputy Purishkevich (a frequent guest of the Abelsons), and other conspirators, lured Rasputin to his house on the Moika River, poisoned him, then shot him, and threw his body in the river. (So maybe it *was* his blood I saw.) Years later it became clear that this murder marked the beginning of the end of the Russian empire.

There was unrest throughout Petersburg. On a wintry day in 1917 Mama sent me to the grocery store. A huge crowd blocked the way on Sennaya Square, so I stopped to look. I will never forget what happened then.

There were policemen everywhere. I saw machine guns in place on rooftops. Cossacks on horseback were ready. Everyone was waiting for something. And suddenly a procession of women came out onto the square. They were poorly dressed, most of them in black, carrying a white sheet on which was handwritten in huge letters: BREAD!

Bread was in scarce supply in those days. Sometimes you had to line up the night before only to be told, at six in the morning when the bakeries opened, "There is nothing left." And if there was any bread it was horrible. It wasn't black, the way good Russian bread should be, but blackish yellow, sometimes even with a light blue sheen. It was impossible to cut except with an ax, although you could break it over your knee.

The procession of women moved calmly, even quietly. No one sang or shouted. And suddenly, without any provocation, the police

started shooting! Without warning! It was horrible! And the Cossacks, the tsar's merciless guards, whom many still accuse of having
been cruel to civilians, reacted in an absolutely unexpected way.

I saw one of the Cossacks bare his saber and, bending over
slightly, cut off the head of a policeman who was shooting. One
blow—and the head flew off! All this was too much for me. Terrified, I ran home.

That's how the revolution to overthrow the Russian tsar began.
Studies at the conservatory were often disrupted now. One time
when I was playing for Auer, a conservatory usher, an old man with
medals, came running in. "Professor, the enemies! They've set fire
to the police!"

He told us that the Kazansky police commissariat was burning.
No time for studies now! We all ran to see the fire. I remember that
it was very windy and that ashes and pieces of paper were flying
around—all that was left of the police files.

Auer left Petersburg in the spring of 1917, after the February
Revolution, which put an end to the rule of Tsar Nicholas II.
Everyone understood that the old professor was leaving Russia forever. (And so it was: Auer moved to New York; he died there in
1930, at the age of eighty-five.) Without Auer there was nothing for
me to do in Petersburg. Mama decided to return to Odessa.

So I never saw the so-called October Revolution, when Lenin
and the Bolsheviks took power. Later, when we were back in Odessa,
I heard rumors of hunger, executions, and other horrors taking place
in Petersburg. The news went beyond anything that had happened in
Petersburg when I was there. The February Revolution, which I
had observed with my own eyes, was somehow not real. Mikhail,
the brother of Nicholas II (in whose favor the tsar had abdicated),
at first walked along Nevsky Prospect looking happy, with a red
bow on his chest: apparently he liked the revolution too. Lenin had
not yet returned to Petersburg from exile. Before leaving Petersburg, I was shown the luxurious palace of the ballerina Kschessinska, the tsar's former mistress. Now the Petersburg Committee of
Bolsheviks was housed there.

But the name Lenin meant nothing to me at the time. Even now
I think of how useless the provisional government, which came into

power after the overthrow of the tsar, turned out to be. It did not give land to the peasants nor peace to soldiers tired of the meaningless war with Germany. The government simply handed power to Lenin.

And so we returned to Odessa. At first life there was convenient and pleasant. I was young, lighthearted, and enjoyed everything: the fact that I had been a pupil of the famous Auer; the fact that the awesome professor was gone and I was my own boss; the fact that I had some money of my own for the first time. The Petersburg Conservatory refunded the money my father had paid for my education and Mama passed it on to me.

I made a glorious purchase with the money, the first of my life. There was a fashionable jewelry store in Odessa, Barzhansky's. It was closing and had a sale: for half price I bought a gold Longines pocket watch, new and elegantly thin. That watch served me for many years. (Later, in the West, I put it in a safe. Then, quite recently, I reclaimed my gold watch and took it to a jeweler in Lausanne to sell it. The dealer was thrilled. "They don't make Longines like this anymore, it's a historical rarity!" I held on to the watch.)

At first, the Bolsheviks' seizure of power in Petersburg and Moscow somehow went almost unnoticed in Odessa. On sunny days, a lively, motley crowd strolled along the streets. Flags of many nations of the world flew on the masts of ships in the port. But such insouciant life was not to last long. Because Odessa was so important as a port, the struggle for it began soon after actual civil war broke out in Russia.

The regime in Odessa changed many times. First it was the White Volunteer Army of General Denikin, then the Bolsheviks, then the Ukrainian nationalist Petlyura. Foreign soldiers came and went: Germans, Frenchmen, Polish legionnaires. Each installed and supported its puppet. The Germans, for instance, put hetman Skoropadsky in charge.

I observed all this from the sidelines, as if at the theater. I especially liked all the new military uniforms, which seemed to fill

Odessa overnight: the Reds had pointy helmets that resembled something from Slavic folktales; the Poles wore red rectangular confederate caps; the Petlyurovites wore Ukrainian *zhupany*, twirled their long mustaches, and tossed their *oseledtsy*, long ponytails on otherwise shaved heads—exactly like punks today on Oxford Street in London. All these colorful warriors vanished from the city just as fast as they appeared.

Some scenes were pure farce. I remember a detachment of Rumanians who had marched triumphantly through the city to help the Whites, then fighting the Bolsheviks about twenty-five kilometers outside Odessa. They set off for the battle sharply dressed . . . and returned quickly—beaten, wounded, all their panache gone. Yes, war is more than parades.

And so, gradually, the farce turned to tragedy. The regime changed almost every week. Groups of drunken anarchists on machine-gun carts, headed by Nestor Makhno, rolled into town from time to time. Also attacking Odessa were bandits without any particular ideology. These dangerous gangs, called Greens, roamed the streets, making robbery and murder the norm. It was said that the bandits, in order to save time, simply chopped off their victims' fingers when they wanted a ring. So it was hazardous to go outside. Come evening the city was dead.

We lived in a five-bedroom apartment on the third floor of a big apartment house on Preobrazhensky Street, where after dark all the tenants locked themselves in and quaked in fear. One night there was horrible screaming outside. It was a gang of drunks dressed in Red Army uniforms. I don't believe they were real Red Army soldiers—when the Reds retreated they left behind a lot of supplies, which were grabbed up by bandits because it was easier to rob if you were wearing a uniform: civilians are afraid of any army.

And so these drunken bandits in uniform demanded that all the tenants come outside. Who knew what that order boded? My father felt the fear so strongly he began to get ready. Something snapped in me. I ran to the kitchen, grabbed a big kitchen knife, and, blocking my father's way, shouted, "If you go downstairs, I'll kill you!"

It was irrational, like the action of a hysterical woman. It's just that I felt instinctively that the robbers were not representatives of the authorities at all. My emotional outburst worked. Papa, as if coming out of a trance, stopped. We did not go downstairs to give ourselves up to the mercy of the drunken bandits. And that probably saved our lives, because apparently no one else came down and the bandits got tired of waiting. They made some more noise and left.

After that the tenants of our building decided that we had to defend ourselves from marauders. Dr. Sherman, elected "commissar" of the building, got several Japanese rifles, which were available on the black market then. (Probably they had been left behind by White Admiral Kolchak, who was supported by the Japanese.) The rifles were distributed to five or six men in the building, who took turns on guard at night. I was included in this self-defense unit, which made me very proud.

We would sit up, behind the gates with cast-iron designs, waiting for suspicious gangs to show up. Dr. Sherman's instructions were "If you see bandits, shoot!" He was right, the tactic always worked. The robbers would hear shots and not come any closer.

The one time I shot, it came as a big surprise how hard the rifle kicked into my right shoulder. It was so strong, it threatened to dislocate my shoulder. I didn't like that, and I turned in my rifle to our stern commissar. So I never did become a great soldier.

In the meantime, our financial position had deteriorated. Before the revolution, the cloth Papa brought from abroad was sooner or later sold to the big stores—Vikula Morozov's or Ptashnikov's. With the onset of World War One, the stores' fortunes went downhill, along with the market for fine cloth, and Papa was left with a lot of unpaid receipts and unsold fabric.

As I described earlier, Papa's bolts of cloth were stored in the cellars of our courtyard. After the revolution, when people realized there was no law and order and the plundering began, our unsold fabric was discovered and stolen by marauding sailors and soldiers with their drunken girlfriends. We couldn't do a thing about it— our building's self-defense unit wasn't meant to stop soldiers and sailors—and soon all our goods were gone.

At first, Papa, who still traveled abroad on business, managed to bring in small pieces of jewelry. There was still demand for such trinkets in postrevolutionary Odessa since paper money was worthless—each regime printed its own currency, leaving Odessa flooded with the provisional government's kerenki (named for Kerensky), the Ukrainian lopatki, and the Denikin "bells" (imprinted with the ancient, giant Moscow "Tsar Bell" displayed in the Kremlin)—and people preferred something more tangible.

But soon even this source of profit dried up. We were bankrupt and could barely make ends meet. Our main food was corn: corn soup, corn cutlets, and corn for dessert. We had mamalyga, or corn pone, every day. (Nowadays my wife sometimes forgets and tells me, "Have some mamalyga, it tastes good!" Of course, I can't stand the sight of it!)

I already had a reputation in Odessa: after all, I was a glamour boy, Auer's student! So people were always coming from various organizations and committees, asking me to play at their meetings. Mama was very unhappy about this. She wanted me to practice and not give hack performances. And, of course, she was right. She even started telling me, "Go, play soccer!" to keep me from meeting with yet another organizer of a concert.

But life was getting harder. Food disappeared from Odessa. First the animals died—dogs and horses, their corpses lying around in the streets—then people. We had to think about survival.

I gave two concerts in Odessa that were very successful. There were no other solo violinists in the city then, so my performances made a splash. And one day Stefan Katz, a former medical student at Novorossiisk University, came to see me. He was a Red boss of some kind now, representing an organization with the name Ubek-ochernaz—something to do with the Black Sea and Azov Sea Fleet.

Katz asked me to play for the sailors. I would get navy food rations in return: meat twice a day, and other good things. This was a generous and, what was more important, timely proposal. If it hadn't been for Katz, I don't know what would have happened to us.

I played that first time at a palace that, before the revolution, had belonged to the Vorontsov-Dashkov princes. Now it was filled with sailors and soldiers and their girlfriends. The sailors—the elite of the times—were well behaved at first. Then they began changing seats, then strolling around the room. The soldiers kept eating sunflower seeds with incredible virtuosity, spitting out the shells in a long wet stream from the left side of the mouth. The shells covered the marble floors in a soggy mess. (Many years later, I saw cowboys in Wyoming chew tobacco this way.) And all the time, the soldiers managed to kiss their girlfriends noisily on the cheek; all were busy flirting. Whenever the girls would tear themselves away, they'd slip on the shells.

At that first concert I played the "Internationale" on the violin. It sounded rather thin, and no one paid any attention. No one even tried to stand up. I told Katz, "It would be a lot better if there were several of us. It'll sound much more impressive, people will stand, and it won't cost you much more." The most important thing was to get additional food rations. I wanted to help my musician friends.

Katz approved my idea and let me put together a string quartet; now there were four of us playing the "Internationale" in my arrangement, with tricky counterpoint. It sounded much better. And people rose for the revolutionary anthem.

The times were so unstable, you could easily get a nervous tic. Once we were playing at the apartment of a local pharmacist, who owned a large shop that I remember well: mysterious vessels filled with yellow and green liquid stood in the shop window. While we were playing, in the middle of the slow movement of the Beethoven G Major Quartet, a powerful bolt of lightning flashed. We were stunned and stopped playing. After fifteen long seconds there came a deafening bang. It was the Bolshevik cruiser *Sinop*, in the harbor twenty kilometers away, firing on the White Army headquarters (and, as we learned later, the Bolsheviks had aimed very accurately). After a few shocked moments, we went back to our music. But you never forget moments like that!

One of my friends in Odessa was Oskar von Riesemann, a tall, solid, and ruddy blond with a small mustache that I would now describe as looking like Hitler's. A man indifferent to women, Riesemann was a Russified German from a line of Baltic barons. He had studied with Hugo Riemann, knew a lot about music, especially Russian music, and was an important critic in Moscow before the revolution.

Riesemann and I played music often in Odessa, with the baron at the piano. His stories about Russian composers—Mussorgsky, Taneyev, Catoire—were very good for me to hear. Riesemann also introduced me to the work of Max Reger, whom he adored. Under the Bolsheviks Riesemann lay low, trying not to be too noticeable. The times were dangerous for the nobility. He lived quietly in a palace that had belonged to the Vorontsov-Dashkov princes. I remember one night when I stayed late at Riesemann's. We were listening to the sound of running motors coming from afar, and the usually cheerful Riesemann was pale. It was said that the Odessa cheka, the Communist secret police, used the noise of truck motors to muffle the sound of shots and the screams of prisoners and hostages.

When White General Denikin took Odessa, Riesemann became involved in providing food for Denikin's Volunteer Army. I think it was a lucrative job. But the Whites did not last long in Odessa. In January 1920 over one hundred thousand White soldiers left Odessa on foreign ships. Riesemann left with them, on an American cruiser.

Eventually the baron moved to Switzerland, where he published several books on Russian music and, what was most important, helped Rachmaninoff write his memoirs. We met again in Switzerland, and our friendship continued until Riesemann's sudden death in 1934.

I was always trying to expand my musical horizons. There were two good orchestras in Odessa: the opera and the philharmonic. The latter's concertmaster was Naum Blinder, Isaac Stern's teacher. Blinder was a very good violinist with a real European education. He had studied in Manchester with Adolf Brodsky, to whom Tchaikovsky's violin concerto is dedicated. I remember Blinder playing Prokofiev's First Concerto. It all sounded fine and solid, but a bit heavy, perhaps; for my taste, it missed the music's bouquet and poetry.

I liked going to the philharmonic's rehearsals and listening to their presentations of new music. The conductor was Lev Steinberg:

I always remember him holding up his slipping pince-nez with his left hand as he conducted.

Once I was at a rehearsal with concertmaster Blinder absent. We learned that he was sick and not coming to the performance that night. They were rehearsing Richard Strauss's *Ein Heldenleben*, a work that I adored. It has an important violin solo. The manager of the Odessa Philharmonic (husband of the pianist Ania Dorfmann, who later taught at Juilliard) asked me to fill in for Blinder; I readily agreed. And so with just one rehearsal I played *Ein Heldenleben* in concert. The audience shouted "Bravo!" and I was very pleased.

Inspired by my first successes as a soloist, Stefan Katz, now my manager, began organizing concerts in Odessa and in nearby places like Balta, where German settlers lived. Katz's managerial activity boiled down to the following: he went off to the designated place a day or two ahead of time, found a hall (it might be a club or movie theater), and then came back for me. These were our terms: half the box office went to me, the rest to Katz, who also paid for the hall.

I was accompanied by my sister Sara. At first our box office was nothing—the tickets were cheap to begin with, twenty-five kopecks—but gradually the Odessa audiences began to attend our recitals regularly and the money started to flow in.

Katz suggested we go to Kharkov, at that time an important cultural center. They had a Young Philharmonic whose director was Staroselsky, son of the candy manufacturer. Kharkov had a marvelous audience, lots of young people who loved music. We stayed at Staroselsky's, and at night our room would be filled with a delicious, unforgettable aroma—because they made candy right at the apartment!

This idyllic atmosphere was disrupted one night by sobs: it was Stefan Katz crying. It turned out he was bankrupt, unable to cover his expenses. In the morning Staroselsky chided me. "Why are you exploiting your impresario?" I tried to explain that I wasn't exploiting him, just taking my 50 percent, as our contract stated. The story ended with Katz being given travel money and returning to Odessa. The Young Philharmonic arranged for me to give an additional twelve concerts in Kharkov, in the public library.

It was in Kharkov that I first heard of the pianist Vladimir Horowitz. His uncle, Alexander Ioakhimovich Horowitz, had been a student of Scriabin's and later of Taneyev's and had settled in Kharkov to become a major musical figure there: I believe he was director of the local music school and wrote reviews of concerts for the Kharkov newspaper. They said that Vladimir Horowitz was so temperamental that he "broke pianos" when he played! That description appealed to me, and I decided we had to meet, but the occasion would not present itself for a while.

After my performances in Kharkov a man named Zinoviev became my new impresario. He organized a touring group that included myself, the pianist Simon Barere, the bass Platon Tsesevich, and the soprano Olga Karasulova. (I already knew Karasulova. In 1916, at Auer's request, I had played in Petersburg at a benefit for the Red Cross. The concert was in the gorgeous white-columned hall of the Assembly of the Nobility, in the presence of the tsar's daughters. The concert started late, after ten in the evening, and I was used to going to bed at eight. So after performing I fell asleep peacefully on the comfortable bosom of Olga Karasulova, who was also appearing in the concert.)

Our group was given two sleeping cars and we traveled in them around the Ukraine. The others members of our troupe not only made money performing but also sold hard-to-get salt, or tried to trade it for as-hard-to-get potatoes. I didn't get into the salt trade, which had a detrimental effect on both my financial and food situations.

After one concert in Kiev, at which Simon Barere accompanied me, I was approached by the chief of the local *politprosvet* (which oversaw political and cultural propaganda among the Soviet populace). His name was Vilensky and he bore an incredible resemblance to the French artist Delacroix. Apparently I had made a good impression on the audience: Vilensky said that he would like me to return to Kiev for two concerts.

I admit that I thought it was the usual blah-blah flattery. But soon I received a letter from Vilensky giving exact dates for both concerts and offering a lot of money. My accompanist was to be the Kiev pianist Sergei Tarnowsky.

I had heard a lot of good things about Tarnowsky: he was a marvelous musician and had graduated from Petersburg Conservatory with the highest award, the Rubinstein Prize. The award itself was a grand piano, which I'd seen at Tarnowsky's house, made of glorious mahogany with a special plaque lettered in gold (or gold plate). I also knew that Tarnowsky taught at Kiev Conservatory. But naturally, I did not suspect that at one time among Tarnowsky's students there had been a young pianist named Vladimir Horowitz.

4. "Children of the Soviet Revolution": With Horowitz in Russia

In the winter of 1921 I gave two recitals in Kiev with Sergei Tarnowsky as my pianist. After the first concert, an unexpected guest came backstage: seventeen-year-old Vladimir Horowitz. I immediately called Horowitz by his nickname, "Volodya." His older sister Regina was with him, and she invited Tarnowsky and me to their house. "Come have tea with us," she said. So I went.

Other musicians were gathered at the Horowitz house. Horowitz's current professor, Felix Mikhailovich Blumenfeld, the famous composer and pianist from Petersburg who had moved to Kiev, was there. So was Heinrich Neuhaus, a handsome blond man with an intriguing face, a marvelous pianist (his Chopin was fantastic), and a relative of Arthur Rubinstein's.

We sat around the table and had tea. Afterward, Tarnowsky,

who was older than the rest of us, engaged in conversation with Blumenfeld, Neuhaus, and Horowitz's parents, while the young people moved to Regina's room.

Regina was very beautiful, but I didn't care about things like that yet. (An outstanding pianist, Regina later married Yevsey Liberman, who became a leading Soviet economist, one of Khrushchev's advisers. It was Liberman who developed a project of economic reform for Khrushchev that remained unimplemented until Mikhail Gorbachev, who is trying to introduce it now as *perestroika*.)

A student of Professor Pukhalsky's, Regina Horowitz was at that time probably a more advanced pianist than Volodya, but she played the standard repertoire, like Chopin's ballades and mazurkas. When Volodya sat down at the piano, he played something totally unusual: his own version of the sword-forging scene from Wagner's *Siegfried*, or improvisations on themes from *Tristan und Isolde*, or enormous chunks from Rimsky-Korsakov's opera *Coq d'Or*. Pianists never performed things like this in concerts! I was stunned, astonished. It was a musical hurricane.

I played too. There was an instant chemical reaction between Volodya and me. We forgot that I had to return to the hotel, and before long Regina asked if I could stay to dinner. Of course I could!

After dinner, I slept over, even though the Horowitz apartment wasn't that spacious. Once upon a time they had had a large apartment, but after the revolution the family had to move to much smaller quarters on Bolshaya Zhitomirskaya Street.

After my second recital in Kiev it was decided that I would live with the Horowitzes. You could say I came to tea and stayed three years.

Horowitz's father, an electrical engineer, often traveled to Germany on business. Horowitz's mother was a good musician who helped develop her son's talent. The revolution had scared her so much that she practically never left the apartment. Once Volodya and I persuaded her to go to the movies with us, to see the famous actor Ivan Mozhukhin. That expedition turned into an extraordinary event.

Mrs. Horowitz started her preparations first thing in the morning. The Polish maid helped her dress. Volodya and I also helped by tightening her corsets. This was not an easy task. We each took a lace and pulled, leaning against her back. She poured several bottles of L'Origan by Coty all over herself, put on a black silk suit (this was June!) of a style fashionable in 1900, applied liberal makeup in yellow and green shades, and topped it all off with an unbelievable purple hat with a veil.

We came out on Bolshaya Zhitomirskaya. The sun was boiling hot. Everyone stared at us. We decided to hail the trolley between stops, because we would not have made it to the next stop. The trolley came to a screeching halt at the sight of Mrs. Horowitz, and with incredible effort we pushed her aboard.

The laborers seated inside stared at her in amazement. But Russian workers are a modest and polite lot. They immediately offered Mrs. Horowitz a seat. She looked them up and down through her lorgnette, resting her gaze on dirty shoes, and said loud enough for all to hear, "And *this* is what rules us now?"

The film with the famous actor had little effect on Mrs. Horowitz. She went home, never to go out again. And really, what can be better than your own room, when you're used to it? We were a bit worried that one of the trolley passengers would report Mrs. Horowitz's counterrevolutionary comment, but fortunately no one did.

At first Volodya and I gave a joint recital in Kiev and then began traveling around the Ukraine, gradually enlarging the geographical scope of our appearances. We went to Poltava, Gomel, Kharkov, Ekaterinodar, Simferopol, and Sevastopol. We were in Taganrog, Novorossiisk, and Nakhichevan. We appeared in the Caucasus, in Batumi, Tiflis, and Baku. There were interesting trips to Saratov and the Tatar Republic.

We liked performing. Our impressions of the trips were almost uniformly pleasant. There were not many touring musicians at the time, and the audiences were impressed that I was a student of the great Auer (Blumenfeld, Horowitz's teacher, was less famous).

The public was starved for music. Even if we were late, they waited patiently. I remember in Rostov we were very late, and as we headed for the stage the audience, instead of booing us, applauded wildly. (Once, long afterward, I was late for a recital in Murcia, Spain. When I showed up, the audience was furious: they shouted and whistled. In Spain whistling is not at all a sign of delight, as it is in America. I started playing at midnight and ended at three in the morning. I don't think anyone left. They even applauded in farewell.)

Horowitz and I played violin sonatas by Franck, Grieg, and Saint-Saëns. Saint-Saëns's D Minor Sonata is almost never included in programs nowadays, but it is a striking and lively work. We did not put Beethoven in our programs, considering his work not very interesting music, and at that time no one at all played Brahms in Russia.

We appeared onstage in tussore silk shirts with jabots, black slacks, and patent leather shoes. In Kiev we found a tailor, Mr. Cooper, who still had supplies of good fabric. He made clothes for us and we looked good. Of course, it was provincial chic. You couldn't compare our Mr. Cooper with London tailors. But in the Russia of those years we stood out.

We invented all kinds of flashy tricks. I remember our performance in Ekaterinoslav. The local English Club gave summer concerts. We played outdoors. The weather in Ekaterinoslav is changeable: there are frequent storms, and gale-force winds can rise quickly.

So Volodya and I came up with this idea. We usually played without sheet music, but here we would set up music stands. A wind would come and scatter the pages. And we would go on playing as if nothing were wrong! And the whole scenario succeeded, with the audience raving afterward.

In our defense I can say that even great musicians stoop to using tricks that impress audiences. The classic example is Paganini, who composed the ''Moses Fantasy'' (on a theme from Rossini's opera) especially to be played on one string. He began playing on a violin with all its strings, and then with a fingernail of his left hand (unnoticed by the audience) he would break one string after another. Strings were made of catgut then and broke easily. Thus Paganini ended triumphantly, playing his composition on a single string! Our little invention was certainly not in Paganini's class, but Volodya and I got what we wanted—the audience's awe.

We became particularly popular when the people's commissar of education (in effect, the country's culture tsar), Anatoly Lunacharsky, wrote a laudatory article about us in the government newspaper *Izvestia*. It was titled "Children of the Soviet Revolution," though of course Volodya and I were not brought up by the Soviet revolution at all. But the article had a major impact. It was reprinted by local newspapers all over the country. We were a sensation.

As a result, the *politprosvety* literally drowned us in invitations to perform. The terms were very good: we did not pay for hiring the hall, or organizing the concerts, or the advertising. The *politprosvety* took care of bringing in the audiences, and we got all the receipts.

We traveled all over Russia without a care. Our joint recitals went like this: first I played, then Horowitz, then we played a sonata together. So I can brag now about having had Horowitz as an accompanist. But we finally decided that we would earn more if we appeared separately, since Lunacharsky's ringing endorsement guaranteed our audiences.

There was one joint concert I often recall. It took place in Nakhichevan, a small town in the south of Russia. Why did we go there? We had all the time in the world, we weren't in a rush to go anywhere else. In general, it was useless to hurry in those days, even if you wanted to. It took eleven days by train to get from Kiev to Rostov, a distance of no more than a thousand kilometers! The train stopped almost every half hour: no fuel, or there was trouble on the tracks, or congestion . . .

We were invited to Nakhichevan by the musician Arseny Avraamov, a colorful figure. A tall blond, he dressed extravagantly: in a Roman toga. But his ideas were even more extravagant. Avraamov felt that if you gave the people the necessary education, proletarian science and culture would blossom in the shortest time, and soon you would have tens of thousands of proletarian Einsteins and hundreds of thousands of proletarian Shakespeares.

In order to reach that radiant goal as soon as possible, Avraamov gave lectures to workers. He invited us to illustrate his lecture on Bach. "Why Bach?" we asked. "The people need the loftiest and the best," replied the Communist idealist.

The lecture was for the workers of a cartridge factory. Several thousand people were crowded into a large barracks. It was stuffy and smelly. You could see quite a few street urchins in the audience. Every Russian city was filled with them then, the flotsam of World War One and the civil war.

The urchins sold cigarettes and newspapers in the streets, shined shoes, begged and stole. They feared no one and nothing. I still can't understand how Avraamov lured them to the lecture. The one explanation I can imagine is that the lecture was free and the kids expected to be amused by something funny. And in the meantime they could help themselves to the crowds.

For a start, Avraamov talked for approximately forty-five minutes about the fugue in Bach's oeuvre. Strangely enough, the urchins listened rather patiently, probably thinking that the real entertainment was still to come. You can be patient while waiting for the fun. Avraamov even got a hand when he finished.

It was my turn, and I played Bach's Chaconne for solo violin. As soon as I began, I could sense that something bad was going on in the audience. And sure enough, before I got through the first twelve bars, the kids began shouting, "Into the booth!" That was a popular slang putdown in those days, something like "Get off the stage."

If it hadn't been for the street urchins, the workers might have sat through the concert quietly. But they picked up the cry, "Into the booth!"

I stopped playing and Avraamov came out. "Comrades, these are famous artists performing for you, musicians Commissar Lunacharsky has called 'children of the Soviet revolution.' They are playing the best music. Let's listen to them attentively."

The noise died down. There was even scattered applause. I started the Chaconne again. But after eight bars I heard "Into the booth!" I stopped again. And again Avraamov appealed to the crowd. "Comrades! Now workers have the opportunity to hear music that used to be available only to the rich bourgeoisie. But if there are insensible, unconscious elements among you who do not wish to take advantage of this opportunity, let them leave!''

The audience was thrilled and applauded. But no one left. As soon as I started the Chaconne, I again heard the familiar ''Into the booth!''

Avraamov screamed at the crowd in despair. ''Why don't you leave? Why are you disturbing those who want to listen to the great Bach?''

The unanimous roaring reply was, ''We can't leave, the doors are locked!''

Well, they unlocked the doors and the crowd poured out of the barracks. The urchins, appropriately, were first out of there. Out of the thousands of workers, about fifty were left, and they looked rather pathetic in that huge, empty place. It was humiliating. I thought sadly, Ah, I should have played something fast instead!

Horowitz played the Bach-Busoni C Major Toccata with some success, because it was a loud piece. Avraamov was horrified by the whole evening: the proletariat did not understand Bach! I think that in those days even the bourgeoisie did not appreciate Bach very much. Even the ''decent'' public preferred Sarasate. *That* was impressive music; Bach didn't have a chance.

Horowitz's father, who worked in a state organization, often went to Moscow on business. One time he came back with the news that he had arranged a concert for us with the famous orchestra Persimfans.

This interesting group is worth discussing. Their name was an acronym for First Symphonic Ensemble. They were the first full-sized symphony orchestra without a conductor. The group was founded by Lev Zeitlin, a professor at the Moscow Conservatory and a marvelous violinist (and another student of Auer's).

In the first years after the revolution Zeitlin played in the Lenin Quartet, whose cellist was our future buddy Gregor Piatigorsky. Later Zeitlin gathered the best musicians in Moscow and came up with this promising idea: Since we were living under new social conditions, in the age of collectivism, there was no need for an orchestra to be subordinate to a dictator conductor. Let's make music collectively, decide everything by consensus, and in this way seek new paths in art.

Actually, I think that Zeitlin (who had been concertmaster for many years in Serge Koussevitzky's Moscow orchestra) realized that good musicians can easily manage without a conductor and decided that he himself would be the music director.

And so it was. At rehearsals of Persimfans, Zeitlin, who became concertmaster, gave instructions to the other members: he set the tempo and showed them phrasing. But in fact, there were also animated discussions and give-and-takes that would have been impossible under a conductor.

The Persimfans members rehearsed a lot—violinists separately, cellists separately, and so on. Then they all got together and the drilling continued. During the concert, the musicians formed a semicircle, the better to see one another, and the violin section sat with its back to the audience. Zeitlin gave the cues with facial expressions, not with his hand, so the audience was unaware of them. Persimfans was constantly displaying polished performances, splendid ensemble playing, and memorable orchestral solos.

I'll never forget the golden sound of Persimfans's first trumpet, Mikhail Tabakov. He was small and plump, and when he played he puffed up and turned red. But his horn's song was radiant, glowing, and at the same time tender. The other musicians of Persimfans were comparable masters.

I remember Beethoven's Ninth in their rendition. A few days later, Oskar Fried, an excellent German conductor on tour in Moscow, repeated the symphony with the same players. And it wasn't any better with a conductor!

At first audiences came to hear Persimfans as a novelty, then the public got used to them, and for many years the ensemble was incredibly popular, giving thousands of concerts. Persimfans fell apart only in the early thirties, when Horowitz and I were already settling in the West. Apparently, music lovers still needed a wizard at the podium, creating something out of nothing, a symbol of sorts. Dictators big and small were springing up all over Europe. Collectivism was clearly out of fashion in the arts as well as in politics.

I think that the obligatory conductor before an orchestra is merely a tribute paid to a relatively recent tradition. In order to create music in performance, you must have physical contact with it, as a performer has with his instrument. A conductor is deprived of such physical contact, and it shows.

I'll try a risqué parallel. When a handsome man and a beautiful woman go to bed to make love, they don't need a prompter to tell them what to do. Unfortunately, the conductor too often plays the role of that sort of prompter. Good orchestra musicians don't need detailed supervision, and bad musicians won't play well no matter who conducts.

Nowadays, more and more instrumentalists are taking up conducting. When you ask such a fresh-hatched conductor why he switched professions, you are likely to hear, "Oh, the orchestral repertoire is so much more profound and interesting." What nonsense! What could be more profound than a Bach sonata for solo violin or a Schubert string quartet?

I often think of Persimfans. It was a brilliant experiment, and it's too bad it wasn't followed up. Of course, an orchestra without a conductor has to rehearse more, so that the musicians get used to carrying on a "dialogue" when they play, the way chamber musicians do. And, naturally, there should be a leader to assume the role of a general music director.

Perhaps this method of working would be uneconomical in our times. But in principle it is possible, and it is Persimfans's claim to fame that it showed it could be done.

When Volodya Horowitz and I reached Moscow, we first stayed in a hotel, then moved into a room his father rented. People were living in very cramped conditions then. It sometimes happened that there were five or six people spending the night in that one room. Among the guests, I remember Heinrich Neuhaus with his wife,

Zinaida, a dusky beauty. Later, she left Neuhaus and married the poet Boris Pasternak.

This was the program for our performance with Persimfans: I played the Glazunov concerto, Volodya Rachmaninoff's Third. We rehearsed twice, which was enough. I found it easier to play the Glazunov with Persimfans than I had under the composer's baton in Odessa.

In the audience that evening were Otto Klemperer and Glazunov himself. We were a big success. Glazunov came out to take a bow and asked me, "Do you play anything from *Raymonda*?" He wanted me to play something of his for an encore. I reminded him that I played his "Meditation," a beautiful piece, in which he had accompanied me once.

They rolled a piano out onstage. Glazunov asked me, "What key is it in?" I couldn't believe my ears: the composer couldn't remember the key of his own work! I croaked out "D major," realizing that Glazunov was completely drunk!

He could barely stand up. He sat down heavily and we started to play and . . . stopped. In his condition, he couldn't go on. Glazunov left the stage in embarrassment. But the audience still continued raving over the old composer. He was that esteemed.

Horowitz and I were in Moscow when Lenin introduced NEP, the New Economic Policy. I was asked to play at a rally at which Lenin would speak. It was an important speech: Lenin was to explain to his confused comrades in arms just what NEP was about.

Forced to retreat by the general ruin and hunger, Lenin decided to permit private enterprise again. This overjoyed enterprising Russians, but many bureaucrats were in a panic. This was a risky experiment for Lenin too. In his speech, he asked, "Will we be able to create a mode of capitalism subordinate to the state?" (Mikhail Gorbachev is posing essentially the same question now.)

I remember another maxim pronounced by Lenin from the rostrum: "We made the revolution not for the Party but for the people." When he spoke, he jerked his head, raising his famous little beard. He looked like an agitated bird. His speech wasn't too electrifying. After his appeal, as he listened to the performances, Lenin looked tired. He left soon after. It was one of his last public appearances.

As soon as NEP began, food miraculously appeared in abundance in Moscow. Horowitz and I had money, so we could go to the famous café on Stoleshnikov Alley, where the capital's elite gathered. We had fantastically delicious pastries and marvelous whipped cream. We were surrounded by beautiful ladies and by rich gentlemen in fabulous furs. Life was wonderful.

Horowitz and I were invited to the best homes in Moscow. We met the artist Leonid Pasternak and his son Boris, the young poet. I didn't like the paintings of Pasternak *père* very much. I felt I could paint like that, though I was probably wrong. The Moscow superstars, like Konstantin Stanislavsky, a founder of the Moscow Art Theater, frequented the Pasternak house.

Pasternak invited us to the less glamorous parties—we were on the B list, so to speak. But those were interesting enough. Imagine the exotically handsome young Boris Pasternak, inspired, otherworldly, eyes glowing, playing his own musical compositions! At the time Boris had not yet decided whether he would be a composer or a poet, and he composed music that was heavily influenced by Scriabin.

The mighty director of the Bolshoi Theater, Elena Malinovskaya, who had an entire floor of a luxurious town house, invited us for musical soirées. (The Adelgeim brothers, famous actors in the Maly Theater, lived on another floor in the same house.) Malinovskaya's lover, the cellist Viktor Kubatsky, was fifteen years her junior. Though he might have been considered handsome in the golden-haired Scandinavian manner, to me his face was unpleasant (now I would say that he looked like a Nazi officer).

Kubatsky was a cellist in the famous Stradivarius Quartet. The other members were the violinists Karpilovsky and Pakelman, and the violist Bakaleinikoff. All played on Stradivariuses from the state collection, run by Kubatsky, who had great power.

Horowitz and I often performed at rallies where the Stradivarius Quartet also appeared. The members were all good musicians, though perhaps they did not have extraordinary technical abilities. The quartet's first violinist, Daniil Karpilovsky, was, like me, an

Auer student. He was one of those who came to class but almost never got to play. Auer usually did not pay attention to them. He didn't even know their names! But he did recognize Karpilovsky— because he was such a longtime nonplayer.

The most talented member of the quartet was the violist, Vladimir Bakaleinikoff. He had a beautiful big sound. Later he emigrated to the U.S.A. He was Fritz Reiner's assistant at the Chicago Symphony and later worked with the Pittsburgh Orchestra. Bakaleinikoff taught young Lorin Maazel, who had started out as a violinist.

After living many years in America, Vladimir, a real Muscovite by nature, still spoke English with a thick Russian accent: "Doan't do dat." I suspect that he kept up the accent on purpose, because Americans love that sort of thing.

Vladimir's younger brother, Konstantin, also went to America. He settled in Hollywood, where he became an important composer of scores for such films as *Notorious* and *Mourning Becomes Electra*.

There were countless rallies during those years in Moscow. Political leaders gave speeches, and various resolutions and proclamations were approved. But people like entertainment more than politics, even in revolutionary Moscow. So the rally organizers always announced an "artistic part": performances by popular instrumentalists, singers, and dancers.

Two great singers often appeared with us at rallies: the soprano Antonina Nezhdanova and the tenor Leonid Sobinov. How they sang! Unbelievable! Nezhdanova's performance of Elsa's aria from *Lohengrin* was a marvel. When Sobinov did Tchaikovsky's song "In the Midst of the Ball," he seemed to be talking to you, not performing. And his rendition of Lensky's aria from *Eugene Onegin*, heartbreaking! Sobinov as Lensky really asked with regret and sorrow, "Where have you gone, the golden days of my spring?" Other tenors, such as Ivan Kozlovsky, popular in the Soviet Union, merely shouted those words without any meaning.

Sobinov had a mark on his cheek like a Prussian dueling scar. And I think he was into cocaine. Sobinov was very anti-Soviet. And once, I remember, he made a rather daring speech at the Bolshoi Theater calling for artistic freedom. We expected him to be arrested.

But Sobinov was too popular and the authorities left him alone. The times were comparatively vegetarian then.

Among the other stars who appeared with us for audiences of soldiers and sailors was the ballerina Ekaterina Geltzer. She did Fokine's famous number *The Dying Swan*, and I played the violin. Geltzer was terribly nervous because she was pushing fifty by then, a considerable age for a dancer. The part of the stage on which she "died" was always damp with sweat and melted pieces of makeup.

One of our most important appearances in Moscow was a concert in 1923, where Horowitz and I presented the Russian premieres of Karol Szymanowski's Violin Concerto no. 1 and Sergei Prokofiev's Violin Concerto no. 1. In both concertos Horowitz played piano reductions of the orchestral score. (I feel that if you have a great pianist like Horowitz playing with you, you don't need an orchestra!)

Our performance of the Prokofiev took place just a few days after its world premiere in Paris. All the artistic elite of Moscow came to our concert, which was under the auspices of Mezhdunarodnaya Kniga, an international clearinghouse. Among the prominent guests was the composer Nikolai Miaskovsky, who, as I learned later, described the event in detail in his letters to Prokofiev, living in Paris then. Miaskovsky told his fellow composer that as a result of the Moscow premiere Prokofiev's popularity was "almost indecent. You've eclipsed even the Moscow idols, Rachmaninoff and Medtner!"

And in fact, Prokofiev's First is one of the best violin concertos of modern times. It is a work of genius and perhaps Prokofiev's best work. I sometimes think that it is a self-portrait. In freshness and originality it can be compared with Mozart's concertos.

Subsequently I played the Prokofiev concerto many times and even made two recordings of it, one with Vladimir Golschmann and another with Carlo-Maria Giulini. Once, during a performance of the concerto in New York, I suddenly dropped the bow in the second movement (I never hold the bow too tightly). I managed to catch it in midair and continued playing. The orchestra thought it was a trick! Alas, you can't learn to do something like that, even if you practice for fifty years. But there are scary episodes in the life of every concertizing violinist.

Prokofiev's Second Violin Concerto is also an excellent work, with an original second movement. But it is more craftsmanship than inspiration. I've recorded it, too. I think that the young Prokofiev was a genius, but that he lost some of it in his later years. Some say that Prokofiev's talent faded because he was uprooted by his emigration. But when he went back to the Soviet Union in the thirties, he did not experience a corresponding lift. Apparently the problem with roots is more complicated than that.

I played many violin pieces by Karol Szymanowski, including his "Myths" and Notturno et Tarantelle. When I met him, I really liked him, a talented and serious musician, very elegant, a typically Polish gentleman.

At the Moscow premiere of the Szymanowski concerto, Horowitz was in his element. In the score the piccolo has complicated virtuoso passages. Horowitz played them in full with incredible brilliance! You could barely hear me, but it's quite possible nobody particularly cared.

Horowitz the accompanist played, as one would expect, with extraordinary brio, but alas sometimes too loud. Of course, you could say the same about Arthur Rubinstein: in sonatas and piano trios he drowned out everyone, including Jascha Heifetz. And even Rachmaninoff in his recordings with Fritz Kreisler was too loud.

I feel that when two stars get together for ensemble playing, they should not argue over who will dominate but instead should see what the composer has written. Beethoven, for instance, clearly indicates that his sonatas are for piano and obbligato violin *("per il Pianoforte ed uno Violino obbligato")* and not the other way around. Only the *Kreutzer* is a real virtuoso work for violin. Consequently, in the Beethoven sonatas the main role rightly belongs to the pianist.

It's my belief that in principle the piano does not go well with the violin. After all, the piano is a percussive instrument, so to speak. So sometimes even the best compositions for violin and piano sound somewhat unnatural. Say, the famous Franck sonata; in the second movement the piano has so many notes that it almost kills the violin. And if the pianist tries to play softer here, the necessary energy is lost. The same thing happens with the violin sonatas of Brahms. It is only in their slow movements that you can say they are written for the violin rather than for the piano.

The intrusion of the piano in chamber music also can create problems. It's enough to compare two quintets by Schubert—the one with two cellos (C Major) and the *Trout* quintet with piano. The string quintet sings divinely and the pizzicato sounds like an invocation. In the piano quintet you keep hearing a percussive, alien element—the piano.

That is why the pianist accompanist, or rather, the partner, plays such an important role in the artistic life of a solo violinist. In that regard I was lucky to meet first Arthur Balsam and then George Pludermacher, both excellent, refined musicians with whom I performed for many years and also made recordings. They and my other accompanists were also interesting and pleasant people. This is very important for artistic collaboration, especially when you are touring.

I had to make adjustments to Horowitz the accompanist. He couldn't stand being in the shadow! On our tours around Russia we often played Sarasate's "Fantasy on Themes from the Opera *Carmen*." Horowitz complained that Sarasate, as a violinist, wrote a virtuoso violin part and gave the pianist a modest role. Volodya could not accept this, of course, and began improvising his own accompaniment. These improvisations gradually coalesced into his own "Carmen Fantasy," which he later recorded, I believe, three times, each one a different version.

5. Our Adventures
in Petersburg
and Moscow

The culmination of my touring with Horowitz through Russia was our appearances in Petersburg in 1923. They were enormously successful. We came at the right time: the civil war was over, the New Economic Policy was at its height, and the Petersburg public was thirsting for music. Many established musicians had left Russia, and the foreigners touring could be counted on one hand.

Besides which, any public loves discovering "new talent." So when Horowitz and I descended upon the Petersburg audiences, they went wild. We could appear as often as we liked and whenever we liked—we were always sold out. We could play the most serious music—from baroque to contemporary composers like Medtner, Prokofiev, and Szymanowski—and it had no negative effect on the box office. We were greeted and treated as rock stars are today.

Crowds of young listeners thronged to every concert, bringing—
in winter!—enormous bouquets of flowers. After the concerts, students tried to get into our dressing room, to ask a question or get
an autograph. Leading Petersburg musicians—the conductor Emil
Cooper, the remarkable Wagnerian singer Ivan Ershov, the respected musicologist Alexander Ossovsky—came to our room.

The two most influential Russian music critics of the time, Boris
Asafiev (who wrote under the pseudonym Igor Glebov) and Vya-
cheslav Karatygin, attended every performance. Neither was at all
flamboyant—they acted modestly and spoke softly (Karatygin tug-
ging at his unkempt beard), but their every word was given enormous attention and respect.

Both Asafiev and Karatygin wrote with great enthusiasm about
our recitals. Stylistically the more temperamental, Asafiev exclaimed, "Horowitz and Milstein heard the tread of our military
units! Their art is replete with invincible energy and invincible conviction!"

Our performances in Petersburg were organized in this way: first
Horowitz gave solo recitals, then I did my solo programs, then we
appeared together—with sonatas and the new concertos of Prokofiev
and Szymanowski. And finally, as announced, for a spectacular
coda the symphonic concert with Glazunov conducting and our
solos.

Recently I reread with great curiosity Karatygin's feature article
about our winter cycle in Petersburg. He liked the way we played
the Franck sonata, but he found our renditions of the Beethoven
sonatas "much more pallid." Of course, he didn't hold the highest
opinion of the works themselves: modernist Karatygin found them
"too modest, too naive."

However, Karatygin was "enormously impressed" by my evening at the Circle of Friends of Chamber Music. That was understandable: I played Bach, Handel, Corelli, and Tartini. Back then
that kind of music was rarely performed, and Karatygin, a bit of a
snob, always enjoyed trying something new.

Besides, he liked the atmosphere of the small hall of the Circle
of Friends of Chamber Music, the former salon of the Schroeder
piano company on the corner of Nevsky Prospect and Sadovaya

Street. The audiences were usually made up of connoisseurs. Sitting in a corner, wearing a coat and muffled in a scarf, Karatygin was in his element there.

Karatygin was even more approving of our Petersburg premiere of Prokofiev's and Szymanowski's violin concertos. And why not! After all, he was practically the first to discover young Prokofiev (for which the composer remained eternally grateful).

Many musicians at that time (including Glazunov) were fiercely opposed to Prokofiev. That's why it is interesting to cite a review of the Petersburg premiere by Karatygin, this early Prokofiev enthusiast.

"Prokofiev is true to himself. His grotesque style, full of broken lines and sharp corners, is so imbued with throbbing vitality, so rich in capricious color play, so juicy in outline, that it is impossible to listen to his music indifferently. You can either be terribly outraged, which many are even now, or listen with bated breath, plunging into the world of fantastic sound images which Prokofiev pours out of his Horn of Plenty. Particularly delightful is the Scherzo, a magical kaleidoscope of unusual combinations, blinding fireworks of melodies and harmonies, one more paradoxical than the last, which, however, for all their strangeness, are crafted with unusual sharpness and conviction."

The Petersburg music critics of the twenties were philosophers. They could never write an indifferent review of a concert. If they liked what they heard, they published a poem, not a dry, "balanced" account.

Karatygin was also delighted by the Szymanowski works Volodya and I played that evening: the violin concerto, the "Myths," Notturno et Tarantelle. I will immodestly quote Karatygin's conclusion: "The perfection of the presentation of this most difficult program by Horowitz and Milstein is beyond praise."

But I think the most memorable of our cycle of performances in the winter of 1923 in Petersburg was the symphonic evening in the Philharmonic Hall.

Our impresario then, Pavel Kogan, had arranged for Glazunov to conduct. Conducting was a favorite pastime of the venerable composer. Rather indifferent to praise for his works, he could get very excited when anyone mentioned his success as a conductor. So it was not hard for Kogan to persuade Glazunov to appear with us. This was the program: first Glazunov's *Solemn Overture*, then his violin concerto, with me; in the second half, Horowitz played the E-flat Major Liszt concerto and Rachmaninoff's Third. Glazunov conducted the whole program.

The orchestra was first-rate. The hall was a dream: the former auditorium of the Assembly of the Nobility, with its imposing white columns. It was there that Franz Liszt and Anton Rubinstein had startled the Petersburg ladies, and Berlioz and Wagner had conducted their works.

So it was a hall with history. We were honored to perform there, but even the likes of Rachmaninoff and Chaliapin had been nervous when appearing on the stage of the Assembly of the Nobility, and we were no exception.

The tickets were sold out instantly. Karatygin later wrote that the hall was crowded as it only was for superstars—Arthur Nikisch, Hofmann, Busoni. He noted, however, that we did not have full rapport with the conductor. It could not have been otherwise. Glazunov conducted, as usual, very phlegmatically, not taking our temperaments into account. I tried to follow him, but Horowitz didn't have the patience. He kept rushing ahead.

Our success was enormous nevertheless. For my encore I played Glazunov's "Meditation"; the composer accompanied me on piano. Asafiev wrote, "An unusual, unforgettable concert, which will long remain in the memory of those who were fortunate enough to attend."

After our performance, Asafiev presented Horowitz and me with two of his books. I got his small work on Dante, with this inscription: "To the outstanding talent Nathan Milstein from the author, who has come to love him sincerely."

The jacket depicted Dante's characteristic aquiline profile. Almost ten years later, when I was appearing in Rome, there was a banquet arranged after the performance. I heard my manager shouting to someone, "Francesco! Come here, I want you to meet Signore Milstein!" I looked and I saw Dante coming toward me. The same clear profile and haughty gaze. And then the man introduced himself: "Francesco Alighieri; nice to meet you." What powerful genes!

I remember the Petersburg concert with Glazunov also because after our performance the old composer introduced me to a young boy backstage whom I would now describe as a Russian version of Rudolf Serkin. He was serious, his thin lips compressed, and wore large old-fashioned glasses on a long, thin nose, and a tuft of hair at the back of his head. Slowly, as always, Glazunov almost whispered, "I'd like you to meet a very talented pianist, Mitya Shostakovich." He introduced the seventeen-year-old Dmitri Shostakovich as a pianist and not as a composer! Of course, this was still almost three years before the premiere of his First Symphony, which made Shostakovich famous the world over.

After the concert we invited Glazunov to dine with us at the Evropeiskaya Hotel, where we were staying. The best place in town, it was right across from the Philharmonic, so all heavyset Glazunov had to do was make his way across the street.

The Evropeiskaya was a luxurious "old-regime" establishment. It even had a rooftop restaurant, where an excellent violinist played Sibelius's best work, as far as I'm concerned: the "Valse Triste." (Much later I would learn that my friend Balanchine had set one of his earliest ballets to that music.)

The customers in the restaurant were wealthy and extremely pompous. They were the NEP (New Economic Policy) men, the nouveaux riches of the times. Disrespectful Horowitz once tried a culinary experiment of sorts on them. There were jars of mustard on the tables. Horowitz, who always carried Vaseline with him, quickly and cleverly smeared it into the mustard jars.

The restaurant was empty at the time. Gradually it filled up with customers, who began putting "Horowitz recipe" mustard on their food. We watched the NEPmen tensely. It was terribly interesting: what would happen? Alas, nothing while we were there. Perhaps the results were felt later, when they got home?

Another of young Horowitz's gastronomic experiments did not end as happily. This was in Kiev. We were taking a walk in Sviatoshino, a resort area outside town, when Volodya suddenly decided that he was a great authority on wild mushrooms. He picked an enormous bunch and when we got back insisted they be cooked for lunch. We all got sick.

At our Evropeiskaya dinner for Glazunov, we were joined by Pavel Kogan and were served in our room. It was a large suite with three rooms, soft armchairs, and heavy velvet drapes on the windows and doors.

At first Glazunov just sat there embarrassed. Then a comical incident occurred. Glazunov needed to use the bathroom and went off to look for it without a word. Somehow he got lost, managing to end up in the corridor, where he unwittingly opened a private door.

We heard a woman scream. Glazunov had broken into the room of our neighbor, a blond Norwegian diva of incredible beauty, who had come to Petersburg like us, as a guest star. The gorgeous singer was only partially clad! Totally embarrassed, Glazunov quietly made his way back to our room.

That evening Glazunov at first spoke cautiously, but after a few glasses of wine he grew more animated. He was pleased with the concert (also, I'm sure, by the fact that he got all the receipts; Volodya and I had not charged for our appearance). In turn, I praised his violin concerto—sincerely, for I liked it very much. I liked other works of his too—his symphonies, especially the Fifth, the ballet *Raymonda*, also his quartets (though I thought Borodin's were better).

And I truly liked Glazunov the man. He spoke shyly about his music, saying very little, but that evening he talked a lot about Tchaikovsky, who had been a friend of his.

Glazunov reminded us that thirty years ago in the same hall where we had just played, Tchaikovsky himself had conducted the premiere of his Sixth Symphony, the *Pathétique*. Its tragic finale made such an impression on the audience that when Tchaikovsky lowered his baton, no one applauded. There was complete silence, except for an occasional sob.

Many who were present on that memorable evening, like Glazunov, felt a strange premonition. Tchaikovsky stood with his back to the audience, head down, as if in a trance. Finally he awakened and began thanking the orchestra. It was only then that the audience exploded with ovations. A few days later, Tchaikovsky was dead.

When he finished his story, Glazunov plunged into reflection. We were silent too. All the wine was gone. It was getting light when Glazunov left.

In memory of our joint concert I have a photograph of myself with Glazunov, in which I am holding a book. I don't remember what the book was. It must have been something the photographer handed me to make me look more respectable.

Like Petersburg, but in quite a different way, Moscow in the 1920s was an exotic place. Horowitz and I lived there like wealthy foreigners. We paraded around in expensive imported suits and even wore spats, a sure sign we belonged to the elite! We also patronized the best Moscow restaurants.

Of course, Soviet restaurants then almost never served patrons what they ordered. I remember one restaurant on the Arbat where we ordered stewed meat and were brought something black and horrible that looked like a skein of wool. Although we were young and as hungry as animals, we couldn't force ourselves to swallow it. We went to another restaurant and got the menu. Whatever we asked for, the answer was the same: "Ah, we're out of that." We stayed hungry that day.

But man does not live by bread alone. In those Moscow days a trip to the theater was a fine substitute for lunch. Volodya and I were ardent theater lovers and tried not to miss a single interesting production. And there was plenty to see in Moscow in the early twenties! I sometimes had the feeling that people lived for the theater there. The Moscow Art Theater reigned. It was founded before the revolution by Stanislavsky and Nemirovich-Danchenko, three of its studios separating after the revolution and functioning as independent entities.

Karpilovsky, first violin in the Stradivarius Quartet, introduced Volodya and me to Grigory Khmara, an actor from the Art Theater. I wasn't wild about Khmara's stage abilities, even though he was popular in Moscow. The important thing for us was that he got us tickets to the choicest productions.

There were theaters in a more traditional vein, like the Moscow

Art Theater and the Maly, also the bold avant-garde troupes of Tairov, Meyerhold, Vakhtangov, and Fedor Komissarzhevsky. But since the times themselves were wild and experimental, the line between traditional and avant-garde theater sometimes blurred.

For instance, Yevgeny Vakhtangov, a student of Stanislavsky's, was an idol of the traditional theater. But Vakhtangov's own staging was very daring. Or take the highly respected Nemirovich-Danchenko. He organized a music studio in which he presented opera productions that were absolutely mind-boggling in their irreverence.

Volodya and I saw everything. We went to the Art Theater to enjoy Chekhov plays. The theater, a pale gray building with beautiful rounded doors with matte glass, was situated in Kamergersky Alley.

People entered the small auditorium reverently, with a special kind of silence. No applause was permitted at the end of the play, and the actors did not come out for bows. That was Stanislavsky's idea; he wanted to purify the performance so that the actors and audience could concentrate on the play and not think about success. In those years, such an ideal did not seem quixotic.

People came to the Art Theater to recall the Russia that was gone forever—to sigh at *The Cherry Orchard*, to weep at *Three Sisters*. Great actors beloved by the whole country performed here: Kachalov, Moskvin, Leonidov. Before, Volodya and I had only heard of them; now we could enjoy them live. Just imagine, Knipper-Chekhova herself sometimes appeared in the plays of her late husband!

Even more traditional was the Maly Theater, which was headed by Prince Sumbatov-Yuzhin. (Everyone continued calling him prince even though the Soviet regime had resolutely done away with titles.) It was easy to find the Maly: it was on the right of the famous Bolshoi. The Maly had its own glorious actors—Ostuzhev, Yablochkina, Prov Sadovsky—but for some reason I particularly remember the actress Vera Shukhmina. She didn't play leading roles—usually she was onstage as a maid or nanny—but she had so much charm that watching her was a pleasure.

But my favorite actress, and perhaps one of the reasons I went to the Maly so often, was Elena Gogoleva. Oh, what a beauty she was! She was gorgeous and talented and had a wonderful voice—deep, low, resonant.

One of Gogoleva's most famous parts was Sophia in Alexander Griboyedov's classic *Woe from Wit*. I remember my horrible disappointment when I got a ticket to this popular production and learned that Gogoleva was sick and had been replaced by an understudy. But I managed to see her in other plays, in Alexander Ostrovsky's *The Forest* and *The Dowerless Bride*, and also in some modern plays.

I fell hopelessly in love with Gogoleva. I even collected her pictures. But when I got the opportunity to meet her, I botched things.

I was playing at the Kharkov Public Library, and the Maly Theater with Gogoleva was performing there too. A local music lover, a dentist named Shepshelevich (who always wore a black overcoat with beaver collar and was so clean-shaven that you thought no hair ever grew on his face) announced that he was giving a reception in my honor. Among the guests would be a group of Moscow actors, including Gogoleva. I played the Bach G Minor Sonata for solo violin, and I remember seeing Gogoleva in the audience, in the middle of the room. I stopped hearing what I was playing: my fingers went on automatically.

After the concert I went to Shepshelevich's party. I was terribly nervous: how would my meeting with Gogoleva go? When she appeared, I realized she was even more beautiful up close. She was given a seat of honor, and I sat next to her. The food was rather extravagant: enormous carafes of vodka and a variety of grapes called "ladies' fingers" in Russia, elongated and sweet.

Sitting next to Gogoleva, I couldn't think of how to start up a conversation. Suddenly I remembered something I had been taught: a conversation with a lady should begin with a compliment. But this was a beautiful actress, all too likely to laugh if I told her she had marvelous hair or pretty shoes.

My wandering gaze stopped at a carafe of vodka. I remembered another rule: if you want to relax, have a small drink. I reached for the vodka, poured myself one shot, then another. The two drinks didn't help at all. So, still determined to relax, I stopped counting.

I woke up in the morning, still at Shepshelevich's house, in an upstairs room: in bed, fully dressed. My head was bursting, my mouth was dry, and I was in despair. Was this the shameful end of my unconsummated affair with Gogoleva?

I left Kharkov for a performance in Rostov, and I stopped at the big hotel there, First House of Soviets. From my room, I heard a resonant voice: "And who are the judges?" (It was a famous line from Chatsky's monologue in *Woe from Wit*.) I looked out the window and saw Gogoleva's husband, also with the Maly, rehearsing on the next terrace. His name was Vsevolod Aksyonov—a tall, handsome blond. So the Maly Theater was now in Rostov, too! I was horrified. How could I even look Gogoleva in the eye? Of course, I ran into her that very evening: Rostov is a small town.

This time I had a conversational opener—I apologized for my disgusting behavior at the party in Kharkov. And Gogoleva confessed that she had felt uncomfortable that evening too, and hadn't known how to talk to me. "You had played Bach so well! I was afraid of seeming like a dilettante."

Her confession made me so happy: Gogoleva liked my playing! We left Rostov in different directions. . . . Much later, in America, I told a Russian friend about my crush on Gogoleva, and he laughed. "You weren't alone. All of Moscow was in love with her."

Recently I was given the memoirs of People's Artist of the USSR Elena Gogoleva, published in Moscow. The preface calls her one of the greatest Soviet actresses. A photograph shows a no-longer-young woman with a Hero of Socialist Labor star pinned to her chest. Sadly, I did not recognize the beauty I had loved so much.

At the Moscow First Studio Theater, Horowitz and I watched Johan Berger's *Flood*. It was a memorable play about a group of people gathered by chance in a fashionable bar, where they are suddenly cut off from the outside world by a burst dam. (Many years later when I saw the movie *The Petrified Forest* with Humphrey Bogart and Bette Davis, I recalled *Flood*, with its similar situation.)

One of the parts, a bankrupt stockbroker named Fraser, was played by the great actor Mikhail Chekhov, nephew of my favorite writer, Anton Chekhov. When actors portray Jewish characters, they often do it vulgarly, crudely, by overdoing an accent. Mikhail Chekhov played his role with a ceaseless nervous tic, but it was very subtle. He was shaking inside, constantly moving his glass from spot to spot, his handkerchief from one pocket to another.

All of Moscow went "to see Chekhov," whose premieres usually turned into public events. I'll never forget him in Strindberg's tragedy *Eric XIV*. Dressed in brocades, Chekhov played the mad king: thin arms and legs, painfully bulging eyes on an elongated, surprised face with a hooked, "Napoleonic" nose. His makeup in that role was unusual, with an enormous zigzag as a left brow.

I also saw Chekhov in a Stanislavsky production of Gogol's *Inspector General*, in which he played Khlestakov. He was brilliant as the young Petersburg clerk "without a tsar in his head," drunk on his own lies and newly acquired power. He seemed to fly across the stage, muttering and singing in his slightly hoarse voice.

Several times I saw Chekhov in a Moscow production of *Hamlet*. The set was a Gothic church, with something like a cut pyramid in the middle. Dressed in a tight black leather suit like some sort of Superman, with flaxen hair unevenly cut down to the shoulders, Chekhov stood in an arc of light, arms raised to the skies. It was a mystical spectacle with infernal music.

Once Horowitz and I appeared with Chekhov at the end of some rally. Horowitz performed Liszt's "Funérailles" brilliantly, while I made a fool of myself by starting to play the Bach Chaconne and forgetting it in the middle. Happily, no one noticed because I quickly moved into another Bach piece for solo violin, his E Major Prelude.

After my debacle I listened in awe to Mikhail Chekhov read Leskov's story "The Left-handed Smith," a satirical tale about a Russian craftsman who put horseshoes on a steel flea and presented it to the tsar. Listening to him, I didn't know whether to laugh or cry. His "smith," called Lefty, grew into a symbol of the enormously gifted Russian people brutally oppressed by authorities. While reading, Chekhov made slight, almost invisible gestures, each indicating a change in scene or character, all appearing magically right before our eyes. It was grand!

Sadly, Chekhov, like his hero Lefty, did not get along with the new authorities. The censors banned his *Hamlet*—"for mysticism"—and tried to force him to perform in new Soviet plays, which he abhorred. So Chekhov left Russia. He died in America. Unfortunately, I never met him in the West. At least not personally. I did encounter him on the screen, however, much later. I had heard that Chekhov had moved to Hollywood, where he coached many famous American actors—Gary Cooper, Anthony Quinn, Yul Brynner. He also appeared in movies.

Once I went to see a new Hitchcock film, *Spellbound*, in which Ingrid Bergman and Gregory Peck played out a rather improbable story involving Peck's amnesia. I watched incredulously as Bergman struggled to portray a learned doctor, acting all the time like a stupid governess. In order to be more realistic, she kept putting on and taking off her glasses. As if glasses were a sure sign of high learning!

Too often Hollywood forces even major actors to play clichéd roles. (For instance, Albert Basserman, the great German actor, for years played the same character in Hollywood movies: the wise man who never makes mistakes.) And it was exactly this kind of role that Mikhail Chekhov played in *Spellbound*: an émigré professor to whom Ingrid Bergman comes for help.

When I went to see *Spellbound* I didn't know that Chekhov was in the film. Like Bergman, Peck was rather unconvincing in his part, and the action did not come alive until an eccentric bearded old man with a funny accent appeared on the screen. The small role of the professor became central for me.

When the closing credits came on, all I wanted to know was who that marvelous actor was. It was Mikhail Chekhov! Fraser, Eric, Khlestakov, Hamlet! And now, even with Hollywood's typecasting, his performance had not succumbed to the clichés and routine, he had not gotten lost in the shuffle. . . .

One of the most prominent avant-garde directors in Moscow in the twenties was Alexander Tairov. At his Chamber Theater you could see both Lecocq's merry operetta *Giroflé-Girofla* and Scribe's grand tragedy *Adrienne Lecouvreur*. I didn't like Tairov's productions much, they seemed too mannered and decadent. But Alisa Koonen in the role of Adrienne Lecouvreur astonished me.

Nor was I thrilled by another idol of left-wing theater, the director Vsevolod Meyerhold. Crommelynck's farce *The Magnificent Cuck-old* at Meyerhold's theater seemed rather crude to me.

What I liked most of all were the productions of Yevgeny Vakh-tangov. He did *Flood* and *Eric XIV* with Mikhail Chekhov at the First Studio of the Moscow Art Theater, and at the Third Studio I adored his interpretation of *The Miracle of St. Antonius*. In Maeter-linck's play, the wealthy old woman Mlle Hortense dies, and her joyous relatives gather to divide up the inheritance. Suddenly St. Antonius appears, performs a miracle, and the dead woman is res-urrected.

Yuri Zavadsky, an actor of great temperament, played Anto-nius. I'll never forget his imperious exclamation, "Rise, Mlle Hortense!" The audience was so tense that when the old woman got up from her bed there was an audible gasp.

Another production by Vakhtangov that made an enormous im-pression on me was *Princess Turandot*, based on the Carlo Gozzi story (music lovers know the plot from the Puccini opera). Vakhtangov's well-trained actors moved lightly and swiftly, swirling bright swaths of fabric that flew up in the air in rhythm to ever-accelerating music. It was unforgettable theater!

To this day I still recall a moment from the play. When the prince (handsome Zavadsky) guesses Turandot's (beautiful Cecilia Mansurova) riddles, her servant girls get incredibly excited. Al-though their faces are covered with silk scarves, we see how pas-sionately they are talking to one another, because those scarves have started swaying wildly from their excited breathing! And all this in time to the music!

My friend Volodya Bakaleinikoff worked as conductor of the Nemirovich-Danchenko Music Studio. Nemirovich, a great and enormously respected director whose specialty was Chekhov, sud-denly got interested in operatic experiments. He totally redid *Car-men*, calling his version *Carmencita and the Soldier*. The episodes from Bizet's opera were reshuffled, with the crowd replaced by a static choir. And Nemirovich-Danchenko did away with Micaela com-pletely. Her aria in the third act was sung by a voice from the chorus, representing José's memories of his mother.

Nemirovich's production was far more daring than any later experiments by such directors as Franco Zeffirelli and Peter Brook. But you accepted it unconditionally because it did not contradict the spirit of Bizet's music!

Nemirovich understood music well, but he also consulted with Otto Klemperer, who was performing in Moscow then. It was Klemperer who thought of the toreador's spectacular entrance in *Carmencita and the Soldier*: the actor leaped onto a table from somewhere above and then sang his famous couplets!

Another astonishing musical spectacle by Nemirovich was based on Aristophanes' *Lysistrata*. I will always remember those slender, elegant columns against the blue sky, a set designed by the talented Isaac Rabinovich. The whole construction revolved, today a cliché, but at that time something new and daring. Nemirovich jammed the moving set with a crowd of actors who fought, scrambled, and jumped. It was fireworks in motion!

The incredibly lovely Olga Baklanova appeared both as Carmen and as Lysistrata. Later she moved to Hollywood, where she made several successful movies, while flirting wildly with my friend Konstantin Bakaleinikoff.

The blossoming of theater in Moscow in the 1920s embodied for me all the freshness and infinite talent of Russian culture and the Russian people. Now I sometimes hear that it was a result of the revolution. I don't think so. Virtually all of the great directors and actors I have described were already famous before the revolution. It's just that the Soviet authorities used them while temporarily tolerating the bold theatrical experimentation. Then the screws were tightened and it all ended. Many emigrated, and the ones who stayed had a hard time. With one or two exceptions, the theaters I have described were shut down in the late thirties. I was already living in the West, and I learned about these theatrical massacres from the newspapers. And my heart ached for the great Russian theater and Russian culture.

6. Horowitz and I
Move to the West

At a party given by Elena Malinovskaya, director of the Bolshoi Theater, I met the top Soviet military commander Mikhail Tukhachevsky, already a legend. A former tsarist officer who rose with astonishing speed through the Red Army ranks, he was handsome, elegant, and self-assured. (What happened to Soviet military men later? They all became short, fat, and ugly.)

Tukhachevsky adored music and played the violin himself. Moreover, his hobby was violin making. Later, in the West, I learned from the newspapers (it was a major story) that Stalin had arrested Tukhachevsky and other high Soviet commanders on charges of espionage for Germany and a Bonapartist conspiracy.

The charges are widely considered to be false, but it seems to me that Stalin had some basis for his suspicions. Marshal Tukhachevsky was very ambitious—you could see it in his every word and gesture—and he was friends with the leading German generals, especially with General Kurt von Schleicher. A plan could have arisen in which Stalin and Hitler would have been removed simultaneously from the scene by military putsches, following which Tukhachevsky and Schleicher would have come to terms. And world history might have changed completely. . . .

Unfortunately, both Schleicher and Tukhachevsky were executed by their suspicious leaders. I think Tukhachevsky would have had a chance for a successful coup in World War Two, if he had been in charge of the troops, as Marshal Zhukov was. Zhukov had the opportunity and the popularity, but he lacked the ambition and genius of Tukhachevsky, whom German and French historians have described as one of the great military strategists of our time.

Along with Tukhachevsky, Commander Ieronim Uborevich was also executed in 1936. I met Uborevich in 1925, when I was asked to appear in a gala concert marking the graduation day of the military academy in Moscow. (The academy continues to this day, now named after Mikhail Frunze.)

That was the first time I saw Military People's Commissar Leon Trotsky. He spoke to the graduating class. Trotsky had an interesting, intelligent face, and he spoke well, much better than Lenin. But one detail made me laugh: Trotsky's Adam's apple and small beard moved in rhythm with his words. I couldn't keep from laughing, even though laughing at Trotsky was definitely not the thing to do.

Fortunately, my disrespectful reaction to Trotsky's speech did not seem to do me any harm. I was introduced to Uborevich, at the time Trotsky's deputy, who spoke with me amiably. Uborevich was also handsome—a tall, blond giant who in his Red Army helmet looked like a Russian fairy-tale warrior, a *bogatyr*, or like ancient Prince Oleg immortalized in Pushkin's narrative poem.

Knowing Uborevich and having him well disposed toward me played a major role in both my life and Volodya Horowitz's. Uborevich gave us an official document from the powerful Revolutionary Military Council. It read: "The Revolutionary Military Council of the Republic has no objections to a trip abroad by comrades Mil-

70

stein and Horowitz for the purpose of artistic refinement and cultural propaganda.''

And we had not even asked Uborevich for such a document! At that time we didn't want to go to the West! Life was too wonderful in Russia: we had universal adulation, lots of money, and whipped cream and pastries at the café in Stoleshnikov Alley.

But with a paper like that in hand, it would have been a sin to miss a chance to be in Europe. Uborevich said, ''Go! Show them how we care about art!'' So Horowitz and I began packing for a trip to the West.

We were told that in order to obtain a foreign passport we had to pay a tax and get confirmation of our political dependability. Well, the political dependability was easy—weren't we ''children of the Soviet revolution''? Hadn't People's Commissar of Education Lunacharsky himself commended our loyalty in an article reprinted all over Soviet Russia?

That left the taxes, but even here fate was kind to us. When I went to the appropriate offices in Odessa, and Horowitz in Kiev, they dug around in their files and announced that our names weren't on the lists. Which meant we didn't have to pay any tax! We could go!

Horowitz left for Germany first. I had to get attestation that I didn't owe the state any money, after which I left for Berlin from Moscow, via Riga (which was then capital of independent Latvia). I'll remember that day for the rest of my life: December 25, 1925. I traveled in a luxurious sleeping car, which I had all to myself!

I was in a marvelous mood. In the pockets of my only suit I was carrying a substantial sum of money. In dollars! (In those days you could still exchange Soviet coins for dollars at the state bank.) Besides which I had bought all sorts of gold items, which I had squirreled away in my pockets. Those trifles kept me from a good night's sleep—they jabbed me as I tossed and turned, unable to find a comfortable position.

I arrived in Riga at five in the morning. At the German border the conductor peeked into my coach and said, ''Fried brötchen!'' The enigmatic announcement inflamed my imagination! What could it be? A food, but what kind?

I immediately headed for the restaurant car that had been added on at the border. It would be my first brush with Western life. I remember thinking as I entered the restaurant, My goodness! Look at all the different kinds of food to eat!

In Berlin, I took a taxi and went to the Fürstenhof Hotel, where Alexander Merovitch, who had undertaken to manage Horowitz and me in the West, had booked me a room. In those days Berlin was an important terminus of the Russian emigration. There were at least one hundred thousand Russians living in the greater Berlin area, most of them former white-collar workers, officers, students, and businessmen.

Berlin was not that far from Russia, and many émigrés hoped they would be able to return home soon. For now, they could find work in Berlin, and the Germans treated Russians fairly well.

The German mark was worthless in those inflationary years. We émigrés with a bit of money brought dollars with us, and found we could buy much more with dollars in Germany than we could in France or Italy.

Berlin was clean and quiet, the stores were filled with goods, and people were dressed decently, even well. It was a real European capital. But it was the abundance of food that made the greatest impression on me.

The violinist Karpilovsky (with whose Stradivarius Quartet I had appeared at rallies in Moscow) had left for Berlin before me and had organized the Guarneri Quartet there. So we met again in Berlin, and now, as an *echt* Berliner, Karpilovsky invited me to a concert at the Berlin Philharmonic.

Wilhelm Furtwängler was conducting Beethoven's *Coriolanus*, Paul Hindemith (an excellent violist) was performing his viola concerto, and Sergei Prokofiev, whom I knew from Petersburg, was playing his Piano Concerto no. 3. Three names like that in one concert! And all for just five marks!

Believe it or not, I was bored listening to the music; in fact, I talked Karpilovsky into leaving the concert—I wanted to wander around Berlin at night. The main attraction was around the corner, Pschorr's, Berlin's "fast-food" chain then. How the Germans enjoyed themselves there: they took a small roll, put a hot dog in it, covered it with mustard, and followed it with a beer! That was chic, that was delight, that was *la dolce vita!*

Horowitz had come to Germany through Stettin with Merovitch, arriving three months before me. Already he had given two concerts, neither a complete success. I got to Berlin just in time for his third, in which he broke a string, as he often had done in Russia. They hurried to find a piano tuner while the intermission dragged on. This was the moment when I appeared, straight from the Zoologischer Garten metro station, the closest one to the concert hall.

There were a lot of people at the concert. Horowitz was riding high. A particular sensation was his Chopin's Mazurka in C-sharp Minor (op. 30, no. 4), which Volodya had played to great acclaim in Petersburg, too. (I always advised Volodya to play small pieces; that was his forte.) The influential critic Adolf Weissmann wrote an ecstatic review, which caused a lot of talk. That's how Horowitz's career in the West began.

My first concerts in Berlin took place at Beethoven Salle and then in Blüthner Salle. No effect at all! The critics wrote something about "marvelous technique," but that didn't help me. Then I went to Hamburg, where I performed with the local orchestra under Eugen Pabst. Nothing special came from that, either.

Russian émigrés lived in Berlin in a kind of suspended state. The intellectuals—journalists, writers, artists, and musicians—didn't want to break ties with the homeland. They heard news about NEP from Moscow, and for a while it looked as if real capitalism was going to be reinstated.

So Horowitz and I did not consider ourselves defectors, and when we were invited to play at the Soviet embassy (in those days the Soviet diplomatic representations abroad were called *polpredstva*) in Berlin, we readily agreed.

The Soviet *polpred*, or ambassador, to England, Leonid Krasin, had died in London. He was a famous Bolshevik, a friend of Lenin's and Maxim Gorky's, and his body was being transported to Moscow for an elaborate funeral, with a stop in Berlin.

Horowitz and I constituted the musical part of a memorial service for Krasin. With mournful mien, I played Handel's Largo. Volodya delivered a brilliant rendition of Liszt's "Funérailles." The enchanted audience, completely forgetting about the deceased Bolshevik, shouted bravo.

Volodya and I spent a relatively short time in Berlin. Even with the acclaim over Horowitz's third concert, we did not make much of an impression on the German public, hardly standing out from the horde of touring musicians. Merovitch, our manager, insisted we move to Paris; we presumed he knew what he was talking about. Indeed, Paris sounded very glamorous.

Already Russian émigrés were moving gradually from Berlin to Paris. Sincere and earnest, Berlin paled before brilliant and elitist Paris. Chaliapin, Stravinsky, Balanchine, and Prokofiev settled in Paris. Rachmaninoff's family lived there, and Rachmaninoff often came to Paris to give concerts.

In Paris you could meet the musical wise men who had fled Russia: Leonid Sabaneyev, Boris de Schloezer, Peter Souvtchinsky, and Arthur Lourié. Each of these marvelous music critics glorified his own idol. Sabaneyev and Schloezer deified Scriabin, Souvtchinsky and Lourié pushed Stravinsky. I appreciated Lourié's taste and musical judgment, since he was also a talented composer. Lourié walked around Paris in a too-long coat, obviously an immigrant. (Many Russian émigrés bought their coats too long, in case it got very cold.)

Sabaneyev, whom I had met back in Moscow, didn't look too glamorous either: he wore a cheap suit and generally seemed pathetic. He even smelled bad. It was hard to believe that in Russia this man had been one of our most influential critics, a man whose reviews decided the fate of many musicians.

Sabaneyev had a brilliant and caustic pen. Before the revolution he attacked every new work of young Prokofiev, year in and year out. Providence gave Prokofiev a chance to get even. Conductor Serge Koussevitzky had put Prokofiev's *Scythian Suite*, just written, on the program for a concert in Moscow. At the last moment Koussevitzky replaced it with another work. Nevertheless, Sabaneyev published a scathing review of *Scythian Suite* the next day. He had not been at the concert and was unaware of the change in program. There was a terrible scandal. Prokofiev gloated. He met Sabaneyev once again in Paris, but there the critic could no longer harm him:

Prokofiev's reputation was by then on the rise, while Sabaneyev had become powerless.

In Paris Prince Alexis Zereteli, an imposing and generous bearded gentleman, became our agent. He was the manager of L'Opéra Russe à Paris, with whom Chaliapin himself performed. Zereteli sought out beautiful ladies for his performances, either as singers or dancers, hoping that their rich lovers would help support the company's season. Still, the Opéra was always in financial difficulties. The prince was dubbed "Zereteli-Progoreli" (a pun on the Russian word for "bankrupt"). Well, in taking Horowitz and me under his wing, Prince Zereteli wasn't risking anything, since he wasn't paying us anything.

Since Horowitz and I had left Russia with a fair amount of money, we never hesitated to help out Russian émigrés in Berlin and Paris, who besieged us with requests: one had an ailing father, another had a daughter who wanted to play the violin but couldn't afford an instrument, a third wanted to learn the language.

In Russia making money had been easy for us, so in Europe we parted with money easily. We invested in diamonds . . . and were cheated every step of the way. And then, when we saw that our money was melting away and we weren't earning any more, to tell the truth, we got scared.

One day Prince Zereteli announced that the famous Spanish manager Ernesto de Quesada, who had an office in Paris, was interested in me. I was offered a recital in Madrid. If it was successful, I would get another fifteen concerts in Spain, and from there would go to South America to do another thirty-five. Quesada was offering five hundred dollars for each concert, which was a large sum in those days.

I went to Madrid with some trepidation. The concert was being sponsored by a local music society. The hall was only half full, but the audience, made up mostly of women, looked refined. The white-gloved ladies applauded listlessly, however. Of course, it wasn't bridge but just some violinist—not a very chic affair!

There was enough applause for one encore, but when I came

out to do a second one, I saw that the audience was leaving faster than I was coming out onstage. I was particularly upset by three men in the second row. They were practically waving me away. I played and they waved so hard, with their legs as well as their arms, they almost fell back in their seats!

Desperate, I went back to the hotel convinced that my recital was a total flop. Suddenly this man came to see me, a representative of impresario Quesada. He was the last straw: when we shook hands I realized he had only two fingers. It gave me the creeps, but I thought, At least this one's giving me all he's got.

And then this person offered me a contract with Quesada, because, it seems, I had been sensationally successful. And the reviews were in fact excellent. But why had the audience fled? And why had those men in the second row tried to wave me away?

The answer came much later. After the Spanish Civil War, I was appearing in Mexico, where there were many Spanish émigrés. One of them, a Mr. Jiménez from Málaga, had a metallurgical plant in Mexico. He was wealthy and often held musical soirées, inviting thirty or forty people.

After my performance, I spoke with the guests. Among them was the famous musicologist Adolfo Salazar (who later lectured at Columbia University), also a Spanish émigré. I was asked if I had ever played in Spain. By that time I had been almost everywhere in Spain, having played in fifty cities, no less, and I told Salazar that I probably knew the country better than he. Then I recounted the story of my Madrid debut and the strange behavior of the three gentlemen in the audience.

"But that was us!" Salazar exclaimed, pointing to two gentlemen standing next to him. "We were three critics, from *La Prensa*, *ABZ*, and *Nacional*! We were thrilled!"

I said to Salazar, "Strange behavior for being thrilled. . . . I was certain that you were disgusted!"

"No, no, we were expressing our extreme delight!"

Salazar must have been telling the truth, because his review and those of his two colleagues had been very good.

Anyway, as a result of my Madrid appearance, Ernesto de Quesada, who also represented Wanda Landowska, arranged for Miss Landowska and me to appear together in Montevideo and Buenos Aires. This is how it went: In Buenos Aires a concert began at 4:30 in the afternoon and ended around 6:30. Miss Landowska and I would return to the hotel, pack up, and board a dirty but very comfortable ship. I particularly liked the fact that the portions of food on the ship, which belonged to a Polish Jew, were ample—that was important to me in those days!

The ship left at 10:30 at night, and by 6:30 the next morning we would be in Montevideo. We were taken to a hotel and would give a recital in the afternoon. In this way we gave six recitals— shuttling between countries each day. The programs were Bach and Mozart violin sonatas accompanied by harpsichord.

A great musician, Miss Landowska was an unattractive woman with a rather long nose. Her favorite pastime was recording all kinds of stories—funny, horrible, and sadistic—in a special book. On board ship she would come to my cabin and read the stories out loud until three in the morning. I was young and impressionable; it was hard to fall asleep after those readings.

Landowska and I barely rehearsed. She played marvelously, but sometimes not too gracefully. Her favorite velvet dress had originally been burgundy, but with time it took on a greenish-yellow cast. A dark spot developed at the end of the train: you could see that people were constantly stepping on it. One time, coming out onstage behind Landowska, I tripped on that damned train and almost fell down. Another time, with my own eyes, I saw a small white cat run out from beneath the hem of that enormous gown.

Touring South America, I met the great German pianist Wilhelm Backhaus. The occasion was a benefit for Polish violinist Bronislaw Gimpel, whose manager had run off to Europe without paying him, leaving the man stranded. Backhaus agreed to appear with me at a Gimpel fund-raiser.

I went to the rich owner of a local radio equipment store—like Gimpel, he was a Polish Jew—and I stressed that he had to help a compatriot. He proved a real businessman. When I suggested renting a hall for the concert, he countered, "What for? We'll have the concert in my house! We'll invite about fifty guests, each will give two hundred to three hundred dollars, and we'll easily get five or ten thousand dollars for Gimpel.''

And so it was. Gimpel could return to Europe. His brother later accused me of thereby getting rid of Gimpel so that he wouldn't get in the way of my success in South America. Whoever said that no good deed goes unpunished was right.

At the fund-raiser Backhaus and I played Beethoven's *Spring* Sonata and Mozart's E Minor Sonata. We became friends and talked a lot about music. Backhaus was not merely a major pianist (even though he sometimes played Beethoven too drily for my taste), he was also a philosopher, in music as well as in life. Backhaus thought unhurriedly, moved unhurriedly, and paid little attention to the world around him.

Once on a trip in South America I had to travel by ship. I was afraid, and to reassure me my manager said, ''Don't worry! Even Backhaus is doing it!'' And in fact, when I got on board (it was a rickety old shoe of a boat), I saw Backhaus in a deck chair, covered with a blanket. He had a book in one hand and his glasses had slipped down his nose. He must have fallen asleep while reading. Just then a pipe burst and the deck was flooded. There was great panic, a hue and cry. Backhaus woke up . . . and calmly went back to his reading.

There were many music-loving Germans and Austrians in South America. Some of them must have written home about my recitals, perhaps even sent my favorable South American reviews. In any case, Paul Bechert, my Viennese manager, decided to take a risk and arranged two concerts for me in a small hall in Vienna.

Bechert was an extremely interesting person, a close friend of the Austrian poet and essayist Karl Kraus. (He later introduced us.) I became a good friend of Bechert's too, which is rather rare between manager and artist. (I'm glad that my current representative, Harold Shaw, has also become a friend.)

Bechert was very popular among European musicians, perhaps because he was a Viennese correspondent for the Boston *Globe*, reporting on concerts, exhibits, and theater premieres. Every performer wanted to appear in the U.S.A., it being a rule of thumb that the only place you could make real money was in America. They all knocked America, but they all dreamed of a U.S. tour. A good review by Bechert in the Boston *Globe* could be a big help.

The program I prepared for my Viennese debut would likely be considered in poor taste these days, even in a small provincial town. I did Glazunov's concerto to piano accompaniment instead of the obligatory orchestra, a few salon pieces I liked back then, and Tchaikovsky's "Sérénade Mélancolique," the latter with "feeling," almost weeping.

The crowd was small and I was disappointed, but during the intermission a happy Bechert came backstage and said that even though there were few people in the audience, they were all part of the Viennese elite. For instance, Arnold Schoenberg, Alban Berg, and a rising star, Karl Amadeus Hartmann, were all there. And most important, Julius Korngold himself, the all-powerful music critic, had come. He was considered the heir to legendary Viennese critic Eduard Hanslick, who in his day had torn even Tchaikovsky to shreds!

I said to Bechert, "I guess all these important people are going to run off now?"

And Bechert, very pleased, replied, "Not at all! They want to hear the encores!" Schoenberg and Berg were staying for the violin encores! Which showed how free of snobbery these people were. They liked all kinds of music. Can you picture, say, Pierre Boulez listening to a violinist play Tchaikovsky and Glazunov?

I remember the encore I gave my highbrow Viennese audience: an incredibly flashy arrangement of Rimsky-Korsakov's "Flight of the Bumblebee." They were enormously pleased and applauded wildly. Korngold wrote a fantastic review, after which my next two concerts in Vienna were sold out. And even though I had already played with good conductors (Willem Mengelberg in Holland, for example), it was after Korngold's review that people began paying attention to me seriously and I was invited to perform in Berlin with such giants as Furtwängler and Hans Knappertsbusch, and in Hamburg with Carl Muck.

Muck was a thin and majestic-looking man who bore a remarkable resemblance to Wagner. They said he was Wagner's illegitimate son. I had the impression Muck was proud of the rumors. He was always elegantly dressed; navy suit, black tie, and shoes of fine leather. And why not, if he was Wagner's son. *Noblesse oblige!*

Muck was old and apparently a bit lazy. When he got to the third movement of the Tchaikovsky concerto, he was hunched over and waved his arms somewhere below the stand; it must have been too much trouble for him to raise them higher.

At rehearsal we had worked on the transition from the cadenza in the last movement. It is a difficult moment, for the conductor has to be particularly attentive and indicate the orchestra's cue precisely, otherwise the musicians could easily miss it. During the concert I saw to my horror that Muck didn't even raise his hand. I had to save the situation by finishing my cadenza in an exaggeratedly slow fashion. And of course I couldn't say anything about it to the great Carl Muck!

He was friendly enough toward me and invited me to his house, where he showed me his pride and joy—a complete collection of Bach's works. I remember him musing that Bach was the most modern composer in terms of harmony. (Muck liked puns. He would ask "Do you know the Hitlervariationen?" meaning Max Reger's "Variations and Fugue on a Theme of Hiller.")

Muck had lived through more than his share of political troubles. He was appointed music director of the Boston Symphony Orchestra before World War One, and at the start of the war he was shamefully fired for being a German spy! Muck a spy! Could anything be more absurd?

In Vienna I met Arnold Schoenberg. We became close, strangely enough, over painting rather than music. I was introduced to Schoenberg by a tailor, Mr. Wolf, who owned a chain of men's clothing stores.

The name Schoenberg was magic for me, even though I wasn't really taken with his music: *Verklärte Nacht* sounded like saccharine Wagner, and his later opuses were just as inedible to my tastes. But while I did not consider Schoenberg a very good composer, he was certainly an important one. (Prokofiev was just the reverse.) Schoenberg was, as they say, a musical authority. Yet we began talking about art. He was an interesting painter. His portraits in an expressionist style were particularly noteworthy.

The back of Wolf's shop was turned over by the kind owner as a studio to amateur artists like Schoenberg and myself. We met there several times. Schoenberg asked me, "What do you draw?" I replied, "Mountains," my favorite theme. I'm not a professional when it comes to art, and I tend to work in "sprees": suddenly I devote a lot of time to drawing, really get involved, and then I work with great confidence. Schoenberg, on the other hand, worked steadily and considered himself a professional artist. I think he valued his paintings as highly as his musical compositions.

At the time Schoenberg was working on a portrait of his mother: an expressionist face, with the kind of eyes you see on canvases by Soutine. Schoenberg did not win me over with his paintings any more than he did with his compositions, but his opinions on various musical matters, in particular on conducting, I found enlightening.

Schoenberg spoke with great persuasion, like a professor, sipping horrible coffee as he held forth, usually in a café near Wolf's shop. He had a strangely ugly face and not a trace of anything artistic in his personality. The man might have been a doctor, tailor, or bank clerk. The Viennese café where we spent our time is gone now. A rather unattractive Soviet monument stands there—a memorial to the catastrophe Vienna lived through in the middle of this century.

When we settled down in Europe, Horowitz and I (as I've mentioned) had no intention of defecting. We still considered ourselves Soviet citizens on an artistic trip in the West under mandate of the Republic Revolutionary Military Council. In Paris, Khristian Rakovsky, the first Soviet *polpred* to France, invited us to his place regularly.

Rakovsky was a charming, educated man. He knew English and French flawlessly and liked to call himself "Dr. Rakovsky." He dressed like a dandy, was popular with the ladies, and basically lived the good life of a Red capitalist in Paris.

Whenever he gave receptions at the Soviet embassy, a town house on rue de Grenelle, Rakovsky invited not French proletarians but wealthy bankers, influential politicians, and the artistic elite.

Another reason I liked visiting him was that he had two lovely daughters who exercised great charm over me (but not over Horowitz).

Rakovsky constantly smoked long aromatic cigarettes imported specially for him from the Ukraine in elegant packaging. The brand was named after Rakovsky! The *polpred*'s celebrated guests also smoked up a storm, so you could slice the smoke at his parties. Rakovsky joked, "The capitalists are trying to smoke me out!"

Horowitz and I performed in many salons in Paris, and I must say that the most fashionable and luxurious place we found in the French capital was the salon of the Soviet ambassador.

Rakovsky was very well disposed toward us. After several years of living in Paris, we came to him with the idea of going back to Soviet Russia, and it was Rakovsky who talked us out of it. He said, "Don't be stupid! You haven't played enough for the capitalists yet!" And so we stayed.

There's little question in my mind that Rakovsky kept us from going back to Soviet Russia because he knew what was going on there and was anti-Stalin. It was not long before he was recalled, then expelled from the Communist Party, arrested, and tried in one of Stalin's show trials. He was shot, of course.

I recently learned of Rakovsky's total rehabilitation in the Soviet Union, unfortunately a posthumous one. His name has been reinstated in encyclopedias, pictures and biographies of him are being published again.

Valerian Dovgalevsky became the new Soviet *polpred* in France. Horowitz and I did not find him nearly as friendly and refined as Rakovsky, but then our performances in Europe were becoming more and more successful, so we had less time to socialize.

Just then the Soviet embassy in Paris became involved in a major scandal: General Alexander Kutepov, one of the leaders of an émigré military organization, vanished in broad daylight. The Paris newspapers carried daily stories about the political kidnapping; the clues in the case led to the Soviet embassy. We stopped going there. And stopped thinking about returning to Russia, forever.

Horowitz and I liked Paris more and more. We were making new friends there; one of the nicest was the American violinist Samuel Dushkin. Through Dushkin we met George Gershwin, who took us to his place and enthusiastically played a song of his called "Mischa, Jascha, Toscha, Sascha," all first names of famous violinists—Mischa Elman, Jascha Heifetz, Toscha Seidel, and Sascha Jacobsen.

This amusing and witty song, with its music imitating a violin played on open strings, was not yet published, but it was already popular among professional musicians, especially violinists. It was sung at every musical party. (I remember that the lyrics mentioned our professor, Leopold Auer, rhyming "Auer" with "sour.")

Gershwin told us, laughing, that when he was a boy living on Second Avenue in New York and began taking piano lessons, his younger brother, Arthur, was started on the violin. But that didn't last long. Arthur complained that it was very unfair that George got to sit when he played, while he, poor Arthur, had to stand. And so Arthur gave up the violin.

Later, when Volodya and I were staying at the Majestic Hotel in Paris, Gershwin had the room above ours. I learned he was there from the roaring sounds of *Rhapsody in Blue*. Gershwin rehearsed hard and persistently, repeating the same passage over and over. Strangely, that didn't get on my nerves at all.

I consider Gershwin a more talented composer than Aram Khachaturian, who also became famous for introducing folklore, albeit of a different kind, into modern music. Music does not necessarily have to be "pure"; the important thing is its quality. Blacks and Jews influenced what we now call "indigenous" American music. And often the influences are so mixed that it is impossible to tell which is which. For instance, they call Ravel's sonata for violin and piano the *Blues* Sonata, but I hear more Jewish motifs in it than blues.

The point is that in the twentieth century composers began treating exotic material more seriously. For Mozart a Turkish march is a joke. (Landowska played "Marcia alla turca" marvelously!) But Ravel took the elements of jazz to his heart.

I met Ravel at the salon of Mme Dubost. He was sitting apart from the other guests, his face buried in his collar, only his big nose showing. Almost no one approached him, he was so forbidding. He seemed to have come from the pages of my favorite writer, Anton Chekhov. A typical Chekhovian character.

Unfortunately, the most popular of Ravel's works is "Bolero," with its depressing tune that gets you everywhere, like a nightmare. Once when Toscanini was rehearsing "Bolero" in Paris, Ravel was in the hall. He thought Toscanini was using too fast a tempo but did not want to tell the conductor himself. So he sent a messenger, the critic Gustave Samazeuilh, who tried to stop Toscanini, not once but three times. The conductor finally blew up and told Samazeuilh to go to hell. Ravel left the rehearsal and did not attend the concert. I think in this case Toscanini was right. If "Bolero" can be tolerated at all, it is only at a very fast tempo.

Both Gershwin and Ravel were fashionable composers in the days of our youth in Paris, and both have preserved their incredible fame to this day, even though fashions in composers usually change. As do fashions in performers—for various reasons, including nationality.

For a long time German conductors and instrumentalists were popular, then Russians. And so, for one example, Carl Muck was replaced by Serge Koussevitzky in Boston. Now, I think, it's the Orientals' turn. For years the Boston Symphony has been under the baton of Japanese Seiji Ozawa, considered by many to be a great conductor (a matter of opinion, of course).

The quick growth in the prestige of Orientals in music is understandable: there's a culture a thousand years old behind them. Russians don't have such an ancient cultural tradition. And there is another important factor: the Oriental cult of education. Oriental students, including those studying violin with me, make incredible strides in short periods. (It is my observation that the Japanese are somewhat more receptive than the Chinese, but I may be mistaken.)

When I hear people say they are amazed by the swift economic development of South Korea or Taiwan, not to mention Japan, I usually argue that the Oriental countries have always been developed and have always had a high level of civilization. Now they are on the technological tracks of the American model and will move with increasing acceleration to greater success, both in culture and economically.

Horowitz and I Move to the West

Paris is impossible to imagine without salons where the elite hail the latest "ism," tear apart the new prime minister or president, debate the newest fashions and philosophical ideas, and gossip and slander at full blast. Frequented gladly even by the biggest snobs, for Horowitz and me they were not only entertainment, they were an education.

Young, talented musicians were welcome guests at any salon, and Horowitz and I were invited to the best. At the home of Elsa Maxwell, newspaper columnist and society hostess, I often met Coco Chanel, cultural arbiter of Paris society. And the artist Pavel Tchelitchew introduced me to Comtesse de Noailles at Maxwell's.

Coco Chanel spoke abruptly and moved abruptly. She was very forbidding, while Elsa Maxwell radiated charm and friendliness, making jokes at her own expense, usually about her weight and looks. Elsa Maxwell was clever, she beat others—who would say all the nasty things anyway—to the punch.

Another place Horowitz and I went to frequently was the salon of Mme Dubost. On Wednesdays or Thursdays (I don't remember which) she would invite as many as two hundred people to her famous *"Mme Dubost chez elle."* Many of her frequent guests are legends now: Stravinsky, Jean Cocteau, Arthur Honegger. I remember the artists Georges Braque and Maurice de Vlaminck. Vlaminck, whose bright, colorful landscapes I adored, was huge and had a wonderful face.

Picasso was at Mme Dubost's often. He was already famous, yet you could buy one of his paintings for a couple hundred dollars. Once in my presence a young American woman asked Picasso, "How can you judge a painting?" Picasso replied, "I don't judge it. Time and history will do that. Contemporaries, mademoiselle, are often mistaken."

Picasso continued, "Take Corot: he was famous for his landscapes at Fontainebleau—small villages, women in red kerchiefs. It turned out they were easy to forge. Corot painted maybe several hundred landscapes in his life, and now in America alone there are over five thousand of them." (How true. I myself was in an American house whose owner had collected almost one hundred Corot landscapes!) The American woman had to agree with Picasso. "Of course, we bought up everything without knowing if they were authentic or forgeries."

"Well," Picasso concluded, "now Corot's landscapes are no longer valued, no one needs them, while portraits by Corot, which no one paid any attention to before, are considered priceless."

I adored Picasso and his work. Cubism as a whole left me indifferent—I simply absorbed it as artistic information, nothing more—but Picasso was more than cubism, or any other "ism." Even if I don't like a particular painting of his, I can still feel the energy, work, and research that went into it. There is nothing "rational" or calculating in Picasso's works; they all radiate and sing.

Surrealism, which I encountered then too, did not attract me either. I considered its illusionism a mere trick and thought Salvador Dali a talented but insincere artist. Later, in New York, I often met him and his Russian wife, Gala, at mutual friends' houses.

Dali talked loudly in French with a terrible Spanish accent. He would wave his arms around, rolling his eyes wildly and almost shouting . . . "I have a beach near Valencia, I go there, lie down, smear honey on my face, and the flies of the whole world fly to me!"

Such boasts had little effect on me. I merely thought, Would a normal person ever do anything like that? Dali, wrapped up in himself, would go on. "And here's what else I do, I throw rocks in the air and wait for them to fall on me!"

Gala, obviously used to all this, heard out his tirades calmly. She was firmly convinced that while her husband was, of course, a genius, she was the one to make his brilliant ideas profitable. Gala Dali and Vava Chagall were smart businesswomen; in Russia we called people like that "iron women."

I simmered happily in the artistic pot of Paris. Trips around Europe also expanded my views. These things happen gradually: you meet articulate, talented people, devour art, read new, fascinating books in history and philosophy—and suddenly you notice that your out-look has changed considerably.

I changed not only as a person but also, at the same time, as a musician, especially in my attitude toward the violin. In Russia I had not really understood what beautiful violin sound was all about, so it didn't matter to me what instrument I played. My violin then was worth about twenty kopecks, and my bow—a gift from Professor Auer—worth even less.

In Moscow Kubatsky had given me a good Guadagnini from the state collection, but I left the instrument behind when I left Russia. I remember coming to a rehearsal in Hamburg with the conductor Eugen Pabst without any violin at all. Someone lent me his, and that evening I performed with his violin! When I think about it, I can't believe it! Now a young violinist wants a Stradivarius, no less, for his debut. But back then things like that didn't matter to me.

My first years in the West I played random instruments, and in 1929 I bought a Guarnerius del Gesù. It was not a good violin—it had a loud and crude sound, and, even worse, it was covered with a horrible chocolate-colored varnish. Then I got a 1710 Stradivarius—not bad, but a bit rough. Gradually I began understanding a bit more about instruments and bows.

A large role in this part of my education was played by Alfred Hill, one of the most brilliant representatives of that dynasty of British violin dealers. Hill often invited me to the best London clubs, like the Savage Club. I met with him readily, since I liked his stories about remarkable violins and their makers.

I also liked going to Hill's shop on Bond Street, where I tried out various instruments from his collection. I played on an astonishing Stradivarius, known as "the Messiah"—an unforgettable experience! That violin was considered a national treasure in England. In fact, it was illegal to take it out of the country!

Stradivarius did not name his instruments, of course. The names, each fancier than the last, were added by subsequent owners. This is how the Messiah got its name: The famous French luthier Jean-Baptiste Vuillaume wanted the violin, which was in Italy at the time. One of the Hills couldn't wait to have a look at the marvelous instrument either. In a letter to Vuillaume he cried out in despair, "When will I ever hold that violin in my hands? When will the Messiah come?" Hence the name.

The violin I play now is one I got in 1945. It is also a Stradivarius, one of the three or four best examples of his "golden" period: 1716, like the Messiah. Following tradition, I gave it a new name, the Maria Teresa, in honor of my daughter, Maria, and my wife, Thérèse.

Alfred Hill was an excellent professional and an honest man. These qualities nowadays are rare among violin dealers. With few exceptions, their professionalism is on the decline, and they make mistakes at least half the time. That is not acceptable.

Of course, the construction and evaluation of a violin are more arts than sciences. Much depends on the personality and artistry of maker and dealer. Even so, there are constants on which to base your evaluation: the wood, the varnish, the instrument's design.

There can be variations here too. Take, for instance, the Stradivarius of Henri Temianka: it was built of bad, knotty wood, but the instrument sounded marvelous. It's nice when a violin has beautiful varnish. But even that is not a prerequisite for a quality instrument.

There are not that many good violins—I mean authentic Italian instruments—and even fewer ones with the original varnish. Varnish is the first thing to go. A Korean student of mine brought me his instrument—also a Stradivarius, and made the same year as mine—but there was a horrible white varnish on top of the original one. Apparently, someone in the provinces had decided that with a new varnish the violin would look better. Or it was done to protect the original varnish, I don't know. In any case, the violin was ruined. An additional, unnecessary layer of varnish suffocates the violin, and the sound suffers.

In the spot where the resin collects, my Stradivarius had a little bit of new, different varnish. Fernando Sacconi, a brilliant master, labored more than three months to remove that varnish. To do so he used a special method, involving a powder made from rubber. It was an exhausting job that required a jeweler's hand. On my Korean student's Strad, it would take years and years of painstaking work to restore the original varnish. And there is no guarantee that what was left of the original varnish wouldn't come off in the process. Particularly since there are no masters like Sacconi around.

Now I always tell my students that a good bow is almost as important as a good violin. But not everyone can afford a quality bow: a fine one today can go for over fifty thousand dollars.

I have several excellent bows. When I tour, they are always with me, in my case. Of course, you have to keep a good eye on them, especially during orchestral rehearsals. On one occasion, when I returned to my dressing room and looked in my case, there were only three, instead of four. There is only one way to prevent such unpleasantness: lock the door when you leave the dressing room!

When I got to the West, I started writing transcriptions for the violin. Back in Russia I had become aware of my appetite for composition. In Moscow, a Jewish cultural organization (still allowed then in Soviet Russia) asked me to play a Jewish work at one of their concerts. They promised to pay me an extra thirty gold ten-ruble pieces, an enormous fee in those days.

I didn't have a single Jewish work in my repertoire, but I didn't want to turn down thirty gold pieces. So I told them that I would play a fantasy on Jewish themes for solo violin. And I improvised right on stage. What else could I do?

Jewish music has characteristic intonations that are relatively easy to imitate. My fantasy was a big success. My colleagues on that program were warmly greeted, too: the bass Platon Tsesevich, who sang some not so arty Jewish Ukrainian songs, and the trumpeter Mikhail Tabakov, who also presented something Jewish for the occasion.

In selecting pieces for violin transcription, I try to follow one rule: don't take music that is too good, that cannot be added to or cut down. In that case, transcription simply does not work.

Jascha Heifetz, who has done some very good transcriptions, sometimes made this mistake and arranged a piece simply because he liked it. For instance, he heard Horowitz playing Hummel's Rondo. The composition seemed attractively flashy, so Heifetz did a violin transcription. But no one plays it, because what makes that kind of piece sound good on a piano cannot be done with a bow.

I took a Mussorgsky piece for the piano, "The Seamstress," nothing special, but it turned out to be quite impressive in violin transcription, and many violinists have included it in their repertoires (especially since they don't have to pay royalties).

Another example. I did a transcription of Chopin's C-sharp Minor Nocturne, which is played beautifully by Isaac Stern, Gidon Kremer, and many other violinists. On the piano long notes without ornamentation do not sound convincing (the reason Horowitz does not play this work), but on the violin those long notes are marvelous.

In a transcription the result is what counts, not the original material. I reworked "Il pleut dans la ville" by Zoltán Kodály—it's only after the last note dies away that you realize what a divine work it is. It's like good chocolate: you fully appreciate how good it was only when you've eaten it. But with bad chocolate you eat it and hope that it will be good, and then you have to brush your teeth.

I also composed cadenzas, for concertos by Beethoven and Brahms. And my "Paganiniana" for solo violin, in which I used themes from *Twenty-four Caprices* and other compositions by Paganini, gained a certain popularity among violinists. Many talented performers play it, including Ruggiero Ricci, Salvatore Accardo, Gidon Kremer.

The idea for "Paganiniana" was in my mind for a long time, but I didn't write it until I was in America. I needed a ten-minute piece for a recital, and I put "Paganiniana" on the program, then forced myself to spend several nights in a row to finish the work. I was still changing it the day before the concert!

It's a horrible habit of mine to keep fussing with my own transcriptions. Sometimes you make a change and then, in the concert, you feel your fingers going somewhere else. Luckily, I haven't had a catastrophe yet.

In their day many violinists did transcriptions. The greatest master of the genre was, of course, Fritz Kreisler. Others did not do as well, but at least they tried, they satisfied their creative appetite. Now young violinists don't bother to do anything. They just want

ung Nathan Milstein in Odessa, the city
his birth and early childhood.

The *wunderkind* Jascha Heifetz. After his
appearance in Odessa, Milstein's fate was
sealed.

Professor Stolyarsky teaching: "Musical *kolkhoz*," but effective. *(Volkov Archive)*

Eugène Ysaÿe came to Odessa
almost every year. He would
become Milstein's teacher.

Professor Leopold Auer: To study with him was every young violinist's dream.

The Petersburg Conservatory in 1916, when Milstein attended. *(Volkov Archive)*

Chaliapin as Boris Godunov: "An overdose of high art." *(Volkov Archive)*

Young Prokofiev: "Touchy, clumsy, and ugly." Portrait by Alexandre Benois. *(Volkov Archive)*

Mikhail Chekhov as Hamlet. *(Volkov Archive)*

With Glazunov and Horowitz: Photo taken
in memory of the joint concert in
Petersburg, 1923.

ɔrgeous Elena Gogoleva, with whom
ilstein "fell hopelessly in love," as Sophia
Woe from Wit. (Volkov Archive)

Milstein with Horowitz (LEFT) and their manager, Pavel Kogan, 1923.

1922 portrait of Boris Pasternak, who had not yet decided whether he would be a poet or a composer.

Khristian Rakovsky (LEFT) with Leon Trotsky: Trotsky allowed Milstein and Horowitz to leave Russia; Rakovsky warned them against returning. *(Volkov Archive)*

Revolution in Petersburg: The burning of the Kazansky police commissariat. (*Volkov Archive*)

"Children of the Soviet revolution": Milstein (SEATED, FOURTH FROM RIGHT) with Vladimir Horowitz (LEANING OVER BACK OF CHAIR), on tour in Kazan, 1923.

Milstein in Vienna: His debut
there was attended by
Schoenberg and Alban Berg.

Milstein in Paris: "Suddenly
your outlook changes
considerably."

to get in front of an orchestra and conduct because that seems the easiest thing to do.

They say that the piano repertoire is richer than the violin repertoire. That's not true! Beethoven's violin concerto, in terms of quality of music and perfection, is superior to all his piano concertos, with the exception, perhaps, of the Fourth. And Brahms's violin concerto, to my taste, is better than his piano concertos.

I am sometimes asked which violin concertos I consider the best, the true classics. In general I don't like making lists of that kind, but the question does start me thinking. Well, I wouldn't head this imaginary list with the concertos by Johann Sebastian Bach. They belong to a different list, of chamber music. But Bach did have a real understanding of the violin. According to Albert Schweitzer, Bach may have been a better violinist than organist. This idea of Schweitzer's is confirmed by the incredible virtuosity of Bach's solo violin works, which Bach himself performed.

If you play the violin cleanly and neatly, Bach will sound good—you won't be able to spoil it—because the violin, as opposed to the piano, is a real Bach instrument. Listening to Bach on a modern piano is like seeing Shakespeare played in French. In English Shakespeare moves in sound waves—higher, higher, higher. In French, he doesn't have that inner rhythm, that springiness.

By the way, Bach's inner rhythmic springiness, like Mozart's, often provokes performers to play too aggressively. They start to play crudely, as if marching off to war. Why?

Mozart's concertos are not real violin concertos for me, either. His piano music is another matter. After all, Mozart—unlike Bach—was a significantly better keyboard player than violinist.

I would put Beethoven's concerto first on my list. It is a miracle, something that seems to have come out of thin air, like some sort of divine message. You can discuss the revelations of his concerto endlessly. One of my favorites is the cadenza in the first movement, in which Beethoven varies the main theme in such a way that the listener keeps waiting for its return with increasing tension. And when it does appear, it's like heavenly song!

Then comes the Mendelssohn. A work of genius from the first note to the last. Then, alas, the Brahms concerto. And at last, the Tchaikovsky: truly a virtuoso concerto. Curiously, these last two works were written the same year, 1878, when Brahms was forty-five and Tchaikovsky thirty-eight.

I feel that Max Bruch's First Concerto is a masterpiece. It has virtues that cannot be found anywhere else. When Joseph Joachim premiered the Brahms, critics and the public often compared it with the Bruch, and many felt that Bruch's concerto was better. I do too, even though Bruch's concerto is not an even work. It has an incredibly spectacular introduction and a marvelous slow movement, but the finale is not so good.

Lalo's *Symphonie espagnole* is a brilliant, very unusual composition. When Tchaikovsky heard it in France, he wrote to his patroness, Nadezhda von Meck, that the work delighted him. Well, what's good enough for Tchaikovsky is good enough for me.

An attractive violin concerto was written by Dvořák. It's a bit heavy, but it is real "musician's" music. Then Saint-Saëns's Third Concerto, which I recorded. It's a pleasant work, which I can't judge too harshly because I'm biased in its favor. I don't admire Sibelius's concerto. Or, for that matter, Elgar's—it's artificial, pompous music, a failed imitation of the Brahms, which in its turn was not too successful an imitation of the Beethoven.

Glazunov's concerto is not an absolute masterpiece, but I like it. Unfortunately, it's too short. When I was young, it was acceptable to perform such short works in a concert. Now you would have to add something like Prokofiev's First Concerto (which I consider a great work). But then the recital would be too long. So there's a dilemma for a performer.

A marvelous and very effective work is Bartók's Second Violin Concerto. I have one objection to it: it's too improvisational, written like an enormous cadenza. The form of a violin concerto can be almost limitlessly original and innovative, but the composer must persuade you that it is a new form and not a shapeless concoction with however many beautiful, expressive moments. I feel this new form in Alban Berg's concerto but not in Bartók's.

I admire the way Bartók, who was a brilliant pianist, plays on his recording of Beethoven's *Kreutzer* Sonata with Joseph Szigeti. Bartók interprets the music extravagantly, more so than Szigeti, and he's right: you can't play Beethoven too academically; it becomes dry and uninteresting. It's like spaghetti. When I order spaghetti in a restaurant, I always ask the waiter not to drain it completely, to leave some of the water; it mixes with the butter and cheese, and it's terrific. But Szigeti was reluctant to play Beethoven "wet."

Szigeti, whom I knew well, was an incredibly cultured musician. Actually, his talent grew out of his culture. In Gstaad we had neighboring chalets, and I would hear Szigeti practicing, playing the same three notes over and over stubbornly. I couldn't understand what he was trying to achieve, but Szigeti apparently had his own ideas. I always admired him, and he was respected by musicians. In his late years he finally got the appreciation he deserved from the general public as well.

I include without hesitation Alban Berg's concerto on my list of great violin concertos. I met Berg in Vienna. He was tall, handsome, and very shy, reminding me of Dmitri Shostakovich or Rudolf Serkin in that regard. His violin concerto, a very important work, is a requiem for a young woman whom Berg must have loved, a woman who died of polio.

In the late 1930s I lived in Paris in a small hotel. The American violinist Louis Krasner used to visit me. Even though he was not rich, he commissioned (or, to put it more bluntly, bought) a violin concerto from Berg, and a bit later one from Schoenberg. Krasner, who came almost every day, kept playing the two concertos for me. I didn't like the Schoenberg very much, but the Berg fascinated me.

At that time the musicologist and publisher Henri Prunières was running a series of prestigious private performances under the auspices of his magazine, *Revue musicale*. It was the Parisian equivalent of the Mezhdunarodnaya Kniga concert series in Moscow, at which Horowitz and I premiered the violin concertos of Szymanowski and Prokofiev.

At Prunières's I played the Prokofiev with pianist Alexander Labinsky, who was married to the ballerina Olga Preobrajenska. (Much older than her husband, she maintained a ballet studio in

Paris.) The Prokofiev was a great success; it is a fairly accessible work. Afterward, Prunières asked me to play again in the *Revue musicale* series. "Not necessarily something new, but perhaps something that is rarely played. Why don't you do Karl Goldmark's concerto?"

I didn't really want to play Goldmark. Prokofiev, even when presented with piano accompaniment rather than an orchestra, was still interesting as a novelty, but Goldmark with piano would have lost a lot. I shared my doubts with Krasner, who suddenly said, "Play the Berg! You know the concerto better than I do by now." When I reminded Krasner that he had exclusive rights to Berg's concerto, he said, "No problem! I play it with an orchestra, and you will be doing it privately, with a pianist. That's an entirely different matter."

I prepared the Berg with a very good French pianist. Even though the French were lukewarm about Berg then, his concerto was a deserved hit in the *Revue musicale* circle. And I was glad to have learned yet another great modern composition.

7. Eugène Ysaÿe and Queen Elisabeth of Belgium

In the summer of 1926, while living in Paris, I went off to see Eugène Ysaÿe, the great Belgian violinist. I remembered Ysaÿe from his performances in Odessa before the revolution, and I thought, Ysaÿe is a marvelous musician who obviously knows a lot. He has a reputation as an innovative artist, a bold experimenter. He was the first to play Franck's sonata and Chausson's *Poème*. That impressed me. I wanted Ysaÿe to tell me his secrets and advise me on my further development.

I went to see him at the resort town of Zout sur Mer—on the coast not far from Ostend. Ysaÿe had a villa there named La Chanterelle. Zout was a rather ugly place frequented for some reason by wealthy tourists, and very proud of its local hero (the street he lived on was named after him, avenue Ysaÿe).

I came to Ysaÿe without an appointment, afraid that if I tried to set a date his secretary would tell me to stay home and not bother the maestro. I spent my last centime on the trip. When I reached La Chanterelle, Ysaÿe's secretary came out to see me. As I later learned, Jeanette, an American from Brooklyn, was his former student. Ysaÿe would marry her shortly.

Jeanette was stern with me: "*Le maître* is tired, he is resting. He cannot see you!" I pleaded, explaining that I didn't have money to return. We argued for a while. Suddenly Ysaÿe came out, enormous and completely naked. "What's all this noise?" He really had been taking a nap, after the beach. Our arguing had awakened him.

"What's the problem?"

"Some kid wants to play for you. . . ."

"Why not? If he's bad, we'll send him home."

Even roused from sleep, Ysaÿe was reasonable. He led me inside and threw on a beach robe, which barely covered his bulging flesh.

(There's a difference between big and fat. The Russian bass Chaliapin was the former, and Ysaÿe the latter. I knew Chaliapin; he had an enormous body, but it was muscled. You could use him as a model for a monument. But Ysaÿe's flabby body evinced a life of excessive food and drink.)

Sitting down, Ysaÿe asked, "What will you play?"

"What would you like to hear, maestro?"

"A Paganini caprice!"

With extreme modesty, I said, "Maestro, which one of the twenty-four would you prefer?" And then I thought, Does that sound too arrogant? But I simply couldn't put it differently, truly! There had been virtually no distractions in Russia—I almost never went to the movies (there was no television yet), and there were no particular amusements. So I practiced the violin! I had learned all of Paganini's caprices, all of Bach for solo violin, and much more.

Ysaÿe asked for the first caprice, a rather difficult one. I delivered. He asked for the last one, the twenty-fourth (also not easy). Ysaÿe didn't hear it through. He interrupted me and asked, "What do you play of Bach?" When I offered him a choice here, too, Ysaÿe didn't believe his ears! Skeptically, he had me play the Fugue from the First Sonata.

I won't say that I performed it well, but I was getting through it, when Ysaÿe interrupted me again. "Why so fast?"

"Would you like it slower, maestro?"

Ysaÿe said hurriedly, "No." Then he said, "Listen, my child, what do you need here? You play Paganini well, Bach, too. What more do you want?" The praise was nice, but I was also disappointed: the maître was sending me home! Noticing my saddened face, Ysaÿe took pity. "You know what, my child, come to my house tonight. We'll play some chamber music."

The maître didn't ask me to dinner, even though the invitation would have come in handy—I was practically starving and had no money; I needed a good nourishing meal a lot more than chamber music.

When I arrived at La Chanterelle at 9:30 that evening, I was led into a large room with about ten guests who had clearly just finished dinner. Dirty plates, glasses, and cups that held the remains of coffee, beer, and wine were heaped everywhere. A horrible sight, a horrible smell. Besides which, the place stank of cigars.

Ysaÿe shoved an instrument in my hands. "Take it!" I thought he was handing me a violin, but it was a viola, which I barely managed to hold: it was big and heavy. Ysaÿe ordered, "Play!" It turned out he wished to play a quartet, and they needed a violist. Ysaÿe was first violin. Second violin was Queen Elisabeth of Belgium, an amateur violinist and a great fan of Ysaÿe's. I don't remember the cellist.

Ysaÿe himself handled the viola and the cello with ease. Apparently he expected every violinist to have a mastery of those instruments. And so he gave me the viola without a word of warning. It's a good thing I had learned the instrument back in Odessa and had played it—fooling around, really—in a quartet at gatherings the local pharmacist used to hold. I had even gone through some serious works as a violist, such as Beethoven's G Major String Quartet.

But Ysaÿe's viola was too big and heavy for me. It was very uncomfortable to play, and I barely handled my part (I remember we were doing a Schumann quartet). My salvation lay in the fact that everyone was playing away with great enthusiasm, paying me little heed, and were having their own troubles. Also, they all apparently thought that since I was young I had to play well, that it was *their* problem Schumann's music didn't fit together. But it was my fault, I was the one failing miserably! Hitting wrong notes all the way!

When we'd have a problem with a passage, Ysaÿe would give Queen Elisabeth a heavy pat on the shoulder and say, "Hold on, *ma petite!*" (He called her "little one" and she called him "papa.") And every time Ysaÿe's powerful paw fell on the queen, who was around fifty at the time, she froze, absolutely thrilled. It was an amazing sight for the uninitiated. I stared and understood nothing!

That is, I understood what Ysaÿe and Elisabeth were saying, having spoken a bit of French back in Odessa (as mentioned earlier, when our family was doing well we had a Swiss governess), but I did not understand the situation at all: Elisabeth was, after all, queen of a European state! And she was being treated—before my very eyes—like an ordinary woman. . . .

Through the musicale, Ysaÿe continued gulping wine. This did not add any polish to his playing. His hands trembled anyway, and after the wine . . .

During those years Ysaÿe appeared as a violinist less and less frequently, and when he did go onstage, more often than not he was no longer the legendary master and inspired musician who had played Bach, Beethoven, and the Romantics with his famed brilliance and transcendence. But violinists went to Ysaÿe's concerts anyway. When he appeared in Paris, you could see all the elite there: Kreisler, Enesco, Thibaud. They conceded freely that Ysaÿe's performing style had influenced them—had encouraged them to a more relaxed interpretation, with improvisational vibrato and freely used rubato. Those marvelous violinists were all, so to speak, Ysaÿe's spiritual students. I don't know what they would have gained from *le maître* if they had taken regular lessons from him. I, alas, learned almost nothing.

At first I was bursting with enthusiasm. I moved to a small

pension not far from Zout and for six or seven weeks came to *le maître* assiduously for instruction. But Ysaÿe said practically nothing to me! I brought him the Brahms concerto. Ysaÿe was not interested in the least in my playing. Instead of hearing me out, he picked up his violin and began playing the concerto along with me, doing the orchestra part. He sawed away enthusiastically, trying to imitate the flute or clarinet, while I was developing a terrible headache!

In order to put an end to this torture, I would start to tell Ysaÿe how I had gone to hear him in Odessa before the revolution. It was impossible to get into an Ysaÿe concert in those days—always sold out. I told Ysaÿe how we young fans of his had come up with the perfect technique for getting into the hall without tickets: as I've described, we would show up in a large band, then half would start a noisy scene to distract the police and ushers long enough for the others to sneak in.

Listening to my stories, Ysaÿe laughed. What I didn't tell him was that I couldn't recall for the life of me *how* he had played! I just remembered that a massive, immensely impressive man with a leonine mane of hair had come out onstage, that everyone had spoken of him ecstatically, gasping: "Oh, the great Ysaÿe!" He was an exciting legend for me, a myth. As for the reality, well, the reality was disappointing.

Others showed up for lessons with Ysaÿe—a violinist from Odessa whose name was Volchikis, a very good American woman violinist named Mitchell, and William Primrose, the famous future violist. Primrose played the violin then. He was a real virtuoso and could rattle off all the Paganini caprices. While fiddling, Primrose literally tore apart his instrument. (When we met in Gstaad a few years later, I said to him, "You can't play like that on a violin, but on a viola—trust me—it'll sound terrific." I don't know whether it was my advice or not, but shortly Primrose switched to the viola.)

When I began studying with Ysaÿe, I was playing a violin I had brought from Odessa. It had been made by the brother of the legendary Odessa aviator Utochkin and was covered with horrible red varnish, with white wood underneath the color of matchsticks. But I liked that instrument. Then, I don't remember how, Utochkin's violin vanished. Volchikis gave me another one—"the work of an anonymous master." Its sound was bombastic! I played that violin with pleasure; I even gave a concert on it in Paris.

Once during a lesson with Ysaÿe a string broke. The master lent me his instrument—a Guarnerius del Gesù. But I didn't appreciate that violin then. (Generally speaking, I feel that one's fortune doesn't lie in the instrument. I am no violin worshiper.) At the end of the summer, however, Ysaÿe let me play on his Guarneri once more, and suddenly the violin sounded marvelous, like Ysaÿe! Juicy, free, expressive, as if I were performing in a large hall. Even the lusty vibrato resembled Ysaÿe's own! And I remember thinking, If a great master plays on an instrument for a long time, it takes on his artistic qualities. How strange. . . .

Well, as I said, I got almost nothing from Ysaÿe, even though he treated me kindly. He gave me a photograph of him standing in the middle of a wheat field, and he inscribed it with a passage from one of his solo violin sonatas. He also gave me the score of his sonatas, inscribed with a real paean in my honor. The photo and the music were in the trunk I left in Paris when I set off for the U.S.A. in 1939. I never saw them again. . . .

Over the years I have played a few of Ysaÿe's solo violin sonatas. There are sections of very good music in them. I particularly like the one called *Malinconia*, dedicated to Jacques Thibaud, with its Dies Irae leitmotiv. But basically, it was fun being with Ysaÿe and playing with him. His presence alone could be an inspiration—that overflowing bulk brought into motion by music! Ysaÿe even tuned his violin with enormous temperament! Yet it wasn't really leading anywhere, and I began to get sick of it. I hung around at Ysaÿe's a while longer and then returned to Paris. Gracefully, Ysaÿe did not forget me and even asked me to perform in a concert honoring Queen Elisabeth, which he was conducting.

As a conductor Ysaÿe was a constant presence in Belgium. He also successfully led the orchestra in Cincinnati, Ohio. Playing under Ysaÿe, the musicians gave their best. In that way Ysaÿe the conductor was like Alexander Glazunov, although certainly a much bolder one.

Not agreeing with your teachers is an art that should be learned!

Toulouse-Lautrec went to Degas for advice, and Degas told him, "Never use black!" Lautrec didn't listen—and became famous. Still, one of Ysaÿe's suggestions, which he made almost in passing, is something I cherish and use all my life. He said, "Never play classical music (including baroque and Mozart) *forte-fortissimo*. Remember: *forte* simply means, 'don't play *piano*'; and if it says '*piano*,' don't play *forte*." And he's right a thousand times over! The music of the baroque and of the classics mustn't be played too loud or too soft. Or too fast, for that matter.

Ensembles playing baroque music on the original instruments are quite popular nowadays. The audiences adore them. They think that they are getting the result of profound research, that it's very stylish work. But in my opinion these ensembles too often serve up Bach in an incredibly tasteless way.

The point isn't in the instruments on which the musicians play but in their approach. I've heard diligent performers on original instruments who played baroque music vulgarly, with a nervous super-Romantic vibrato. And those superfast tempi! In the Bach suite with flute, James Galway, who has a marvelous tone, takes insane tempi, which totally perverts the music. But the audience is in raptures and you can't get tickets to Galway's concerts. . . .

Ysaÿe adored Russian music and had a deep understanding of it, and his interpretations of the Tchaikovsky and Glazunov concerti were inspired and affectionate. He particularly appreciated the Canzonetta from the Tchaikovsky concerto. Russian music at that time was highly regarded among the French elite, thanks to Claude Debussy (who dedicated his string quartet to Ysaÿe, by the way).

People forget that Debussy lived in Russia as a young man. He taught music to the children of the notorious Nadezhda von Meck, and so his Russian experiences must have been a major influence on Debussy's music. Listen to his *La Mer*: it comes from Rimsky-Korsakov's opera *Sadko*. (Rimsky-Korsakov was a genius at capturing the element of water in music; his *Scheherazade* is confirmation of that. I always wondered where this Russian composer got those musical flows and breaking waves.)

And take Mussorgsky. Some of Debussy's pieces seemed to be modeled after Mussorgsky's! For instance, "Chevelure" from

Chansons de Bilitis. Naturally, in Debussy the Russian influence is passed through the fine sieve of French taste: the French were elegant and precise, refinements the Russians, alas, often lacked.

Queen Elisabeth of Belgium was a great fan of Russian music and Russian violinists. She lived in a palace between Brussels and Ostend, to be closer to Ysaÿe, and in 1937 she organized the Ysaÿe International Violin Competition, which David Oistrakh won, with the four other Soviet competitors all winning prizes too. After that, Elisabeth became so enthralled by Soviet violinists that she gradually came to the conclusion that communism couldn't be so bad if it produced such musicians. Fortunately for Belgium, the government is not an absolute monarchy. (Though I doubt that Elisabeth would have experimented with communism in Belgium; she did, however, learn Russian.)

I would meet Elisabeth and her husband, King Albert, in the home of a wealthy Swiss, Professor Kramer, an orthopedics manufacturer, who had made his fortune during World War One producing prostheses for arms and legs. His wife, Frau Professor Kramer, liked music and musicians and was in love (platonically) with my friend from our Odessa days, Baron Oskar von Riesemann, the music critic.

King Albert was impressive: slim, tanned, with curly hair. He wore the aura of "martyr king," acquired when the Germans invaded Belgium during World War One. The relationship between Elisabeth and Albert was cozy and comfortable. Each was warm and attentive to the other, and at first it was hard to tell who set the tone in the family. Things like that are revealed in trifles, details. Once after lunch, Albert was picking his teeth with his fork. Elisabeth slapped his hand immediately: "Albert, shame on you!" A scene from bourgeois family life, not royalty.

Albert took me aside one day and asked confidentially, "My wife likes the Russian cellist Barzhansky. Is he a good musician?" Barzhansky came from a family of Odessa jewelers, from whose store I'd bought my marvelous gold watch. He wasn't a particularly handsome man, and he wasn't a very good cellist, either. He and his sculptor wife used to visit the royal palace as if it were their own home. I was surprised Elisabeth was so taken with him—as a musician, of course.

But naturally, I couldn't say anything bad to King Albert about my compatriot, so my answer was rather evasive: "Your Majesty, I have never heard Barzhansky play, but my colleagues describe him as a good cellist." My answer apparently satisfied Albert.

I could explain Queen Elisabeth's attitude toward musicians this way: Surrounded by people who constantly wanted something from her, she longed to escape that suffocating circle—so she relaxed in the company of artists. She found it interesting and pleasant to be with them.

I remember one time when my friend the Russian musician Issai Dobrowen and I were sitting with a group that included Elisabeth. She told us, "Smoke, talk about whatever you want, don't talk, leave, come back! Don't pay any attention to me! Forget I'm here!" Although her outburst went against all the rules not only of royal etiquette but of ordinary good manners, it was so sincere! Elisabeth wanted to be just "one of the guys" among us musicians.

Queen Elisabeth attended virtually every concert of violinists appearing in Brussels, and never missed those of performers who were connected to Ysaÿe or his name. Elisabeth considered herself a pupil of Ysaÿe's and honored his memory.

Once (this was before World War Two) I played in Brussels with an orchestra, doing the concertos of Mendelssohn and Saint-Saëns. I appeared at the end of the program (the conductor was afraid that once it heard me the audience would leave). Audiences in Brussels in those days were not as refined as, say, those in neighboring Amsterdam, but they still applauded me politely. I played an encore, packed up my violin, and came out for a final bow.

When a violinist comes onstage without his instrument, this is usually a signal for the audience to make a break for it. But Elisabeth would not leave; she stood in her box and applauded! And since the queen wasn't leaving, the rest of the audience had to stay. They stood and brought their palms together feebly, looking exhaustedly not at the stage but at the royal box, preparing to rush for the doors at the first opportunity. Seeing the situation, I immediately grabbed a violin from one of the orchestra members (who were still onstage) and started another encore. But the violin sounded terrible!

That is one of the dangers traveling soloists face. They have to pray that the concertmaster has a good violin in case something happens to their own instrument. Once when I was playing the Brahms concerto in Los Angeles under the baton of the talented Zubin Mehta, I had to grab the concertmaster's violin practically on the run. Luckily, it was a Strad. But that doesn't always happen. Even in wealthy America, the quality of violins in orchestras outside the big cities is not overwhelming. I remember playing with the New Jersey Symphony. When I broke a string, the concertmaster's violin turned out to be totally inadequate. I had to interrupt the performance again and ask if any of the orchestra players had a good instrument. One of the second violins, a rich dentist in his professional life, had a good one—a Guadagnini, I believe.

Back in Brussels that time, I sort of accommodated myself to the miserable violin. When the concert was over, I followed etiquette and went to the royal box. Elisabeth said, "Milstein, after your own violin, that one sounded like a wooden box with ropes strung over it!"

I replied, "Your Majesty, why did you make the poor audience suffer through an additional encore?" Elisabeth's answer was memorable. "I did that on purpose. The listeners are ingrates. They don't understand how much musicians give them. By applauding, I force the audience to pay attention."

That's how Queen Elisabeth helped create a good reception for visiting violinists. Of course, this was eccentric on her part, even quixotic. But what would the world do without Don Quixotes—both male and female? Elisabeth was perfectly altruistic in her love of the art of the violin. In that sense she was perhaps the best of Ysaÿe's students, embodying his ideals and devoting herself completely to music.

In our day monarchs and politicians rarely appear at concerts of classical music. And if they do, they are usually there not for the music but out of considerations of charity or as some important political gesture. Why not love classical music for its own sake? We live in an era of dilettantism. Dilettantes have taken over every-thing—culture, industry, politics. And they have done so trying to look like professionals.

But I think of Queen Elisabeth with great sympathy, even though she was an amateur in the field closest to my heart—music. The purity of her ambitions was obvious. She tried, as best she could, to influence the taste of her subjects, to change it for the better. And she may even have succeeded, against all odds. Elisabeth was one of the rare exceptions in this crude, cynical, and calculating world. She loved, to paraphrase Stanislavsky's famous line, music in the self instead of the self in music. And part of that love she left to us.

8. Rachmaninoff
as I Knew Him

I adore Rachmaninoff, both as a performer and a composer. I love all his compositions. As a composer, he is unabashedly emotional and forms his works almost instinctively, like Schubert. And, as in Schubert, Rachmaninoff's compositions are sometimes too long. I readily forgive him that because of his sincerity and depth of emotion, even though some music professor in Liège will raise severe objections. (The French do not understand Rachmaninoff or Tchaikovsky. In France, if people hear music coming in from the street, they shut the windows. In Russia, on the contrary, they fling them open wider.)

Here I should say a word about Tchaikovsky, too. I consider him a composer of genius and believe that in terms of talent he may be the equal of Beethoven. But, unfortunately, Tchaikovsky, a typical Russian, was sometimes not as organized in his compositions as Beethoven and other great German composers.

The same trait is manifest in Rachmaninoff. It sometimes seems that he has too much melody! In order to fully appreciate the beauty of this melodic overabundance, you have to love Russian folk songs. I was born in Russia and I feel that beauty. That's why Russian musicians have a special affinity for Rachmaninoff. And that's why it was Horowitz who did such powerful interpretations of Rachmaninoff's Third Piano Concerto and his other works for piano: the *Etudes-tableaux*, *Moments musicaux*, preludes, Second Sonata (in which the composer himself permitted Horowitz to make some cuts). But of course it is not just a question of one's origins; the congeniality of the "emotional profiles" of the music and its interpreter also plays an enormous role.

I particularly love Rachmaninoff's Second Piano Concerto. It's a masterpiece. What a divine beginning! The more you listen to that concerto, the more you find in it. Not only is the piano part a work of genius, but the orchestra is exquisite too. Or take Rachmaninoff's colossal work for orchestra, chorus, and vocal soloists, *The Bells*, based on the Edgar Allan Poe poem. Or his three marvelous symphonies—each epic, majestic, monumental! Bruckner may be deeper, but Rachmaninoff is more emotional and natural.

As a performer Rachmaninoff was, on the contrary, very analytical. In his own interpretation, the form of his works seemed impeccable. Rachmaninoff's overall forte as a pianist was shaping the form. He erected a work's form right before your eyes, with unbounded imperiousness. Of course, he was helped by his mighty technique—an unbelievably powerful sound, enormous dynamic range, and rhythm that was at once iron and hypnotically flexible.

The first time I heard Rachmaninoff was back in Petersburg in 1915. He played his Second Piano Concerto. It was a matinee, and the audience was full of youngsters who, like myself, had come with their mothers. But I wasn't looking around, Rachmaninoff made such an impression on me when he appeared onstage. He was extremely serious, even grim, as if he were not yet quite awake. He settled on the chair, looked at the audience from under his hairy brow (a characteristic mannerism, as I was to learn), as if to check that all the tickets had been sold. (At least, that was my impression then.)

He seemed in no hurry to start playing, and after some thought, he apparently came to the conclusion that his chair was too far from the piano. He decided to move it closer. So he reached out and grabbed the piano, then tried to pull the chair, with him on it, toward the instrument. Instead, the piano moved toward him. The audience, up till then breathless, gasped. Rachmaninoff didn't need to play after that, he could have gotten a standing ovation right there. (Chaliapin in Boris Godunov's death scene, appearing on the stage even before singing "Wait! I'm still the tsar!" had a similar effect.)

Many years later I told Rachmaninoff how I had heard him perform when I was a child and how he had won over the audience even before he started playing. He loved the story and laughed. Rachmaninoff, despite his grim appearance, was a merry man. You can hear it in his music. There are powerful lyrical moments when his soul is singing, if I may put it that way. And there are other moments when you can see his humor. He liked to be amused. I idolized him and loved to make him laugh.

I met him in 1931, when I was twenty-seven. We were introduced by my old Odessa friend Oskar von Riesemann, with whom I became reacquainted when I arrived in Switzerland. All the musicians there knew Riesemann. When I came for the summer to Gstaad, he called and drove over in his car to see me.

Rachmaninoff lived on the shore of Lake Lucerne in Hertenstein. Riesemann lived in Kastanienbaum, about forty minutes' drive from Rachmaninoff's villa, Senar. Not only was he a friend of Rachmaninoff's, he subsequently published a book called *Rachmaninoff's Recollections*. Riesemann brought Rachmaninoff to my concert, and Rachmaninoff, as I recall, liked my playing. In any case, I became a frequent guest at his house.

I remember amusing Rachmaninoff with stories about my luck at gambling. Really, I won at everything—blackjack, roulette, and, mostly, carambolle. Carambolle differs from roulette by having only nine numbers, rather than thirty-six. In Montreux and Lausanne you were allowed to make only two-franc bets, but by betting only on four and seven (mostly on seven), I would end up winning seventy-five to a hundred francs every evening. As I returned to the Hotel Excelsior, where I was staying, I jingled the silver pieces victoriously in my pocket. Rachmaninoff was greatly entertained by my gambling tales.

Once I was performing in Lucerne and Riesemann brought Rachmaninoff, his wife, their daughter Tatyana, and Tatyana's husband, Boris Conus. They had dined before the concert, and after eating, Rachmaninoff dropped by the casino, where, following my system, he bet on seven and won a lot of money. After the concert Rachmaninoff came backstage, jingling the silver victoriously in his pocket!

At that concert I played the Bach E Major Partita for solo violin, and apparently my performance acted as an impulse for Rachmaninoff to do a wonderful piano transcription of some of the movements—the Prelude, the Gavotte, and the Gigue—which he subsequently published as a suite.

Then came the day when Rachmaninoff said to me, "Nathan Mironovich, I'm giving a concert in Paris. I'll be playing the Bach prelude in my transcription for the first time there. You come hear it. And in the intermission, tell me your opinion." Oh, I was so proud. For days I looked down my nose at everybody, I didn't want to talk to anyone: Rachmaninoff was interested in my opinion of his work!

I went to the concert and listened attentively, all ears. There was one passage in the transcription of the prelude that I didn't like; I didn't think it sounded "Bachian" enough.

After the first part of the concert, I went back to see Rachmaninoff, as he had requested, and now I was afraid! Afraid to tell the truth. But I just couldn't not tell it. Only what should I say? I made a bashful face and began, "Sergei Vasilyevich, I have some doubts: in the prelude, it seems to me, you have a chromatic sequence, which doesn't sound just right—" Rachmaninoff interrupted angrily, "Go to hell!"

Oh boy, I thought, this is coming to a bad end for me. Of

course, going to hell was not obligatory, but staying around Rachmaninoff was uncomfortable. There was the distinct possibility of a scene. . . .

After the concert Rachmaninoff's daughter was giving a dinner party. I didn't know whether to go. My God, Rachmaninoff was going to hate me now! His wife, Natalia Alexandrovna, saw me still at the theater, clearly in despair, and came over to me. "Do come with us. Sergei Vasilyevich didn't mean to offend you. He was just nervous after performing." I went, feeling as if I were headed for the guillotine or for questioning by the Soviet cheka. When I got to their house, I stayed in a corner, fearing Rachmaninoff's wrath.

His friends were all there: the composers Glazunov, Medtner, Grechaninov, and Julius Conus (father of Boris). Rachmaninoff still seemed to be in a huff at first, but then, after dinner, he called me into the library: "Nathan Mironovich, come along, come along!" I felt resurrected!

In the library a discussion began, with Rachmaninoff asking Glazunov: "Sasha, did you hear any clumsy chromatic sequences in my Bach transcription?" Apparently Glazunov had not listened too closely during the concert. No, Glazunov hadn't heard anything like that. Then Rachmaninoff turned to Medtner. "Nika, did you?" But Medtner must have been thinking about the dinner and wine to come after the concert. He hadn't noticed either. So I had been the only interested listener! And I knew that partita well from my own playing. Of course, now I was no longer so certain that I was right—maybe I had been spoiled by Leopold Godowsky's transcriptions and my bad taste had let me down.

Still, I saw that Rachmaninoff was no longer angry with me, and no longer wished me to go to hell. I was pleased. After dinner I went to my room at the Hotel Majestic on avenue Kleber—Rachmaninoff was staying there too—then went outside to pick up a copy of *Poslednie novosti* (The Latest News), a Russian-language newspaper published by the émigré Pavel Milyukov. When I returned, the concierge stopped me. "M. Rachmaninoff would like you to go to his suite."

I was afraid: what if he cursed me again? I meekly opened the door to his suite—just a tiny bit, not daring to enter—and he shouted, "Come in, come in! You were right!" I was ecstatic!

Rachmaninoff's musical authority in Russia was immense, to such a point that when Vladimir Horowitz and I came to know him, we felt it was our incredible good fortune: he was a classic, like Bach or Beethoven, and here we were, meeting with him, playing for him, fooling around!

We visited with Rachmaninoff often in Switzerland, usually around four in the afternoon. Volodya amused Rachmaninoff with his imitations of various pianists. For instance, he would do the elderly Ignacy Paderewski, who comes out on the stage and can't find the piano, or figure out which way to go, all the while looking bewildered. It was quite accurate; I had seen Paderewski like that! (I remember a concert in Dallas: expensive tickets, loads of people. Paderewski wandered around the stage exactly as Horowitz had mimicked him, then sat at the piano. He started to play, and you couldn't hear a thing! He played so softly. . . . But a lady near me sighed with delight, "How divine!")

Horowitz also parodied the pompous Artur Schnabel. Or Walter Gieseking: how Gieseking raises his arms for a powerful attack, lowers them forcefully on the keyboard, and gets only a mezzo-forte sound.

Rachmaninoff adored those caricatures of Horowitz's . . . until Volodya did his Rachmaninoff imitation for him. Volodya came out, hunched over, heavily dragging his feet, then sat down and rubbed his face in a characteristic gesture. Rachmaninoff took offense. And that was funny too!

I remember another occasion when he took umbrage—this time at both myself and Gregor Piatigorsky. We had decided to play a joke on Rachmaninoff: we came and told him we were going to play for him a new duet by a contemporary Italian composer, Gian Francesco Malipiero. I knew Malipiero wrote operas, and I was also familiar with his transcriptions of Monteverdi and Vivaldi, but I wasn't aware he had ever written a duet for violin and cello.

So we began improvising according to an agreed-upon outline: Grisha Piatigorsky began with something in the "recitative and fantasy" style, and I followed with a chromatic accompaniment (which always works and doesn't sound too dissonant because you can't tell where it's eventually going to lead). We fooled around in this manner for a rather long time. It sounded good, very convincing. Finally Piatigorsky decided it was time to finish and quietly led the melody upward. I followed, adding something along the way. I got up so high that I didn't know what to do next. I burst out laughing hysterically. It was awful!

Rachmaninoff got up silently and left, obviously insulted. For the rest of the evening he wouldn't come out to see us. Eventually, of course, he got over it and made up with Grisha and me. Rachmaninoff forgot things like that rather quickly.

Once, I made Rachmaninoff happy by teasing Volodya Horowitz. This is the story: The three of us were in New York at Horowitz's Riverdale house. We started talking about whether too much concertizing was harmful for a performer. I maintained that it was. Rachmaninoff agreed. Horowitz argued that you can get used to frequent performances. "You can get used to mistakes too," I noted. If you play a work constantly, you overplay it and stop monitoring yourself. I said to Horowitz, "Take yourself, for instance. You have great temperament, but sometimes, going after an effect, you sort of lose control."

"Where do I lose control?" exclaimed Horowitz indignantly.

I suggested that Horowitz show Rachmaninoff how he played a certain passage in the last movement of Tchaikovsky's First Piano Concerto. "You have a fit there, like an epileptic," I said, imitating Volodya convulsively bunching up the rhythm. (Like many other great artists, Horowitz often didn't play what is written in the notes. Sometimes it was brilliant, sometimes not.) Of course, I was grossly exaggerating his "mistake," to make it look funny and to amuse Rachmaninoff. Volodya fought back, maintaining that I was inventing it, that he didn't play that way.

Rachmaninoff said, "Why bicker?" He turned to Horowitz. "Vladimir Samoilovich, I know that you make recordings of everything you play. They tell me you've done two of the Tchaikovsky. Let's go listen to them." We played both of Horowitz's recordings. Sure enough, he sounded just as I had imitated him. Rachmaninoff was pleased. "I knew that Nathan Mironovich would not be mistaken, he has a good ear." Was he recalling the Bach prelude incident in Paris, when he was so angry with me? Oh, I was in seventh heaven from Rachmaninoff's recognition and trust!

That trust was also expressed before a performance of his *Rhapsody on a Theme by Paganini* with the Philadelphia Orchestra under Stokowski, when Rachmaninoff handed me the orchestra parts for the violins and violas and said, "Make it so that the violinists and violists don't complain—put in bowing so that it's comfortable for them to play." I worked assiduously and returned the edited scores to Rachmaninoff.

It is not widely known that in 1924, when Koussevitzky sought the mantle of music director of the Boston Symphony Orchestra, held for some years by Pierre Monteux, he had a powerful competitor. The Bostonians were seriously considering inviting Rachmaninoff. But then, it was widely rumored at the time, Koussevitzky's wife made a large donation to the orchestra at a strategically important moment. As a result the vacancy went to Koussevitzky.

One might think that this maneuver of the Koussevitzkys would have been a blow to Rachmaninoff's American career. But I once discussed this question with Piatigorsky, and we came to the conclusion that it was a blessing in disguise. There are many conductors but only one Rachmaninoff. Once he became a music director Rachmaninoff would most certainly have cut back his piano playing. And the members of the BSO board would have driven him crazy with their opinions on budget and repertoire. So it was better for music that Rachmaninoff continued actively performing as a pianist.

However, Rachmaninoff's wife, Natalia Alexandrovna, could not forgive Koussevitzky on principle. When Rachmaninoff died and his body was brought to New York from California, Koussevitzky showed up at the funeral. Their relations had always been rather cool, and here was Koussevitzky, pretending deep grief and sobbing demonstratively.

Natalia Alexandrovna was outraged. "What a clown! That snake Koussevitzky! He had the nerve to show up at the funeral after what happened with the Boston Symphony!"

When I met Rachmaninoff he was almost sixty. Looking at him, you would think that he never ate—he was so thin, so dried-out. But still he was handsome—of course, not like Gary Cooper, more like a Russian nobleman (Rachmaninoff's grandfather was a famous tsarist general in his day, commander of the Cadet Corps in Petersburg).

Rachmaninoff was tall, and though not a giant like his friend Chaliapin, he looked imposing. (It was his way of holding his head, his manner. Elisabeth, Queen of Belgium, was not a tall woman, but she rose above everyone else wherever she appeared.) I sometimes thought that Rachmaninoff resembled Alexander Kerensky, who became the Russian premier after the overthrow of the tsar. Kerensky fled Russia and settled in the U.S.A. I met him at Oberlin College in Ohio. He had the same peculiar shape of the face, and the same crew-cut hair. But Rachmaninoff had a more artistic look. The slight slant of his eyes suggested that somewhere in the Rachmaninoff line there was Tatar blood.

Rachmaninoff always appeared in the same suit. He smoked Sano cigarettes, using a glass cigarette holder. At one point there was a hysterical campaign about the dangers of smoking Sanos, but Rachmaninoff did not give up his favorite brand. What he did was break each cigarette in half. Eventually he would smoke the second half, but everyone—including Rachmaninoff—thought that he was smoking less.

At least he was stretching out the time for each cigarette. He made a ritual out of it. Everything he did turned into a ritual, and everything he did was attractive. What made it so were his amazing, marvelous hands: big, powerful, beautiful.

Rachmaninoff understood all kinds of machinery. And he loved to drive. "I can cover a thousand kilometers behind the wheel and not get tired!" he would boast. He often traveled to his concerts in Europe (and later in America) driving his own car. Every year he bought a new Cadillac or Continental, the most expensive cars. (He could afford them.) He did this because he didn't like to fuss with repairs. The old car was taken to the dealer; Rachmaninoff added fifteen hundred dollars and got a new automobile.

The pride of his estate on Lake Lucerne, Senar, was the embankment he had built. One of his favorite pastimes was rowing. I lived in Bürgenstock, on a hill. Rachmaninoff came to visit several times by boat, rowing it himself. (Later, when he inscribed a photograph for me, he wrote the town as Regenstock instead of Bürgenstock, because whenever he came to visit it always seemed to rain; it was a pun, of course, on *regen*, meaning "rain.") Rachmaninoff used to take Horowitz and me for rides on the boat, and he amused himself by stopping in the middle of the lake, standing up, and enjoying the view. The boat would rock terribly, and I would be in a panic, thinking we'd all drown. But Rachmaninoff didn't care.

Before the revolution Rachmaninoff had lived on a large estate in Russia, and in Switzerland he continued to be an avid gardener. He developed some exotic black rose. It was very beautiful, even though it wasn't truly black but rather dark burgundy, or dark purple. It became a major event. Photographers came and pictures of the rose appeared in newspapers and magazines, but since it was so dark a color and the photographs were black-and-white, it was hard to see what was so special about the rose.

Rachmaninoff had good business sense and was always investing in various enterprises. Of course, he had business advisers. Every artist who makes good money is besieged by people with advice on how to invest it. But Rachmaninoff found the time and patience to sort out the advice and to act accordingly, which made him rather an exception.

Rachmaninoff didn't require any special entertainment to relax. Like a child, he was amused by the simplest things and adored all kinds of gadgets. He enjoyed poker and would delight in peeking at other people's cards. He'd get up from the table, walk around the players, bend over and say, "Honest, I won't tell, I won't tell anyone!" And it wasn't all that important for him to win. Horowitz, when he played with us, also peeked at the cards. But he needed that in order to be a winner. Rachmaninoff was simply having fun and being amusing.

As a great and famous male artist, Rachmaninoff had female fans galore. (I remember he once told me that he liked women in black stockings.) But at home his wife, Natalia Alexandrovna, reigned supreme. She protected him and did so with great dignity and tact. With a wife like that Rachmaninoff could sometimes pretend that he was a lamb, while actually he was a lion. And there were occasions when he showed his claws!

Piatigorsky told me of one such occasion. He was playing in a salon in Berlin with the young Polish pianist Karol Szreter. Rachmaninoff was there, too. After the performance, Szreter wanted to approach Rachmaninoff and ask for his impressions. Piatigorsky warned, "I don't recommend it. Rachmaninoff might tell you the truth!" Piatigorsky knew that Rachmaninoff was not overly generous with praise—a simple "good" was about the highest encomium one could expect from his lips.

But Szreter simply had to find out Rachmaninoff's opinion. Trembling, he approached him and said, "Sergei Vasilyevich, how did I play?" The reply was brief and to the point: "Very badly."

I remember another episode. One time, in America, where Rachmaninoff had settled permanently in 1939, a lady persistently asked me to introduce her to the maestro after an upcoming concert in Chicago. I tried to explain that Rachmaninoff was always tired after a performance and would be unlikely to give her the "musical conversation" she was hoping for. And was I right!

I was in the dressing room when the lady burst in; Rachmaninoff was sitting in a deep armchair, head on his chest; his heavy arms hung loosely. He was resting. She came up to him, and with a shrug I said, "Sergei Vasilyevich, I'd like to introduce Mme N. to you. She loves music very very much!" Without moving his head or lifting his eyes, barely rising from the chair, Rachmaninoff offered her his long hand. "How do you do," he said in thickly accented English. And fell back in the chair. The audience was over. Behind Rachmaninoff's back I mouthed to the stunned lady, "I told you so!"

The circle of people around Rachmaninoff was relatively small. The center, naturally, was the Rachmaninoff family: his wife and two daughters. The elder, Irina, married Prince Peter Wolkonsky, but he died very young. It was a great tragedy. Boris Conus, the husband of the younger daughter, Tatyana, was a rather colorless fellow.

One of Rachmaninoff's best friends was Nikolai Medtner, whom Rachmaninoff valued highly both as a pianist and a composer. I played his excellent violin sonata with Riesemann. I also had a pretty good knowledge of Medtner's piano music, because Horowitz absolutely adored it. He played his concerto and his *Fairy Tales* for piano, some of which are simply marvelous. Unfortunately, Medtner's music is not popular now, even though its qualities are unassailable. I want to do a transcription for violin of one of his fairy tales. Heifetz already tried, but he wasn't very successful because in his transcription the violin doesn't sing.

Medtner, like Rachmaninoff, left Russia because of the Bolsheviks. Rachmaninoff tried to promote him as much as he could, helping to organize concert dates for Medtner in the U.S.A. and elsewhere.

Another émigré supported by Rachmaninoff was his cousin Alexander Siloti, in Russia a famous and wealthy pianist and conductor. Siloti was one of Liszt's favorite pupils; they say that he was his illegitimate son. Siloti in profile really did resemble Liszt. I think he was proud of the resemblance, making the most of a birthmark on his cheek, à la Liszt.

I met with Siloti several times in the New York home of Alexander Greiner, of the Steinway company, who was also a friend of Rachmaninoff's. Steinway has a tradition of supplying famous musicians with pianos, often for free. They do it for the publicity, and at the time this was one of Greiner's duties. (I very much needed a free Stradivarius then, but alas Steinway didn't have one.)

Rachmaninoff, who wrote marvelous songs, had vocalist friends, one of whom I remember well—the beautiful, large, and very tall Nina Koshetz, who looked like a painting by the Russian artist Philip Maliavin, and in other respects was like a dignified edition of the actress Dagmar Godowsky, daughter of the famous pianist (and at one time Stravinsky's girlfriend). I met Koshetz in Paris, where she had moved from Moscow. She was a great soprano, and Rachmaninoff, utterly charmed by her, dedicated his immortal "Vocalise" to her.

And of course, one of Rachmaninoff's most famous friends was the bass Feodor Chaliapin. The two musical giants adored each other. Rachmaninoff spoke of "Fedya," as he called Chaliapin, with unusual tenderness. Chaliapin was such an impressive figure of a man that simply seeing him was an experience.

I remember Chaliapin walking along the boulevard des Madeleines in Paris, stopping at every store window and studying the display with his monocle raised to his eye. Chaliapin was like a walking monument, creating a sensational effect wherever he went. Everyone turned around to stare at him, young and old: Who was that extraordinary man? And I must say that Chaliapin, who was a great artist not only onstage but in real life, did everything he could to get attention. He liked to wear colorful, bright ties, and a white panama suit, and to carry a heavy walking stick. He reigned over the crowd like a gigantic Martian!

I was at Chaliapin's house in Passy, on rue Renoir, invited there by his son, Boris, a good friend of mine. Boris became an excellent portraitist and later did a painting of my wife, Thérèse. When he moved to America, he did hundreds of covers for *Time* magazine. In my New York years, Boris Chaliapin, Balanchine, and I stayed up till three in the morning at the Russian Tea Room many a time. . . .

Chaliapin *père*, like Rachmaninoff, was a willful artist, shaping a musical work as he saw fit, creating the impression of genius in compositions that perhaps were not so powerful to begin with. For instance, I heard his performance of Alexander Grechaninov's religious music: Chaliapin sang divinely, with such dramatic impact that you were literally torn to pieces. I'm not so sure that the score would have the same effect in anyone else's interpretation.

I once heard Chaliapin perform at the Salle Pleyel in Paris, at a benefit concert for needy Russian émigrés. The newspapers publicized the concert by announcing that he would perform songs and arias at the audience's request. And, in fact, the program listed approximately three hundred musical compositions from which the audience could choose and call out their selections.

As it turned out, Chaliapin had no intention of presenting a program according to the whims of his audience. His strategy was different. Say he wanted to sing Mussorgsky's "The Flea." There might be calls from the audience for "Beethoven!" "In questa tomba oscura!" "Rachmaninoff's 'Lilacs'!" Chaliapin would stand majestically and calmly, surveying the crowd through his monocle, and wait until someone shouted, " 'The Flea'!"

Then he'd announce in his resonant bass, "I hear a request for 'The Flea.' "

The crowd immediately grew still, because whatever Chaliapin sang turned into a polished diamond. So they ended up hearing a concert of Chaliapin's war-horses. And of course, no one was upset about being tricked by the publicity gimmick.

Both Chaliapin and Rachmaninoff were very right-wing. Each lost a significant fortune in Russia because of the revolution. In the West they had to start over, almost from scratch. And, being great artists, they achieved financial security. But they had no intention of losing it again to another revolution. Besides which, both were extremely independent, in their work and by temperament. Neither would have tolerated government interference in his artistic affairs.

Although they hated the Soviet regime, Chaliapin and Rachmaninoff remained fierce Russian patriots, almost chauvinists. The Russian roots and character of their work are indisputable. And the Soviet authorities understood that quickly. In the first years of the revolution they were hostile to Chaliapin and Rachmaninoff: after all, they were "white émigrés." But with time that hostility faded. And in the 1930s, Rachmaninoff's compositions gradually returned to Moscow concert halls.

Rachmaninoff was very ambivalent about coming back into favor. The famous Red Army Song and Dance Ensemble had appeared in Paris several times, and their programs had included works by Rachmaninoff. But in those years, going to see the singing and dancing Red Army men would have been against his political convictions, even though he really wanted to hear Russians performing his compositions.

Rachmaninoff did not like talking much about music, but I tried to get him going every time we met. He was such an authority for me, his opinions on subjects I was unsure of were very important to me. Sometimes his replies were brief and enigmatic, but they were always extremely stimulating.

For instance, I once asked Rachmaninoff what he thought of Mussorgsky's *Boris Godunov*. He responded, "Marvelous music, but not Russian." At first I was confused: how could Mussorgsky be not Russian enough for Rachmaninoff? Eventually I figured out what he had in mind. Apparently, he didn't like the presence of Oriental motifs in *Boris*. Say, the monk Varlaam's famous aria, "Kak vo gorode bylo vo Kazani"—after all, it bears an incredible resemblance to the chorus of Polovtsian women in Borodin's *Prince Igor*. And that chorus is a vivid example of "Oriental" music.

Rachmaninoff taught me to listen closely to music, to find various connections and influences in it. The most amazing discoveries await a musician on that path.

I remember my pianist Tasso Janopulo and I were rehearsing Beethoven's *Kreutzer* Sonata. This was in Paris on the rue du Faubourg St-Honoré. It's a marvelous place, a quiet cul-de-sac inhabited by film stars and artists. It was late June, and quite warm, so we opened the window into the long inner courtyard.

The celebrated French actor Louis Jouvet lived opposite. He had an exotic servant—a Turk in a fez. Rehearsing the *Kreutzer*, we had gotten to the characteristic closing theme of the exposition of the first movement when suddenly the Turkish servant called to us across the courtyard, "You're playing my people's music!" Out of the blue, it seemed, he was holding a tambourine, then singing along and dancing while beating the rhythm on the tambourine!

At first Tasso and I were astonished, but then I thought, Of course, the theme is Turkish in character! That's why it's so inconvenient to play, by the way. We are so used to hearing it in the context of the Beethoven sonata that we do not notice its exotic roots.

I also played the *Kreutzer* (and other Beethoven sonatas) with Rachmaninoff. Interestingly, Rachmaninoff admitted that he did not like the *Kreutzer*. He joked about a young lady violinist back in Moscow who had pursued him, offering to play the *Kreutzer* for him, but he had avoided her.

Rachmaninoff as I Knew Him

One time in Chicago, Rachmaninoff and I were the guests of Dr. Maurice Cottle and his wife, the pianist Gitta Gradova. Rachmaninoff liked both very much and he had high esteem for Gradova as a fine musician. That evening Rachmaninoff was in a good mood. He had already performed his ritual: he'd had his vodka and had broken a Sano cigarette in half. Seeing the sheet music for the *Kreutzer* on the piano (I had been rehearsing it with the pianist Arthur Balsam for a coming concert), he unexpectedly asked me, "Do you have your violin?" When I told him my violin was right there, he suggested we play the *Kreutzer*.

We looked through the first movement, and Rachmaninoff noted, "That Beethoven was a good composer. He knew what he wanted and realized it precisely. He may have given the wrong tempi sometimes, perhaps because tempo is a relative thing that depends on the metronome: that is, on a machine. But the notes, they are his own, they come from within, and so they are written with extreme precision."

Then we played through the whole sonata. It was obvious that Rachmaninoff knew the work thoroughly. He played majestically, as if composing this music, shaping the form freely, focusing on unexpected details. It was an unforgettable experience!

A few of the things he showed me then have stayed with me ever since. Say, the piano *tutti* in the first movement, which he played softly and which gave me goose bumps. Or the tremolo at the end of the first movement, which he used brilliantly to prepare for the chorale episode that follows.

Before I played the *Kreutzer* with Rachmaninoff, I confess that I didn't consider the second movement very interesting music. In form, the second movement is a theme with variations, and everyone, for some reason, plays the theme faster than the variations. But the variations are very effective when played fast—that's their point. In Rachmaninoff's hands, they bubbled like champagne! He wasn't afraid of quick tempi. Everything was coming to a boil, more and more—and then he led up to the finale, which he played, contrary to tradition, quite slowly!

In Russia, where Rachmaninoff was a popular composer, he performed almost nothing but his own works. So when I met him in the West, he didn't have the traditional pianistic repertoire "in his fingers," paradoxical as that may sound. He had to study Beethoven, even Chopin, because Western audiences would not attend recitals consisting only of his own works. And Rachmaninoff was not ashamed to ask advice of his great colleagues Leopold Godowsky and Josef Hofmann, whom he respected greatly.

Rachmaninoff approached any new music with great curiosity. I remember how once in Switzerland I showed him the sonatas by Pergolesi for two violins, transcribed for violin and piano.

There is a story to that transcription. Alessandro Longo, the wonderful musician and specialist in early music, came to a concert of mine in Naples. Afterward, he took me to a museum that held material on early Italian music, including manuscripts of Pergolesi's. I looked through them and exclaimed, "Ah, why doesn't someone transcribe those sonatas for violin and piano!" And Longo did.

Rachmaninoff and I played through the Pergolesi sonatas. He was delighted both by the music and Longo's work. Truly, Longo managed it beautifully; rarely do the violin and piano sound so good together. Subsequently the music became widely popular, and Stravinsky used it in his ballet *Pulcinella*.

We also played Schubert's sonatinas for violin and piano. Rachmaninoff especially liked the first—it was the simplest and most direct. He did a transcription of Schubert's "Wohin?" from the cycle *Die schöne Müllerin*, but it wasn't as interesting as his transcriptions of other composers. Such as his reworking of Kreisler's "Liebesleid" and "Liebesfreud" for the piano—which are brilliant! I should say that any interpretation by Rachmaninoff of any piece of music by another composer amounted to a kind of transcription, because he changed so much. And he was seldom criticized for it, because he did it so powerfully.

For instance, he played Beethoven in a very Russian way, but it didn't shock anyone. Even that notorious purist, Artur Schnabel, would say, "The only one who plays Beethoven well—after me, naturally—is Rachmaninoff." Rachmaninoff's Beethoven was muscular—a bit crude, with a pockmarked face and dressed in mussed work clothing.

Or take Schumann's *Carnaval*, which is usually played like a game of Ping-Pong. Even Arthur Rubinstein makes it sound merely flashy. But Rachmaninoff's *Carnaval* is a series of grand pictures, of luxurious, impressive canvases: mysterious ladies, extravagant gentlemen, the whole Romantic era.

And how Rachmaninoff played a Chopin waltz or mazurka—like Genghis Khan, like a Cossack with saber bared! Chopin's *Fantaisie* falls apart in the hands of other pianists, but Rachmaninoff sculpted it like a Michelangelo, out of a single block of marble. When he played the "Funeral March" from the Chopin sonata it was completely different from what was written in the notes but no less grand. The last movement sounded just like wind blowing in a cemetery. Here too Rachmaninoff created a tragic picture, a whole Romantic landscape. What imagination he had!

Rachmaninoff's recordings, though marvelous, do not convey all the magic of his playing. Unfortunately, in those days the technology of sound recording was primitive compared with today. Rachmaninoff told me this story. In 1940 he was recording his Third Concerto with Ormandy and the Philadelphia Orchestra. In the transition to the third movement the piano has a big cadenza, with a grand passage across the entire keyboard.

Rachmaninoff complained, "I did fifteen takes of that passage. Everything was fine with the whole passage, except that final B-flat! So we left the passage for the next day. . . . I worked and worked at home. The next day the B-flat was okay, but the rest of the passage was a catastrophe!" Now, of course, they would have fixed it for him. The modern recording industry has lots of tricks at its disposal.

It wasn't easy talking with Rachmaninoff. Deep down, he was an extremely private person. At times it almost seemed that nothing interested him. Occasionally Volodya Horowitz was actually afraid to talk to him. For him Rachmaninoff was a god; he adored him. And the adoration made him reluctant to start a conversation. I, on the other hand, always tried to make Rachmaninoff laugh, and gradually we developed a relationship that was simpler than his relationship with Horowitz. It also helped that I was a violinist, which precluded any possibility of professional jealousy. Yes, Rachmaninoff was jealous of Horowitz!

He used to say that Volodya played his Third Concerto better than the composer himself. I don't think that Rachmaninoff believed that completely. If he had, he wouldn't have said it. This way, it was better for him to say it than to hear it from others. (Rachmaninoff also suggested that the pianist Benno Moiseiwitsch, whom he liked very much, played his *Rhapsody on a Theme by Paganini* better than the composer.)

The moments when I played with Rachmaninoff or for him are unforgettable. And Rachmaninoff himself, I think, derived some pleasure from his meetings with us. When he invited us—Volodya Horowitz, Grisha Piatigorsky, and me—he usually wanted us to play for him, and as a rule he did not have other guests.

Once Piatigorsky and I arrived in Hertenstein to see him—as usual, around four in the afternoon but without an appointment. Piatigorsky had his cello, I had my violin. A servant opened the door, "Quiet, quiet, the master is sleeping. . . ." Rachmaninoff usually took a nap after his Russian lunch. The house was completely still then.

Piatigorsky and I tiptoed into the living room. On the music stand we saw the sheet music for Rachmaninoff's "Vocalise," which we both knew well. Without discussing it, we took out our instruments and began playing the "Vocalise," standing up, very quietly, in unison, an octave apart.

Suddenly Rachmaninoff came into the room. Sleepy, he looked like a prisoner with his crew cut and striped pajamas with raised collar. Without a word he went to the piano and, also standing, accompanied us—and so beautifully! When we got to the end, Rachmaninoff left the room still without a word, but with tears in his eyes.

We never spoke about that episode with him: we were afraid. But later, in New York, Alexander Greiner of Steinway told me, "Milstein, what have you done to Rachmaninoff? He can't forget how you and Piatigorsky played his 'Vocalise.' He says it was marvelous." Coming from Rachmaninoff, even indirectly, this was incredible, wild praise. . . .

Too bad that Rachmaninoff never wrote a violin sonata. On second thought, maybe it's for the best. If he had written one, I would definitely have played it, and I would not have been heard over the massive accompaniment. Just recall his cello sonata, where the cello literally drowns in an avalanche of piano sounds.

One time Horowitz, Piatigorsky, and I were sitting with Rachmaninoff. I asked the composer why he didn't write for the violin. Rachmaninoff replied sternly: "Why write for the violin when there is the cello?" He wrote the sonata for his friend the cellist Anatoli Brandukov. And that friendship was, probably, the real reason for his preference of the cello over the violin.

The music of some Russian composers is little-known in the West. For instance, Alexander Borodin's grand symphonies and quartets are rarely played. But you can't say that about Rachmaninoff. His compositions were and still are enormously popular. More and more people are not ashamed to admit that they like Rachmaninoff.

The point is that for a long time he had a reputation for writing sentimental, salon music—music in poor taste. In that sense he shared a fate with Chopin, who once was considered a "composer for governesses." Just recently Mahler was considered in poor taste, but look at his reputation now. And I feel that Rachmaninoff is a better composer than Mahler, who could often sound superficial and empty. In Rachmaninoff, everything comes from the heart. Unfortunately, there are music lovers today who fear music that comes from the heart.

But prejudices and fashions change, while art filled with real emotions remains. And Rachmaninoff will remain, because he is a legendary figure in twentieth-century music. Rachmaninoff created his own myth. And there are no more myths today.

9. Stravinsky
and His
Interpreters

For me Igor Stravinsky is a tragic figure. I regard him as a great composer but a man with major flaws in his personality. I was one of the first performers of his violin concerto, and I played some of the violin transcriptions of his compositions. I met with him rather frequently, especially before the Second World War—in Paris, Berlin, and, for some reason, rather often in Venice. And we had all kinds of conversations, serious and lighthearted.

(Experience shows that the most important thing in dealing with composers is to go heavy on the compliments. And it doesn't even matter whether you know their music thoroughly or not. A composer is like a woman: whether she's a tall beauty or a short frump, the moment you tell her "You have a lovely hat!" she is won over, pleased with herself and you. It's the same with composers: even indirect praise makes them happy. Stravinsky was no exception to this rule.)

When I moved to Europe from Russia, it was very hard for me to establish my attitude toward Stravinsky unambivalently. He was so changeable, all the time turning this way and that. That's why a conversation in the early thirties with Rachmaninoff about Stravinsky became so important for me.

I asked Rachmaninoff: "What do you think of Stravinsky?" He replied, "I adore *Firebird* and *Petrouchka*. Sheer genius! But after that came artificial works. Say, *Les Noces*—there are a lot of good things in that, especially the ones derived from Russian folk ditties. But on the whole, it's an artificial work. And now, all those terrible *Apollon musagètes*!"

Rachmaninoff's words had an enormous impact on me, for my whole life. Rachmaninoff had the position and the authority to be able to tell the truth about Stravinsky. But I was a young violinist, and I was afraid to, even though many of my reactions coincided with Rachmaninoff's. His words prompted me to think independently in my evaluation of Stravinsky, disregarding the fashion of the day.

Relations between Rachmaninoff and Stravinsky were complicated. Even though both were Russian composers, they represented different schools. Rachmaninoff's roots were in Moscow, Stravinsky's in Petersburg. Stravinsky was very sarcastic about Rachmaninoff as a composer. Rachmaninoff, naturally, was immediately informed of Stravinsky's caustic remarks. He preferred not to criticize Stravinsky in public, but in our conversations he often repeated, "Stravinsky has lost his genius."

Later, I was told, Rachmaninoff and Stravinsky made up, at least for the sake of appearance. There could be no real rapprochement because the differences were too great between them, both as musicians and as human beings.

Rachmaninoff was not only a significant composer, he was a marvelous musician as well. You can't say that about Stravinsky. As a composer Stravinsky elicited colossal respect. Stravinsky the musician was another matter. His musical verdicts were often dubious and trendy. I'll talk more about that later.

A comparison of their human qualities is not in Stravinsky's favor either. No matter what he was talking about, Rachmaninoff was always totally honest. Stravinsky's insincerity was striking. Sometimes he even showed it off. He behaved differently with different people. He prevaricated and wheedled, always trying to squeeze the maximum benefit from everyone. Rachmaninoff was the total opposite: direct, severe, honest. His opinion of a person usually was formed instantly and forever.

As we get closer to the end of the twentieth century, we see better the importance of modern Russian music. Earlier, Stravinsky's authority over that music dominated. Now Rachmaninoff, Prokofiev, and Shostakovich are gaining. At the same time, beyond Russian music, the position of such former authorities as Schoenberg and Webern is diminishing. Alban Berg is another matter. He managed to combine twelve-tone technique with Viennese folklore, so Berg's music is still played.

Russian twentieth-century music is probably the most substantial and also, it seems, the most popular. Richard Strauss and Alban Berg, as I said, are widespread, but basically as opera composers, and putting on operas is an expensive business. The French composers are played mostly for entertainment. Say, Francis Poulenc, whom I met and performed with. He was a witty, elegant man— and that was how he composed. But when you listen to his music, you can't get away from the impression that it was written for adult children. It is so simplistic.

Of course, Poulenc and some other French composers imitated Stravinsky. They were under his heel almost literally. And no wonder: Stravinsky's imagination and inventiveness seem inexhaustible. Sometimes I think that Stravinsky and Picasso invented so much that they ruined twentieth-century art. In order to resist them, you need to be titanic. And I don't see any titans around, especially in the second half of the century.

Russian music is edible. But even here Stravinsky is an exception. Traditionally, Russian composers have been inspired by string instruments, but Stravinsky was carried away by the piano. He even composed at the piano, which he spoke about with pride. But that's not the point. The main thing is that Stravinsky perceived the piano basically as a percussion instrument.

Stravinsky and His Interpreters

For Stravinsky rhythm was God. The rhythmic variety of Stravinsky's music is astonishing. That's why he was generally drawn to percussion instruments. In Stravinsky's orchestra, the percussives tend to dominate. It makes me think of the rhythms of modern Russian poetry, like Vladimir Mayakovsky's. People rarely bring up the possible influence of Russian Futurists on Stravinsky. But having seen the avant-garde theatrical productions in Moscow, I have no doubts about that influence.

At the same time, I see Stravinsky's very character in his preference for percussion instruments (and sudden blows!). As a man Stravinsky was what the Germans call *bissig*: he liked to sting and jab and hurt. (You often see that in short people, and with the years Stravinsky got shorter and shorter, as if he were being washed in hot water; he kept shrinking.)

I think that Stravinsky's genius as a composer is best manifested in his small chamber works. And it's interesting that Stravinsky prefers various combinations of wind instruments, also the piano. He did new editions of his old ballets, "shrinking" their orchestrations. There was an economic reason in that (as there was in everything Stravinsky did), but there was also the influence of the composer's physiology and psychology.

Stravinsky and his times are swiftly receding from us. There are fewer and fewer people left who knew Stravinsky back in the thirties, as I did. For young people, Stravinsky is a museum waxwork, someone out of a textbook. He exists in airless space for them, interacting not with living people but with all sorts of "isms": modernism, neoclassicism, serialism, and so on.

But in real life, people's sympathies and antipathies are at least as significant as lofty aesthetic principles, perhaps even more so. In any case, psychology and life's daily problems often prompted Stravinsky (and many others) to make decisions that were explained retroactively with purely aesthetic reasons.

Stravinsky wrote a lot of instrumental works, but it's clear to me that he never found a great performer to champion his music. Nor many conductors.

Paradoxically, the greatest interpreter of Stravinsky's music is a choreographer, George Balanchine. If not for Balanchine, many of

Stravinsky's works, especially of the late period, would have been forgotten. If contemporary audiences know *Agon*, that's thanks solely to Balanchine. Which is natural, since we're talking about a ballet, after all. But the same could be said about Stravinsky's piano concertos and his violin concerto. You're more likely to hear them at the New York City Ballet than in a concert hall.

I think that is Stravinsky's tragedy. He adopted a hostile attitude toward his performers. And nothing good came of it. Stravinsky tried to create a myth of the composer who knows—exactly and definitely—how his music should be performed. As if music were a science! Now they say that Stravinsky's mistrust of performers came from his "objectivist" aesthetic. That may be so. But only in part! Psychology played an important part too. Stravinsky was jealous of performers. It seems he had a powerful performing impulse he couldn't realize, and that was one of the reasons he was so often angry at other musicians.

Besides which, Stravinsky, in my experience, didn't understand at all how his music should be played. Few composers do! Even Beethoven didn't understand how his music should be presented. Composers don't know how to make their own music sound good. That's why they need cooperation, not confrontation, with performers.

But instead of cooperating, Stravinsky spent decades fighting musicians who tried to play his works their way. There were so many clashes, scandals, sarcastic letters to the editor of so many newspapers! And all in vain.

Instead of fighting with the performers of his old music, Stravinsky could have been composing new music. But he wanted to control everything. The man had a control mania! He thought that once he let a composition out of his hands, he could still control its fate. But that's just an illusion.

It was Stravinsky's character to manipulate people. And that also affected his relations with performers. Stravinsky regarded his compositions as a product, and new works were given not to the one who could play it best but the one who offered the highest price. There are many examples of this.

One is the story of the premiere of Stravinsky's opera *The Rake's Progress*. I heard about it from my friend Issai Dobrowen, the Russian composer, conductor, and pianist, who once played the *Appassionata* for Lenin.

After World War Two Dobrowen and his charming wife, Manya (of Baltic-German descent and a relative of the violinist Georg Kullenkampf), moved to Sweden, where Dobrowen did a lot of conducting and recording. A talented and witty man, Dobrowen had an incredible resemblance to Pushkin: the sideburns, the impulsiveness . . . His ears stuck up through his hair like a poodle's.

I had performed with Dobrowen often—both when he was pianist and conductor—in the U.S.A., Scandinavia, and Switzerland. He was a marvelous musician and a sweet man (I called him "Dobroweichik"), albeit a nervous one. I remember a joint recital in Stockholm, which included a sonata and the lovely "Fairy Tale," both by Dobrowen, and Beethoven's *Spring* Sonata. Furtwängler came to our concert. The next day Dobrowen was conducting the opera *Eugene Onegin* and Furtwängler showed up again. That was an enormous compliment on his part.

In the early fifties I went to Stockholm, on my way to Oslo and then Bergen; Dobrowen was going to conduct all the concerts. In Stockholm, he and Manya invited me to lunch. And it was then that Dobrowen filled me in on all the details of the backstage story behind the celebrated premiere of Stravinsky's long-awaited new opera, which he composed with W. H. Auden as librettist.

Stravinsky had written *Rake's Progress* with La Scala in Milan in mind. They were going to pay him seven thousand dollars. But Nicholas ("Nika") Nabokov, the writer's cousin, got involved. Nabokov, who came from a family of famous Russian liberals, was a talented composer himself. In his youth he was one of Diaghilev's last protégés. I believe he even wrote a ballet for him. I became good friends with Nika Nabokov in the late twenties in Paris, lounging in cafés and restaurants with George Balanchine and Grisha Piatigorsky and the artist Pavel ("Pavlik") Tchelitchew, discussing the latest musical and political news.

Nabokov was an incredibly witty and erudite conversationalist.

No wonder he charmed Stravinsky. But Nabokov's most important function stemmed from his understanding of musical politics: he was invaluable in getting the best terms for Stravinsky's commissions.

After World War Two Nabokov was something like musical adviser to the American government in European cultural affairs. He had numerous useful connections and could push the right button at the right time and organize a moneymaking contract for Stravinsky.

And that was how he helped with *Rake's Progress*. Dobrowen recalled that Nabokov entered into negotiations with Venice's La Fenice theater, despite La Scala's interest. The Venetians were eager to win from Milan the premiere of an opera by the famous composer, and it came down to a question of money. A large amount was raised from local hotel owners, who wanted the publicity, and La Fenice came up with a sum of twenty thousand dollars, much more than La Scala's offer. Stravinsky gave *Rake's Progress* to Venice.

Nabokov came up with a clever trick in this case. The money was not offered formally for the opera as such but for the composer's willingness to conduct its premiere! That way, Stravinsky pocketed the entire fee instead of sharing it with his librettist, Auden.

Compare that with the dedication and altruism of Balanchine! It's hard to imagine Balanchine giving his ballet to another theater at the last minute because it was offering more money. In fact, Balanchine often let theaters other than his own perform his ballets for free.

Not Stravinsky. He never forgot his financial interests, under any circumstances. I think that Stravinsky's heightened interest in money also helps explain his tense relations with performers. He always wanted to play and conduct his own works himself so he could collect the entire fee.

Of course, you can't reduce to psychology alone a question as important and complex as Stravinsky's relations with his interpreters. Stravinsky's musical tastes also pushed him toward confrontation. He tried to create "objective" art, comparable in spirit to baroque music, where light and shadow lie evenly, without blending. That's why Stravinsky was repelled by the "Romantic" style of interpretation, with all its excesses. But even here, it seems to me, he overdid it.

At some moment Stravinsky decided that you could simply do away with interpreters and he began composing for the pianola, a mechanical instrument fashionable in the twenties. But then the fascination with the pianola quickly passed, and Stravinsky was forced to admit it had been a stupid idea.

This is another instance of the complex intertwining of aesthetics and personal motives. It is why I feel it necessary to recount my meetings not only with Stravinsky but with a few of his interpreters. All these people, each of whom was important in his own way in the history of the musical culture of our times, are gone. Some of them did not leave memoirs. And those who did publish something left a lot out. In the meanwhile, the many and varied worlds of Stravinsky are vanishing forever. . . .

I met Igor Stravinsky in Paris, in the early thirties. We were introduced by the violinist Samuel Dushkin, an American Jew of Russian descent. Dushkin understood a little Russian but was embarrassed to try to speak it around me. I only heard him speak French to Stravinsky—probably it was easier for him.

Stravinsky's French was not bad, and his German was excellent. I don't think he knew English then, but later, in America, he mastered it as well. Speaking with Stravinsky was a kind of linguistic challenge, since he had an unusual interest in language and enjoyed various linguistic tricks and problems. His Russian was always filled with puns and unexpected turns, not always suitable for print.

I want to recall Dushkin since people rarely remember him now. He was a good musician, and as a violinist he was a thorough professional, but he lacked temperament. And even though he played quite decently, I always felt that his performance was wrapped in cellophane. Dushkin performed comparatively rarely, and I think did not depend financially on his concerts. (An important circumstance that must have eased his collaboration with Stravinsky.)

Dushkin was friends with a very good pianist named Beveridge Webster. Both were supported by the American musician Blair Fairchild, who was, I think, an amateur composer. In any case, Fairchild must have been wealthy, since he rented an apartment in a very good area of Paris, on the rue l'Université.

Fairchild was almost always away, and the inseparable Dushkin and Webster lived there. It was a marvelous apartment: chic but understated. It had the style typical of wealthy emancipated expatriate Americans.

Dushkin was a nice man and we became good friends. In those years Stravinsky wasn't paid big fees yet as a composer. In order to make money, he performed his own music, both as a pianist and a conductor. He invited Dushkin to participate in these performances.

They began working on transcriptions for piano and violin of various Stravinsky works, to be performed in recital. Stravinsky's reasoning was simple: it was much easier to organize a dual recital than a solo evening or, especially, a symphonic concert. And it demanded much less effort and rehearsal. Orchestral rehearsals, even in those pre-union days, could cost a pretty penny.

Working in collaboration with Dushkin, Stravinsky wrote his violin concerto. It could have been so marvelous! Stravinsky is a great composer and he had enterprising taste. But I don't think he understood the violin as an instrument very well, and Dushkin lacked imagination as a violinist. At least such was the final evidence of their joint effort.

Dushkin was somehow neutral and colorless as a person, too. Still, he did have one great turn in his repertoire. When we went outside and needed a taxi, Dushkin whistled so sharply that cabs stopped in their tracks. He whistled masterfully: with two fingers, like a hooligan, with minimal effort and maximum effect. I envied him and tried to imitate him, but in vain. By the time I got all my fingers in my mouth and sucked in air and got ready to blow my pathetic little whistle, the taxi had sped by.

Why did Stravinsky choose Dushkin for a collaborator? Why didn't he approach a more interesting violinist? Because, characteristically, he wanted to keep the reins in his hands completely. He was afraid that a major artist with a strong personality would interfere in the composition, make suggestions, insist on changes. Stravinsky could not allow that. He was an autocrat without the slightest desire or ability to delegate power.

It was evident in everything Stravinsky did. Take his conducting. He wanted to control everything here too, just when he should have let go, instead. He indicated every rhythmic figure from the podium. And that's a mistake. The orchestra members often sense the music better than the conductor does. They shouldn't be led by the hand.

Toscanini conducted the music, not the rhythm. He knew where to let go. On the other hand, I remember Sir John Barbirolli, with whom I played Prokofiev's Second Violin Concerto at a festival in Lucerne: like Stravinsky, he tried to give all the details of a rhythmically complex moment—and botched things up.

A composer should not be too stubborn when he is collaborating with a performer. Nothing good can come of it. Once again I have to recall Glazunov, who was so generous in spirit that he said to me, a youngster playing his violin concerto, "Play it any way you want!" His composition did not suffer from my performance and his authority was not decreased. Everyone ended up winning: the composer, the performer, and the audience.

And here's another example of just the opposite: The Austrian composer Gottfried von Einem, author of the grand and incredibly dramatic opera *Dantons Tod*, is a friend of mine. (There used to be a joke in Vienna: "*Aber die Musik ist von Andern!*"—a play on the name von Einem, "von Andern" meaning "by someone else." That wasn't true, actually—von Einem is a very gifted composer.) He wrote his violin concerto especially for me, coming to Paris, where I was living at the time, so we could work together.

Von Einem's concerto had exceptionally interesting elements, but it was too long—five movements, fifty minutes of music. (By comparison, Brahms's concerto lasts about thirty-six minutes, with the cadenza.) I suggested some changes in the third movement, the Adagio. Von Einem seemed willing. But his wife, who tended to be very jealous, worried that I might spoil something in her husband's work. So I got a letter from him that said, "Unfortunately, I cannot agree to your proposed changes, my wife won't let me."

I replied, "Unfortunately, I am very busy and cannot continue working on your concerto. I wish you success."

So what happened? Ruggiero Ricci, a brilliant violinist, played von Einem's concerto—just once, I think. And no one plays it anymore. Too bad. Von Einem often comes to my concerts in Vienna, and every time he sighs, "Nathan, you were right." Well, Glazunov accepted that possibility in Odesssa right away; it took von Einem a lot longer.

The first time I heard Stravinsky's violin concerto was in 1931 in Berlin, played by Dushkin. It might have been the premiere. I liked the composition very much and found the thought of playing it appealing. So when Dushkin's exclusive rights to the concerto ended, I learned the work.

I was supposed to play Stravinsky's concerto in Boston with Serge Koussevitzky. Stravinsky and Koussevitzky had a complex relationship. Both were émigrés from Russia—Stravinsky left for the West in 1910, and the conductor arrived ten years later. I don't think that Stravinsky liked Koussevitzky as a conductor, and he would complain to me about Koussevitzky as a music publisher.

Koussevitzky came to the West as a very wealthy man. Back in Moscow, when he was famous as a bass player of unmatched brilliance (probably the greatest of modern bass players), he married Natalya Ushkova, daughter of a tea magnate. His wife's fortune permitted Koussevitzky to develop in two directions at once. First, he put together an orchestra in Moscow of top-class musicians and became its conductor. He invited great soloists to perform with them, ensuring box-office success. Second, Koussevitzky founded a music-publishing house to print the scores of the best new Russian composers. It was announced that all the profits would go directly to the composers, and that Koussevitzky would get nothing, which of course created a great deal of publicity for Koussevitzky.

After the revolution, Koussevitzky moved to Paris and resumed his wide-ranging conducting and publishing activity. It was obvious that he had somehow managed to smuggle his "tea money" abroad. But the days of his Moscow extravagance were over, and Stravinsky complained to me that even though it was generally thought that Koussevitzky was publishing Russian composers like Rachmaninoff, Prokofiev, and Stravinsky at a loss, actually he was making a profit on their work while they were not being paid in full.

It should be noted that Koussevitzky was not involved in the day-to-day publishing activities. The executive director was a certain Gavriil Paichadze, with whom Stravinsky had to haggle over every centime. So it's quite possible that Koussevitzky knew nothing about it.

Nowadays Koussevitzky is remembered mostly as the longtime director of the Boston Symphony Orchestra. He loved it, and the BSO returned the affection. As its conductor, Koussevitzky did a lot. He founded the Tanglewood Festival and created a composers' aid society. And he commissioned the *Symphony of Psalms* from Stravinsky, the *Concerto for Orchestra* from Bartók, and the opera *Peter Grimes* from Britten.

Some composers, including Stravinsky, were unhappy with Koussevitzky's conducting, complaining that he could not easily read orchestra scores, especially modern ones. For me, however, it's the results that count. And the results of Koussevitzky's work with the BSO were often first-class interpretations.

Koussevitzky was a real showman, sometimes even a clown, and that affected his performance, which could be too temperamental, with a strain of gypsy style. But he was also a sober, calculating businessman who liked to say, "I'm soft enough to make promises but firm enough not to keep them!"

Stravinsky reproached Koussevitzky for being two-faced and evasive, even though he was as evasive as a snake himself. Well, it takes one to know one. As for Koussevitzky's attitude toward Stravinsky's music, let me get back to what I witnessed when I came to Boston to play Stravinsky's violin concerto.

In those days concerts were given in Boston on Thursdays, Fridays, and Sundays. We rehearsed three times. At the first rehearsal Koussevitzky looked miserable, because he didn't know the score at all. Somehow he got through the rehearsal—probably hoping to catch on as we went along.

At the second rehearsal, as we were repeating something for the umpteenth time, Koussevitzky suddenly stopped and turned to Richard Burgin, his concertmaster, and exclaimed piteously, "Richard, I can't conduct this music. You take this concerto— you're the specialist!"

Burgin, a cultivated man, had studied in Petersburg with Auer.

He was Koussevitzky's friend and assisted him in conducting. Burgin adored modern music and therefore knew Stravinsky's score. I knew it too. Burgin got on the podium, and we had a very fruitful third rehearsal on Thursday morning. In the end it was Burgin who conducted Stravinsky's violin concerto.

Burgin reminds me of something else. Russian émigré musicians weren't of a single political opinion, as people today for some reason think they were. There were some who were conservative in outlook, like Stravinsky and Balanchine; there were political opportunists, like Prokofiev; and there were people with leftist opinions. Richard Burgin was a leftist.

Burgin kept repeating, "The future belongs to the Soviet Union!" No arguments could convince him otherwise; he was totally blind on the subject. In 1956 Burgin went with the Boston Symphony to perform in the Soviet Union. I ran into him in London after his return, at the shop of violin dealer Alfred Hill. He looked troubled. I asked him, "What happened to you in the Soviet Union? An earthquake?"

Burgin replied, "No one laughs there!"

As they say, it's better to see something once than hear about it a hundred times.

Of course, Burgin wasn't the first fellow traveler who was disillusioned in the Soviet Union. The same thing happened to André Gide in the thirties. Also to Arthur Koestler. The love of these intellectuals for the Soviet Union was abstract, in their minds. It's a good thing they had enough emotion and talent to see, once they were in the country of their dreams, that they had been unconscionably duped. Others, even when they saw with their own eyes, continued to insist on their misapprehension. It's just that they're not talented people. Intellect without talent is a dangerous, destructive thing.

Stravinsky had little respect for conductors as a caste, remarking once that conducting, like politics, rarely attracts original minds. I feel the same way. Each of us has his accounts to settle with conductors. Stravinsky probably had to deal with a hack attitude toward his works more than once. I am also surprised by how reluctant many conductors are to work at a new score. Even the best of them can be simply lazy; the incident with Koussevitzky, unfortunately, was not exceptional. In Philadelphia I played Stravinsky's violin concerto with Eugene Ormandy, a marvelous musician. But he didn't know the music at all, either; he was absolutely terrified.

I did know two loyal and intelligent interpreters of Stravinsky's music. One was Pierre Monteux, a major conductor and an extraordinary musician, who was the first and perhaps the best performer of Stravinsky's most outstanding works: *The Firebird, Petrouchka*, and *Le Sacre du printemps*. I performed a lot with Monteux, one of that rare breed of conductors with whom it wasn't dangerous to appear even without a rehearsal.

Once I was playing Lalo's *Symphonie espagnole* in San Francisco with Monteux. They were expecting me to arrive by plane, but in those days I didn't fly at all, and so I arrived by train the day of the concert. I called Monteux immediately and said, "What do we do?" The old man answered calmly, "Don't worry, Milstein, don't worry. Come to me before the concert and play a bit." I came and saw to my relief that he knew and understood the music perfectly. That evening everything was fine.

Speaking of Monteux, memory retains amusing details. Once I was traveling by train from Paris to Venice, with a change in Trieste. At the station in Paris I observed this scene: two ladies carrying a load of baskets overflowing with foodstuffs—eggs, fruit, millions of bags and sacks. I thought they were going to sell their wares to the passengers. But it turned out one of them was Monteux's wife (always cooing *"mon Pierre"*) and the other, I think, her sister. I asked, "Where are you going?"

"Pierre is going to Trieste to conduct the best orchestra in Europe!"

Actually, the orchestra in Trieste was notoriously bad. Oh, those conductors' wives! They believe what they want to believe.

From 1936 to 1952, Monteux was music director of the orchestra in San Francisco, at the time one of the best in the United States.

When Mrs. Monteux began saying that Pierre no longer wanted to run the orchestra, that he was tired, the board, taking her at her word, didn't plead with Monteux to stay. So he had to leave.

Monteux was over seventy-five by then, but he continued making guest appearances all over the world—he was so beloved that he could have had any orchestra he wanted. In particular, the Bostonians chose Monteux for their first trip to the Soviet Union in 1956 (the one that changed Richard Burgin's world view). Monteux died at the age of eighty-nine, at the time head of the London Symphony. He had lived long enough to conduct the fiftieth-anniversary performance of *Sacre du printemps*.

In his youth Monteux was a conductor for Diaghilev's Ballets Russes. It was there that Ernest Ansermet, one of the most ardent champions of Stravinsky's work, began his career. He was a very good conductor, and we were friends. It was always interesting talking and playing with Ansermet. He was a mathematician by education and had even taught math. I don't know if this helped him in his conducting, but there is no denying he interpreted Debussy, for instance, like no one else. Debussy's *La Mer* by some conductors is nothing but water, while with Ansermet it was French champagne!

Ansermet was striking looking: he could have played the role of Christ in the movies without makeup. But his character, it seems, was far from Christian. After Ansermet and Stravinsky broke up, he published a book (I think even two volumes) attacking the composer vociferously for his surrender to serial composition. He was convinced that Stravinsky had betrayed his own genius.

Ansermet was definitely neurotic, as I had opportunity to see for myself. Once I was playing Beethoven's concerto in Geneva with the Suisse Romande Orchestra, which Ansermet founded and conducted for fifty years. It was considered a good orchestra, though I can't say I agreed. Anyway, at rehearsal the musicians were tired and limp, having just returned from a tour. I tried to turn them around somehow. Suddenly Ansermet said, "Stop it, Nathan, we're all tired. . . ." And then, really unexpectedly: "Go to hell!" Why? I hadn't meant anything bad.

But since I was being sent to hell. . . . I put away my violin and left. That evening I arrived at the Victoria Hall forty-five minutes before the concert, as I always do. An usher ran to meet me. "Maestro Ansermet is waiting for you!" Ansermet was in his dressing room, and when I went in he began weeping and tried to kiss my hands. I never did understand what the problem was. After the concert Ansermet and I went, as usual, to a theatrical restaurant not far from the concert hall, where our friendship was renewed.

Clearly, even the most elementary clashes between artists, their arguments and reconciliations, have a note of irrationality. Things can't be explained completely—it's impossible. Both Monteux and Ansermet had been friendly with Stravinsky at first. Later, when Stravinsky began conducting his own works, he started finding more and more character traits in the two conductors that annoyed him. We can only speculate as to what degree Stravinsky's aesthetic judgments were the result of his personal relations with musicians and vice versa.

Monteux, Ansermet, and Koussevitzky were brilliant personalities. Unfortunately, I can't say the same about Samuel Dushkin. Yet Stravinsky, as far as I know, did not consult with the conductors when he was composing, and he did consult with Dushkin. And at least to my taste, Stravinsky's violin works are to a substantial degree not Stravinsky but Dushkin, even though the notes per se belong to the composer. Stravinsky was prickly, sharp, but the violin transcriptions of his works are soggy and limp. Of course, when Stravinsky himself was playing, they acquired a rhythmic sharpness. I remember Stravinsky accompanying Dushkin in his "Chanson russe." (That's a transcription of the Berceuse from his opera *Mavra*.) Stravinsky accentuated the rhythm so much that I asked, "Igor Fedorovich, why are you striking the keys so loud and making the accompaniment so percussive?" Stravinsky just smiled smugly.

There's another story regarding "Chanson russe." I was recording it in 1949 in New York for RCA Victor, with Arthur Balsam at the piano. At the same time, in a nearby studio, Stravinsky was recording something else of his as a conductor. When he learned that Balsam and I were working on his piece, he came over to see how we were doing.

After listening for a while, Stravinsky expressed his displeasure. "Very fast, Nathan Mironovich! Too fast!" I acquiesced to Stravinsky and we recorded "Chanson russe" at a slower tempo. Too bad: it wasn't as good as it could have been. The piece has something Byzantine about it: beneath the mask of calm there is incredible inner tension. That's why its tempo cannot be placid.

At a subsequent concert in Los Angeles I put "Chanson russe" on the program. Of course, I played it at my tempo, with more movement than Stravinsky had recommended. Other violinists play "Chanson russe" for an encore, but I don't agree with that. I always put it in the main program—and they always ask for a repeat! That's the way it happened this time, too. The audience shouted "Encore!" And I gladly repeated the piece.

What I didn't know was that Stravinsky was in the audience. (He lived in L.A. then.) After the concert he came backstage and said enthusiastically, "Oh, Nathan Mironovich, it was marvelous, just marvelous! Your tempo is better!"

I was amazed, because I knew that Stravinsky was an extremely stubborn man who usually did not change his opinion. The secret was, of course, that "Chanson russe" had been a success that evening, and I had had to play it again. Composers love hearing their own music. Stravinsky may have been stubborn, but he could also be gratified.

What Stravinsky needed to transcribe his works successfully was an authoritative adviser, and Dushkin was not that. I was present, however, at one such fruitful collaboration for Stravinsky—with my friend Grisha Piatigorsky.

It took place on board the SS *Rex* headed for New York from Europe. Stravinsky and Piatigorsky had worked together on *Suite italienne*, a transcription for cello and piano of the suite from *Pulcinella* (a ballet in which Stravinsky had already "transcribed" a few works by Pergolesi), and as everyone knows there's nothing to do on a ship. So after lunch I would accompany Grisha to Stravinsky's cabin, where they fussed with the cello part of *Suite italienne*. Piatigorsky was very daring and persistent in his suggestions, and Stravinsky listened to him. It was fascinating to watch them work.

One of the most daring innovations in the suite is the stunning moment when the cellist tosses the bow behind the bridge, creating a special sound—an unforgettable, fantastic effect! That brilliant idea came about quite accidentally.

Tea was served at 4:45 on the ship. Lovely young women joined Piatigorsky and me for tea. (To tell the truth, he was the main attraction. I was the dummy.) That day, I remember, we were expecting a particularly beautiful young woman. And Stravinsky, of all the rotten luck, was engrossed in the work, with no sign of ending the session. Piatigorsky was beside himself. He was afraid he'd be late for our date but didn't have the nerve to tell Stravinsky about it. And because he was so nervous, the bow jumped out of his hand and slid behind the bridge of the cello! An unusual, whistling sound resulted. Stravinsky literally jumped up. "That's it! Marvelous! I like it! How did you do it?"

After a few tries they decided to use and write down the accidental discovery. I have to give Stravinsky his due here: his wit, his speedy reaction, his readiness to experiment. Clearly, Stravinsky was delighted. And so were we: at last we could go off to have tea with the beauty.

The weather on the crossing was horrible. The SS *Rex* was an Italian liner, with lovely wooden furniture and trim. But it creaked terribly in bad weather. The waves crashed threateningly against the sides—Bang! Bang!

There was quite a bouquet of musicians on board: Stravinsky, the pianists Josef Hofmann and Ignaz Friedman, Dushkin, Piatigorsky, and I. We were all on our way to America to make money. If the SS *Rex* had sunk, there would have been a lot of work for musical journalists—all those obituaries to write!

It was scary in the cabins: you couldn't see anything, everything creaked and howled, especially in first class, with that damned wooden furniture! (I have always traveled de luxe—even when I didn't have the money. I adored it! Of course, it wasn't very practical. The violinist Joseph Szigeti tried to set me on the righteous path—a more rational man, he always bought second- or third-class tickets.)

For Stravinsky and me on that trip, the deck was our refuge. Some sailors would come to scrub the deck, spreading the stink of their alkaline solution. We would put up with it, getting up obediently when the sailors needed to move our chaise longues.

One evening I hurried out on deck. Stravinsky was already there. (In general Stravinsky was a dandy who loved to dress fashionably, even to the point of caricature. But he didn't bother with evening dress on that crossing. I, on the other hand, was forced to dress formally—I was with my first wife, Rita, and she insisted that her husband look proper.) I sat down next to him. Stravinsky understood me and I him. Stravinsky was afraid! How I loved him for that! And Stravinsky returned the sentiment. Our horror of the sea brought us together. The ship pitched and rolled and I kept thinking in terror, Oh-oh-oh! I tried to strike up a conversation about music. Through gritted teeth, Stravinsky made frank, quite short comments about other composers that made me stop in embarrassment.

Stravinsky's terror increased. Compared with him I began to feel like a hero. I did his bidding and even tried to calm him down. "Milstein, give me your hand," he said. That was too much! I started to think he was performing a play with me entitled "Stravinsky Is Afraid."

My suspicions of a grand act grew when, in response to a waiter's offer, "Would you like me to bring you some water, gentlemen?" Stravinsky replied, "A little wine, I suppose." He also ordered some white chicken meat, boiled potatoes, and, to top it off, a tomato. I couldn't even think of eating and watched Stravinsky in horror. He dispatched the food with great enjoyment and appetite.

But then he sagged again. "I want to see Ignaz Friedman. He'll calm me down! Milstein, find Friedman!" Fortunately, I knew where to find him, since his cabin was not far from mine. Holding hands, Stravinsky and I headed for Friedman.

Stravinsky was right. If anyone could calm him in the face of raging nature it was Friedman. He was a serious, sedate gentleman, very wise, who resembled the pianist Wilhelm Backhaus. Friedman always wore a tuxedo. And his wife was a Tolstoy (I'm not sure if she was a countess, however). It had been Friedman who helped Rachmaninoff, whom he adored, with two thousand dollars in 1918 to move from Scandinavia, where he was stranded, to New York.

Rachmaninoff was grateful to Friedman all his life for that kindness. He told me about it often.

But what was most important, Friedman was an astonishing pianist, who played Chopin like no one else. I also admired him as the ideal bridge partner, and we spent many hours playing.

When we got to Friedman's door, we knocked. No one replied. Stravinsky pushed the door and it opened. We went inside. Friedman was lying down and, completely ignoring the tempest, was fast asleep. His eyeglasses had slipped from his nose, and an open book lay near his side.

We woke him up. Friedman ordered some wine, and he and Stravinsky drank it. I just watched them with envy. Stravinsky knew what he was talking about: Friedman had a magical effect on him. He was absolutely calm now. But what was I supposed to do?

Stravinsky loved wine and drank a lot of it—as if he were a real Frenchman. And, also like a Frenchman, he couldn't stand water.

Interestingly, many of his habits were French. Even his stinginess was more French than Russian—it was so demonstrative. A Russian wouldn't show off his money-grubbing that way. But Stravinsky showed off his greed. (Yet there was nothing French in Stravinsky's music. It was totally Russian.)

Grisha Piatigorsky one day told me how Stravinsky came to him with a contract to divide up royalties for the *Suite italienne* (which they had worked on in my presence on the SS *Rex*). When Stravinsky announced that they would share fifty-fifty, Grisha was thrilled. But not for long, because practical Stravinsky explained that as the composer he got 90 percent of the royalties, and they'd share the *remaining* 10 percent fifty-fifty. In other words, Stravinsky got 95 percent and Piatigorsky, 5 percent.

I think this manner of dividing up royalties was yet another reason why it was Dushkin who collaborated with Stravinsky on the violin transcriptions and not, say, Jascha Heifetz. I doubt that Heifetz would have acquiesced so easily. But Dushkin (and Piatigorsky) put up with it.

Stravinsky's views on religion were very Russian. He created the impression of being an extremely devout person. I recall one conversation when religion came up and Stravinsky spoke with fire and enthusiasm of the necessity of faith. I don't know if he attended church often, but I do know that in his everyday habits he was— like Diaghilev—superstitious and prone to believe omens.

Stravinsky composed a lot of sacred music, but with a strange quirk: almost all of it is written for Catholic services or with Latin texts, even though Stravinsky himself was Russian Orthodox. This Catholic orientation is curious when you bear in mind that in the nineteenth century the Orthodox Church's greatest enemy was the pope.

He had another rather Russian trait. A small man, Stravinsky (who seemed even shorter than he really was; of course, he was very muscular and sturdy) adored big women with voluptuous curves.

I recall his onetime girlfriend Dagmar Godowsky. She was an actress who loved music and, consequently, musicians. Dagmar was plump, merry, and aggressive. She spoke loudly and with temperament, cultivating a gypsyish style and always making scenes. I can't imagine Stravinsky liked that, being basically quite bourgeois.

I did not know Stravinsky's first wife, Catherine, but I adored his second, Vera. When we met, she was still Vera Sudeikina, wife (although separated) of the artist Sergei Sudeikin. But Vera accompanied Stravinsky everywhere. She was so big and so beautiful! Like a portrait by Kustodiev or Maliavin: endless shawls with big bright roses. Vera was witty and lively, but much more proper than Dagmar. There was nothing bohemian about Vera; she was created for marriage.

Vera had refined tastes, and she was a gifted artist. Later, in California, she opened a small art gallery, and I dropped by whenever I was in Los Angeles. Vera rose like a monument amid the fragile works of art. Even in her later years you could see how beautiful she had been.

Vera and Stravinsky were the perfect pair—perhaps because they were opposites both in appearance and personality. Big, kind, generous, always calm and smiling, Vera spoke melodically and in measured tones; and next to her, short Stravinsky, sharp (as if made from angles), calculating, nervous, always aggressive, and spewing paradoxes.

Even Vera's quintessential Russian looks (actually, she wasn't

Russian at all) made a glaring contrast with Stravinsky, who was often taken for a Jew. I remember early in the Nazis' rise to power, I performed Karl Goldmark's concerto in Karlsruhe. An orchestral work of Stravinsky's was also on the program. The review in the local paper began like this: "The soloist of yesterday's concert was a Jew. The whole program was also Jewish. How could this calamity happen?" So at this time, Stravinsky often had to prove that he wasn't Jewish.

By the way, about other allegedly Jewish composers: Contrary to legend, neither Bizet nor Ravel was Jewish (even though Ravel did compose a work called *Hebrew Songs*). And Max Bruch, author of the marvelous "Kol Nidrei" for cello, was not Jewish either, even though most Jewish music lovers seem convinced that he was.

In his later years Stravinsky composed *Abraham and Isaac* on commission from the Israeli government. That reminds me of a story making the rounds a long time ago. A Jew from Brooklyn is standing in front of a Rembrandt in the Hague Museum, a painting depicting a Jewish family, as so many of Rembrandt's works do. And the Jew comments, "Typical Jews! They didn't have any money, but they had to have a portrait by Rembrandt!"

As I've mentioned, Stravinsky liked dressing up. He was extremely interested in everything to do with clothing and fashion. I remember a meeting with him in Venice, after the war. I was coming out of a store where I had had incredible luck: I had found and bought a jacket I liked. (I should explain that it's very hard for me to buy a jacket in Europe: it'll be short somewhere. But Italy is the land of what I call Mediterranean fashion: wide in the seat, too wide in front, but not too long in the sleeves. Which suited me fine!)

Still, the jacket was a bit tight in places. I decided that since it was a double knit it would stretch. It was quite spectacular with its red color. Anyway, I bumped into Stravinsky, who immediately exclaimed with envy, "Milstein, what a beautiful jacket!" We went to have tea in a café on San Marco Square and Stravinsky could talk about nothing else. He kept repeating, "What a jacket! What a great color!"

Stravinsky spoke about jackets, shirts, and ties with sincere enthusiasm, and I believed him completely on these topics. But when he talked about music, I sometimes doubted his motives. There was so much mixed in: marvelously fine perceptions, opportunism, and attempts to *épater les bourgeois*.

For example, Stravinsky would suddenly begin to sing the praises of Gounod and Chabrier. Now, I doubt he was that crazy about those composers; he simply knew that no one would suspect him of poor taste. On the contrary, they would respect him even more: Stravinsky finds high quality where no one else can!

Once Stravinsky told me that Beethoven was essentially a primitive composer. That seemingly outrageous statement does capture something; in fact, when you are in the dressing room and you hear only the melody and bass of a Beethoven symphony being performed onstage, the music can sound rather bare. But, as was often the case with Stravinsky, pointed observation was turned into paradox. And paradoxes are easier to grasp—both by a mass audience and by snobs. Which is just what Stravinsky wanted.

Or take Stravinsky's paeans to the operas of Cimarosa, Bellini, and Verdi. Perhaps his raptures were unfeigned, but you began to take them with a grain of salt when you realized that this extravagant praise of Italian music coincided with his own flirtation with Mussolini and Fascist Italy.

Still, for all his contradictions Stravinsky remains one of the most interesting people I have ever met. It's a shame, of course, that his instrumental music is not among his great achievements. It is my profound belief that it would have been better and certainly more successful if he had fully and sincerely cooperated with performers. Experience shows that great interpreters can make the best music even better. That is the peculiar nature of music. For better or worse, it is a performer's art.

10. Music and Politics I: Furtwängler, Toscanini, and Other Conductors

Often you hear people say something like, "Let musicians play well, but they should stay out of politics. It's none of their business." I always reply, "Politics is too important to leave to the professionals." The natural growth of musicians (and all artists) depends on the environment in which they live. Therefore we must try to make those conditions beneficial. The totalitarian regime in Russia destroyed the gifts of my friend Prokofiev. Another friend, Balanchine, developed his genius precisely because he moved to a democratic society.

I tend to be dubious when a musician's fame is blown up purely out of political considerations, often without the artist's concurrence. An example is the great cellist Pablo Casals, whom I knew.

Casals was advertised as a great antifascist and fighter against

149

General Franco. Of course Casals was anti-Franco, but not because the Caudillo was a fascist. Casals hated Franco because he would not give Catalonia its independence. A sweet man, Casals was a fiery Catalan, and all Catalans—no matter their political convictions—hated Franco. Contemporary Spain is democratic, but many Basques plot against the Spanish government. Those Basques are not leftists or rightists, they are nationalists, as Casals was.

I also don't like it when they try to destroy a musician's reputation solely out of political considerations. That happened to Wilhelm Furtwängler, a very conservative man with right-wing views, but certainly not the Nazi he was depicted to be. People forget that many right-wing Germans hated Hitler.

Once, in Stockholm before the war, Furtwängler came to one of my concerts. The next day we went to the opera, to *Eugene Onegin*. A conversation on the political situation in Germany started, and I remember how Furtwängler openly expressed his dissatisfaction with Hitler: "I am a German, but what's going on in Germany now is *Schweinerei*."

Some Americans could not forgive Furtwängler for staying and conducting in Nazi Germany. I saw a photograph in some American magazine with the caption: "Furtwängler bowing to Hitler and Goering." What nonsense! The picture shows Furtwängler after a concert, responding to the applause of the audience, among whom are Hitler and Goering. What if there had been a gorilla in the audience? Would Furtwängler's bow then have meant, according to the logic of his critics, that he was also for gorillas?

A rather unpleasant incident in which those critics tried to involve me occurred when Furtwängler was invited to be director of the Chicago Symphony in 1948. Several famous American musicians announced that they would boycott the Chicago orchestra if he took the job. I did not join the protest, even though some of my best friends had signed the anti-Furtwängler proclamation.

Soon after that incident I appeared in Chicago, and a journalist came backstage to see me.

"Did you sign the protest against Furtwängler?"

"No, and why should I? Furtwängler is a great musician, absolutely not a Nazi, and if the protest succeeds, it's the Chicago Symphony who will be the loser.''

Edward Ryerson, the orchestra's presiding trustee, was present during this conversation. He probably related it to Furtwängler, because when I came to Lucerne, where I was to do the Dvořák concerto with Ansermet, Furtwängler came to the rehearsal, which he had never done before. During the break he came over and said with great bitterness and passion, ''You are a nice fellow [*netter Kerl*], but some of our common friends are not.''

And so Furtwängler didn't come to America then. It's too bad, because if he had headed the Chicago Symphony, his influence would probably have been strongly felt in American musical life. And I am still convinced that the depiction of Furtwängler as a Nazi by some Americans was deeply unfair.

Herbert von Karajan was another story. He was a member of the Nazi Party for at least eleven years. But even here the question was not as simple as it seems. Membership per se in the party proves little. The brilliant Soviet violinists Oistrakh and Kogan joined the Communist Party during Stalin's lifetime. Does that mean that they supported Stalin's crimes? No, they were just surviving, and in the West, as far as I know, no one ever condemned them for it.

My appreciation of Furtwängler as a conductor grew gradually. As previously mentioned, when I first heard him in Berlin I was drawn more by the delicious sausages and beer than by his performance. This was in 1926, when the German *Würstchen* had a much greater attraction for me, a young émigré from hungry Russia, than did Furtwängler's profound interpretations.

I began attending his concerts more and more frequently. Gregor Piatigorsky, at the time first cello in Furtwängler's orchestra, the Berlin Philharmonic, introduced us. Piatigorsky performed sometimes as a soloist with the orchestra—in Richard Strauss's *Don Quixote* and Schumann's concerto. Those were memorable occasions.

After my successful concerts in Vienna, my agent, Paul Bechert, said, ''I guarantee that in a short time you will play with the Berlin Philharmonic and Furtwängler himself will conduct!'' And so it happened. Furtwängler asked me to play the Dvořák concerto. Three days before the performance I got sick, with a high fever! But naturally I could not decline to appear, and I was given special shots to get me on my feet.

I could not have imagined that the Dvořák would have particularly interested Furtwängler, who composed complex (and not very attractive) music himself. But it turned out he knew the composition note-perfect.

Being a young, brash musician, I used to make a cut in the slow movement of the concerto. Furtwängler did not approve. Another giant of German music, Richard Strauss, reacted the same way to this cut of mine in the Dvořák.

One time I had to play the concerto in Frankfurt. My manager told me, "You'll be performing with Strauss, I hope you don't mind." It never occurred to me that he was talking about the famous Richard Strauss, who had been considered a classic back when I was at music school in Odessa. I loved his bright, crafty, masterly symphonic poems *Till Eulenspiegel* and *Don Juan*. *Ein Heldenleben*, which I knew from Odessa (and had even played its violin solo, replacing the orchestra's ailing concertmaster), I then considered a major work (now I don't like it, it's too bombastic for my taste). In Odessa in those years, *Death and Transfiguration* and *Salome* were often performed. In fact, Strauss was more famous in our country than Brahms.

By the time of that concert in Frankfurt, I was sure he had died. So I paid no attention to the manager's words about the prospective conductor—Strauss, Schwartz, what difference did it make?

When I saw the maestro and realized it was *the* Richard Strauss, I was almost in shock. I was certain that Strauss would not know the Dvořák concerto—how could music like that interest him? But as soon as the rehearsal began, from the first minute, I realized that he knew it, every note of it! And of course I made the same cut in the slow movement, forgetting to warn him. Suddenly he said reproachfully, "But this is the most beautiful part of the concerto!"

So they both said it, Strauss and Furtwängler! And naturally, they were right. Since then I have always played—and recorded—the concerto without cuts.

Several years later, when I was appearing in Munich, I was told that Strauss would be happy to see me. I was the one who was happy! We met at the restaurant of the hotel Vier Jahreszeiten: Strauss after conducting his opera, I after my concert. Strauss had not forgotten how we had played the Dvořák! The place was cozy, the food was excellent. We sat and talked about music. Strauss spoke about Mozart, Beethoven, and Tchaikovsky with such wisdom that after our meeting I was too agitated to fall asleep. (After the war that restaurant became expensive—and was not nearly as good.)

Of course, Strauss was primarily a great opera composer. I loved his *Salome* and his later operas, *Der Rosenkavalier, Ariadne auf Naxos, Die Frau ohne Schatten*. I will even say that Strauss was a better musician than Wagner, although Wagner was a greater genius. And naturally, I adore Strauss's late opuses, especially *Four Last Songs*. At that time he could have stopped composing and enjoyed life, but instead he gave us the gift of those masterpieces.

Strauss, like Furtwängler, was in the Nazis' employ for some time. In their case I use the word "employ," because "collaboration" would be too strong. Both Strauss and Furtwängler considered themselves German patriots. As musicians they felt themselves inseparable from German culture, that it would suffer in their absence. So they lacked the self-confidence of Thomas Mann, who, emigrating to the U.S.A., proclaimed, "German literature is where I am."

Strauss and Furtwängler, by remaining in Germany, tried to defend the dignity of German music. Both were in conflict with the Nazis constantly, and in the end they were dismissed from leadership in musical affairs.

Neither man was proud of what was happening in Germany in those years, and in that sense could not be compared with Walter Gieseking, a brilliant pianist but a dyed-in-the-wool Nazi. Gieseking even boasted of his party membership; when he came to perform in America before the war, and an immigration clerk on Ellis Island asked, "Are you a Nazi?" he proudly declared, "Yes!"

The story of Herbert von Karajan's Nazi sympathies has also been blown up out of proportion, it seems to me. Karajan was a nationalist. When Hitler came to power, Karajan was young, Germany was strong, dictating to the world, and Karajan must have liked that. But as far as I know, he was never anti-Semitic, even though they tried to make him out to be an anti-Semite. Those accusations all came out of intrigues among conductors!

There were always obstacles in Karajan's life: first, the gigantic figure of Furtwängler; then the purge of denazification, in which I think the Allied authorities treated him and Furtwängler too harshly; then tenure in Berlin, a split city in a split country. And finally, Karajan lost his famous battles with both the Vienna State Opera and the Berlin Philharmonic.

Karajan was a major conductor and great worker. He was also a talented poseur, though not in the same class with the legendary Russian bass Chaliapin. For all that, Karajan did not overdo pantomime, like some conductors. At rehearsal he worked honestly with the orchestra (I was a witness to that), and the result of that hard work shone in his concerts. The world fame of the Berlin Philharmonic is the fruit of Karajan's work. And his personality gave the orchestra a certain glamour that helped considerably in its guest performances and record sales.

Karajan used his authority to support young musicians, for which many have been and will ever be grateful. He created success for them without diminishing his own. He also left a rich legacy of performances in various media.

When music and politics mix, you get "musical politics," in which personal rivalry can play a large and sometimes fatal role. I think that such a role was played in Furtwängler's musical career by his rivalry with another giant, Arturo Toscanini.

It is hard to imagine two more opposite individuals than Furtwängler and Toscanini. They differed in almost every respect. Short Toscanini always amazed one with his earthy creative vitality. Tall Furtwängler seemed to inhabit the clouds. Toscanini, when conducting, tried to dictate and to structure every detail. When Furtwängler came out to lead the orchestra, his gestures were vague. The orchestra players did not understand when they had to come in, but they did it, somehow. I always wondered how Furtwängler managed that.

Toscanini was a Catholic, and Catholics are always *sachlich*. He conducted Verdi's full-blooded, down-to-earth music grandly, unforgettably. Furtwängler was a Protestant, a Romantic. He was great in the German classics, which he understood better than anyone. And each man knew exactly what he wanted to get from the orchestra—and got it, working ferociously until he was exhausted. How different from today's conductors, under whom good orchestras play well and bad ones badly—so much for their "conductorial craft."

Yet despite the fact that Furtwängler and Toscanini were so different and music is so large a field, they still couldn't share. Each was jealous—sometimes childishly so—of the other's success and fame.

I remember well how in 1930 Toscanini brought the New York Philharmonic to Berlin. It was their European tour, which was incredibly successful. I was an observer of the audience's electric expectations. There sat Bruno Walter, Otto Klemperer, and Erich Kleiber. Piatigorsky, Horowitz, and I were together in a loge box. Toscanini was conducting a Beethoven symphony when Furtwängler, who was in the next box, suddenly jumped up and ran over to see us, exclaiming, "Horrible acoustics, don't you think so? Monstrous!" It was all too obvious what he meant by "acoustics."

Here's another typical story, on the other side of the rivalry. Furtwängler often appeared in Paris with his orchestra, or to conduct at the Grand Opéra. Horowitz and I went to hear him do Wagner's *Die Meistersinger*. The overture sounded, and I saw Maestro Toscanini enter the hall with his wife, Carla, daughter Wally, other relatives, and Mme de Vecchi, a large woman who always accompanied the Toscanini family.

As soon as the overture was over, Toscanini jumped up from his seat. *"Dilettante, canaille!"* That's how upset he was by Furtwängler's conducting! And then the maestro walked out! Like baby swans following a parent on Lake Geneva, the family proceeded behind him. Oh those grand temperamental conductors!

It is no secret Toscanini had complaints of a political nature against Furtwängler. In fact, he began expressing them rather early, and by 1937 everything was over between the two maestros (I would call them "unwilling rivals"). How much of that was real political indignation and how much jealousy on Toscanini's part, I don't know. We can only guess. . . .

The same sort of conflict existed between Toscanini and his compatriot, conductor Victor De Sabata, another artist criticized for his political views. De Sabata—like Furtwängler—was a marvelous musician (he was also a composer) and no fascist at all.

(An amusing family incident involves De Sabata. Maria, my daughter, attended one of my concerts for the first time when she was seven. It was a matinee at Carnegie Hall and De Sabata was the conductor. After the concert he asked Maria, "How did you like it?"

"I liked it," she replied. "But not what you did. You make too much noise." She was sticking up for me! She was particularly offended by the cellists and bass players: "Papa played on a small violin and all the others had big ones!")

While playing at La Scala in Milan, I saw a curious concert series advertised: four requiems, by Mozart, Berlioz, Brahms, and Verdi, to be conducted by Karajan, Furtwängler, De Sabata, and Toscanini. From Toscanini's point of view it was three fascists and one antifascist: himself. Strictly speaking, he should have refused to perform. But he did not, and as far as I know everything went smoothly.

Incidentally, Toscanini's own political position was not immutable—it evolved, as happens with many people. Everyone knows that Toscanini was vociferously opposed to Mussolini. Less well-known is the fact that in earlier years the maestro rather actively supported Mussolini and his party. Mussolini had started his career as a militant socialist. In one of Lenin's letters you can read about his meeting with the "very intelligent" Benito Mussolini. Once in power, Mussolini rather cleverly tried to get the sympathies of avant-garde writers, artists, and musicians. He patronized the Futurists and Stravinsky. Mussolini's attitude toward Jews also differed sharply from Nazi racism. Until 1938 there were many contacts between Mussolini and the Jews.

Before the war I often performed in Italy, and I had friends among influential Italian Jewish families. Once, when I appeared in Naples at the San Carlo Theater, the director told me that a letter had come from Mussolini's secretary: Could I come to tea with Mussolini tomorrow? I happened to be free the next day, and it was only an hour and a half by express train from Naples to Rome. I was quite curious to see Mussolini in a home atmosphere, so I accepted.

I had seen the Duce several times, delivering speeches from the balcony of his palace on Piazza Venezia in Rome. It was an amusing sight: Mussolini was like a flashy conductor overdoing the pantomime. It was clever on his part: when appealing to the crowd, politicians (like conductors) work on the emotions, not reason. In that situation mimicry and gestures are more important than words. Mussolini's audience was clearly thrilled and shouted as one, *"Viva, Duce!"* It looked like a sideshow; the dense atmosphere of menace typical of German political rallies was almost completely absent.

So I went to Rome. Mussolini's apartment was not far from via Appia, and there were no guards. The apartment was furnished in the most run-of-the-mill way, like the dwelling of some modest bourgeois type. The secretary presented me to Mussolini, who was dressed in a shabby dark suit, and to his wife, Rachele.

At first we had tea with lemon, then I played the Bach Chaconne. Afterward, Mussolini started a conversation, which we carried on in a mix of French and Italian. He smiled frequently, revealing blindingly white teeth: even in that situation, he was trying to win over his audience.

I remember being astonished by Mussolini's hands: they seemed strangely inanimate, as if made of plastic. I had the feeling that they would break if I touched them. So I was a bit frightened when Mussolini asked to hold my violin.

"I've loved the violin since I was a child. You know, I almost became a violinist," Mussolini said.

With hands like that? I thought, but said nothing.

(Stravinsky also visited Mussolini, and on learning of the Duce's love of the violin thought of Nero fiddling while Rome burned.)

Seeing that Mussolini's interest in the violin was genuine, I asked him why there were so few examples of marvelous Italian violins left in Italy, home of great instrument making. After all, the violins of Stradivari, Amati, and Guarneri were national treasures and glories. Mussolini agreed that something should be done about it. Well, something was done about it, but not by Mussolini. After the war there was a major international exposition of valuable Italian instruments at Stresa—instruments brought primarily from America, England, and France—and the Italian government acquired several excellent ones. . . .

I remember one time when I was to play the Mendelssohn concerto with Toscanini. Particularly I remember that Rita (my first wife) and I had tickets for the wonderful musical *Lady in the Dark*, with music by Kurt Weill; it starred Gertrude Lawrence and Danny Kaye. Suddenly Rita came in to tell me that Toscanini had called, inviting me to dinner and asking me to bring my violin. He wanted to exchange ideas on Mendelssohn before the performance.

At first I was somewhat upset—having to forgo the pleasure of seeing Danny Kaye! But then I decided that this was a marvelous opportunity to learn what Toscanini thought about the tempi in the concerto. Now, when I think back on that invitation, I am impressed by the maestro's sense of responsibility toward the performance and the soloist. Conductors of incomparably lower stature wouldn't even think of consulting with the soloist before the orchestra rehearsal. . . .

To my taste, the Mendelssohn concerto is the most perfect of the violin concerti. It may not be as profound as Beethoven's, but art does not necessarily have to be "deep." The Mendelssohn is three-quarters classical and one-quarter Romantic. It's harder to play than the Beethoven concerto—you can't drag it out or abuse the *ritenuti*—but if you limit yourself to delivering "just the notes," you get bilberry kvass, as they say in Russian. (Which is not to disparage that divine Russian drink; I still remember Babushkin's kvass in Petersburg: it was so marvelous, so delicious!)

After dinner, Toscanini sat down at the piano, and I picked up the violin. As the maestro started his accompaniment, it sounded somewhat fragile. Clearly Toscanini conducted with much more assurance than he played the piano. But he explained to me how to hold the form in the concerto's cadenza, how it is structured and develops. He understood the nature of violin-singing very well, because he was an incomparable opera conductor. And he knew what to do with that cadenza! To this day I teach it to all my students à la Toscanini. And all of them play it better as a result.

Toscanini was a real, formidable musician. But he wasn't perfect in everything. His Beethoven was sometimes too fast and his Wagner was not romantic enough for my taste. Toscanini's genius was most vividly manifest when he conducted opera: there he could let loose his temperament, his enthusiasm and drive. He could display fully his meticulous attention to detail, and his organizational talent.

I've been to Radio City, where in legendary Studio 8-H Toscanini rehearsed Verdi operas with the NBC Orchestra, created especially for him. I particularly remember the rehearsals of *Otello* and *Falstaff*. He would become so engrossed in working with the vocalists that he sometimes forgot about the orchestra. He could do that because NBC got him the best musicians in the world.

The concertmaster was the brilliant violinist Misha Mishakoff. Frank Miller sat as first cello (when he played the solo in the Brahms Second Piano Concerto, the audience didn't want the piano to start). The orchestra musicians caught Toscanini's every look, every hint. I remember in *Falstaff* he began conducting an episode instantly, without any preparation, and they all picked it up, as one! Unbelievable!

I was introduced to Toscanini by Vladimir Horowitz, who became the maestro's son-in-law in 1933 when he married his daughter, Wanda. Horowitz was accused by some of marrying to further his career, but actually Volodya was already famous by then. For me Horowitz is as much a giant of the piano as Toscanini is of conducting. But Volodya was rather cowed by Toscanini: he was reluctant to play for him or talk to him.

I remember how Horowitz performed the Rachmaninoff Third Piano Concerto with Toscanini. Rachmaninoff had been Horowitz's idol even back in Russia, and Volodya had an understanding of him like no one else. Toscanini, on the other hand, was not very passionate in regard to Russian music. (In Italy the veneration of Rachmaninoff and Tchaikovsky is limited. Even Italian musicians who are Communists, who adore everything Russian, are not such fans of Russian music.) As I remember it, Toscanini was waiting for Horowitz to give him some clue as to what to do with the Rachmaninoff concerto, how to approach it, but Volodya was reluctant to appear impertinent.

Many people considered Toscanini and Horowitz the ideal pair: "best conductor" and "best pianist." And both had wanted to perform and record together. First they did a record of the Brahms Second Concerto, released by RCA Victor, which was a great commercial success. So they decided to record the Tchaikovsky concerto.

In spring 1941 Wanda called me with a request to come to the Toscanini house to listen to the recording of the Tchaikovsky her father and her husband had recently made. "You come, and if you don't like it, tell Papa. I don't like this recording, but I'm afraid that RCA will pressure Papa and Volodya to allow its release. Because RCA will make money on it no matter the quality. And you must understand, Volodya doesn't want to offend anybody. But you are impartial. So, come and tell Papa!"

Wanda, a woman of character who likes things to be done right, wanted Volodya to be at his best on the record. But alas, he was not. I knew and loved the Tchaikovsky piano concerto. It can sound at once brilliant and poetic. The divine second movement is like a scene from *Eugene Onegin*! But that evening, when the recording was played in the presence of Toscanini, Horowitz, and guests, the performance seemed not so great to me. Volodya even botched the famous octaves from the first movement. Usually, when Horowitz reached those octaves, the audience jumped up, not understanding where that squall of sound was coming from. I was a witness to that myself! It would come like a hurricane, an avalanche of sounds. But not this time.

Wanda, who possesses great wisdom and taste, had sensed this herself, but rather than get into an argument with her father, she wanted me to tell him. When the recording was over, a chorus of praise was heaped on Horowitz and Toscanini. None of the other guests expressed any objections. Suddenly Toscanini turned to me. "Milstein, what do you think?" As if daring me to criticize it. I hadn't expected the question and was so caught off guard that I blurted, "Maestro, I don't like it!"

Perhaps that was exaggerating, for the recording did have its good points: two great artists like that cannot fail completely. But I was irritated by the sycophancy of the others. In any case, my careless remark was ignored; everyone just pretended that nothing had happened. The RCA representative, to smooth the situation over, said something to the effect that, well, maybe they'd have to look into it. . . .

The record of the Tchaikovsky concerto was released without any extra work and was a colossal commercial success. It was a sure business, Horowitz and Toscanini in tandem. But what Wanda told me later is interesting. At his Christmas parties, Toscanini liked to play his recordings at full blast so that the music could be heard throughout the house. That year he played his recording of the Tchaikovsky concerto with Horowitz. And after listening to it, he told Wanda, "You know what? Milstein was right!"

Once I spent a night with Toscanini, from two A.M. until nine. It was again on board SS *Rex*, sailing from Europe to America in 1933. It was December and it was cold. There was a terrible storm. I was on deck, terrified, wrapped in a luxurious fur I had bought in Frankfurt. I saw Toscanini appear on deck pacing back and forth, conducting with one hand and twisting his famous mustache with the other.

"Maestro!" I hailed him.

"*Che? Eh, caro Milstein!* Any *problemi?*"

(My "*problemi*" were simple—I was seasick!)

"Sit down, I have blankets."

And I began asking him about the *grandi maestri*—Verdi, Mascagni, Puccini. And about the *piccoli maestri* also. I was interested in Toscanini's opinions on the famous conductors of the past. So he began telling me about Hermann Levi, who was the first to present Wagner's *Parsifal* at Bayreuth. "Oh, there was a profound musician!" And what about the legendary Arthur Nikisch, had he known him? *"Dilletante!"* What about Carl Muck? *"Grande, grande maestro!"*

In later years, I had the opportunity to learn how drastically Toscanini's opinions could change. All of us—Horowitz, the Toscanini family, and I with my second wife, Thérèse—were settled in New York. This was a period when relations were strained between the Horowitzes and Toscanini, when they did not meet or speak. I pleaded with Wanda and Volodya to make up with the maestro. "Toscanini is an old man, there is no time for animosities between you. If something should happen to him, you will regret your present attitude. Make up with him!" Finally, Wanda and Volodya invited the maestro for dinner and he accepted. Peace was made. I was invited too as sponsor of the reunion.

The family dinner went well. Toscanini drank the soup with gusto, slurping noisily as usual and spilling half of it. Then he drank champagne, got a little tipsy, and bitterly exclaimed, *"Vecche uomo, vecche uomo* [old man, old man]!" Wanda responded, "Papa, don't advertise it, we know it anyway."

After dinner Toscanini headed for the library. Horowitz, as ever in awe of his forbidding (though *vecche*) father-in-law, nudged me. "Go on, go talk to him!" When I approached him, Toscanini once again began reminiscing about the conductors he had known. Hermann Levi? *"Grande musicista!"* Arthur Nikisch? *"Formidabile maestro! Gigante!"* Well, what about Carl Muck? "Eh? Muck? *Niente."* Toscanini shrugged. *"Tedesco."* As if saying, What could you expect from a German?

Toscanini's legendary temperament, well known to musicians and the public, exploded once in my presence in a very funny way. In New York in 1939, a benefit was held for the Chatham Square Music School. The star attraction of the program was the "children's orchestra," as it was advertised. The orchestra's violinists included Heifetz, Adolf Busch, Oskar Shumsky, and me, and I remember that one of the violists was William Primrose. The cellists included Emmanuel Feuermann, Piatigorsky, and Alfred Wallenstein.

All eighteen or twenty of us "children" came out onstage in

shorts, even Busch, a big, red-faced man who was almost fifty then, yet looked younger than the rest of us.

(Adolf Busch was an excellent violinist who could perform Paganini's caprices brilliantly and Beethoven's concerto with profundity. But he had heart trouble, and toward the end of his life he had difficulty playing with the old intensity. I remember a concert in Town Hall, when he presented Beethoven's E-Flat Major Sonata with his son-in-law, Rudolf Serkin. He had to stop the concert because his heart was acting up. An announcement was made: Is there a doctor in the house? There were several dozen—right there they could have done any operation under the sun! New York doctors love music. . . . A half-hour later Busch came back out and finished the performance.)

The conductor of our "children's orchestra" was none other than Toscanini. We played Ferdinand Ries's "Perpetuum mobile." Heifetz said before the performance, "Let's surprise the maestro! He'll be keeping a strict beat, as usual. But we'll start an incredible acceleration. Let's see how Toscanini reacts."

The maestro came out to his "children's orchestra" in a long, old-fashioned coat, like a schoolteacher. He began conducting and we followed Heifetz's plan and played faster and faster. Toscanini could not understand what was going on! He was so angry that he dropped his baton and ran off!

The "children's orchestra" was a great success; the audience loved it and thought that the trick with the tempo had been planned that way. The maestro, however, was furious and would not come out for a bow. Instead Wanda came out, dressed in a man's suit (she had borrowed my pin-striped pants) and with a hat in her hand. She even "twirled" a drawn mustache, as if she were the maestro. The audience was certain that this too was part of the grand design and went wild.

Despite a certain eccentricity, Toscanini was a fascinating conversationalist, and I liked visiting him in his marvelous house in suburban Riverdale, north of the George Washington Bridge. There were usually many people at dinner at Toscanini's house: the family, relatives, and guests. They served spaghetti, which I adore.

Toscanini liked to sip champagne and converse in his mixed English-Italian. After dinner he usually went to his library. Horowitz and I would follow. Toscanini, gradually falling asleep, would mutter at us, "What you do is difficult! In order to play the violin or piano, you have to work, to think. For us conductors, others play. And I don't have to do anything!"

As it applies to him and perhaps another dozen or so conductors, Toscanini's words were, of course, a blatant exaggeration. But in principle I think he's right.

Every decent orchestra has at least ten or twenty marvelous musicians. Good orchestras have violinists who could be the soloists in the Brahms concerto. Often they perform chamber music beautifully and manage perfectly without a conductor. When I released a record in 1965 with two Mozart concertos, the critics wrote how unfortunate it was that there was no mention of the conductor. They could not believe that the record was made without one. But Mozart, in my opinion, doesn't need a conductor at all. And there are many other instances when you can do without a conductor.

There was an era when personalities who had already made a name for themselves in music became conductors: von Bülow, Richard Strauss, Rachmaninoff. Now people start conducting without having proved themselves in any other way. Many of them have talent, but that's not enough. They are not ready to work with an orchestra, they can't imagine how well the orchestra knows music. Some conductors consider orchestra musicians ignoramuses, while actually the real ignoramuses are often the conductors themselves.

I like the comparison between conductors and prompters. The artists know their roles, and the prompters merely remind them. The basic function of the conductor is to remind the orchestra, and therefore during a concert the conductor should behave as discreetly as a prompter.

Instead, conductors attract the audience's attention to their person and distract it from the music. Of course, all this does impress the ladies who sit on orchestra boards: a tiny movement of the baton, and the trombones blare!

For the audience, the conductor is the commander in chief. In

England the most mediocre conductors of second-rate orchestras get knighted, yet Benjamin Britten was never given the honor. Government bureaucrats in most countries admire the fact that a conductor has a hundred people under him.

As a solo violinist, I have particular complaints against conductors. Many of them do not study the scores of violin concertos. They just look through them, which can lead to monstrous lapses. For a symphony that the orchestra and the conductor already know by heart, they routinely have three to five rehearsals, yet they play a violin concerto with just one rehearsal, sometimes two, even though the music presents the same problems as a symphony, plus certain tensions related to the soloist.

The word about me among conductors is that I'm difficult. I once played Lalo's *Symphonie espagnole* with the great George Szell and his Cleveland Orchestra. Szell was hardly known as a great Lalo admirer, yet he knew the score to the last note, and at rehearsal we went through the *Symphonie espagnole* from beginning to end, almost without stopping. Highly pleased with himself, Szell said to me, "There, you see, and they say it's difficult to please you!" To which I replied, "Unless it's the Cleveland Orchestra with Szell." Flattered, the orchestra applauded. (I always say something like that at rehearsals, to make the orchestra members play better; it's one of my small tricks.)

I had the luck to perform with such giants of conducting as Carl Muck and Franz Schalk. The public does not remember them now. Better known are Furtwängler and Toscanini, because of their recordings. Still, people today cannot even imagine how these two were adored, envied, and imitated.

As for Koussevitzky, his energy and ambition knew no bounds. He wanted to dominate the American scene, even over Toscanini.

I witnessed an amusing scene once. As happens to many superstars, Koussevitzky was always surrounded by spongers and sycophants. Among his constant admirers was the pianist Petya Luboshits, born in Odessa. (He had two sisters: Anna, a cellist, and Lea, a violinist. Lea, a student of Hřimaly's, was rather famous in Russia. She specialized in Glazunov's concerto, which she played boldly and with fire. Later she moved to America, where the ending of her name didn't sound very nice, so she changed it to Luboshutz.)

Petya was an oily character who never stopped complimenting Koussevitzky, for which the maestro kindly called him Luboshutz rather than Luboshits, and Mrs. Koussevitzky frequently invited Petya to tea.

And this is what I saw at tea one day. The scene is the Koussevitzkys' Boston residence. The maestro, relaxed by the tea, inquires, "Petya, what's new down in New York?" Loyal Petya struck the right note. "O, Sergei Alexandrovich! Why do you perform so rarely in our city? Without you New York is a desert!"

Pleased, Koussevitzky responded, "Don't say that, you have lots of conductors down there. . . . Natalya!" He turned to his wife. "What's that old man's name? . . . The conductor . . . Italian . . . ?" He had wanted to be generous and mention Toscanini, but, you see, he just couldn't remember the name!

Eugene Ormandy loved it when I criticized other conductors: he would invite me to dinner for good schnitzel and good wine, and listen with delight to my barbs. But once he warned me, "Just don't pick on my god—Toscanini!" So I started telling Ormandy how the pianist Arthur Balsam and I were at the NBC studio, where Toscanini was conducting the Brahms Third Symphony, and it was . . . I was about to say "marvelous!" but Ormandy interrupted me and shouted to his wife, "Gretel, did you hear? The only symphony conducted by Toscanini that I don't like either is Brahms's Third!"

Among the things I treasure are two presents Toscanini gave me. Once for my birthday he sent, via Wanda, an original letter from Tchaikovsky to von Bülow, in which the composer wrote something like, "Respected maestro, I heard that you would like to play my piano concerto; it is not ready yet, but I would be pleased if you played the completed first movement."

The other gift from Toscanini is a fascinating letter of Paganini's that mentions Berlioz. Paganini was Berlioz's champion, and in the letter he asks the recipient to put in a good word for Berlioz in

Warsaw. And in the same letter Paganini writes about a man in prison: "Maybe you could help obtain his release?"

That's the kind of people musicians are—it's not enough that they have a lot of problems with their own art, they have to get involved in other people's business, in politics. They strive to help mankind. It was that way in the last century, and it continues to be so in ours. I hope it will stay that way in the future, too.

11. Fritz Kreisler

For my friend Vladimir Horowitz, the god of our profession was Rachmaninoff. For me, it was Fritz Kreisler. He appeared in Russia before the revolution, but I did not hear him play there. Yet Horowitz and I had all his records. (One time years later, I told Kreisler that I saw a program of his performances in St. Petersburg, when he played in a trio with Pablo Casals. Kreisler nodded happily. He liked recalling his concerts in Russia, and in particular the fact that he composed his famous piece "Schön Rosmarin" for his performance in Odessa, the beloved city of my childhood.)

When Volodya Horowitz and I decided to leave Russia for the West, Horowitz went first and sent me a letter from Germany. He told me that he had attended a concert by Kreisler and hadn't liked it, and as a result he was considering going back to Russia. That's how earnestly we took our musical idols!

When I joined Horowitz soon after, the two of us went to a Kreisler concert in Paris. We paid six dollars per ticket—a huge sum in those days; we could have had two rooms in the best hotel for that! I remember we were seated in a box of the Grand Opéra among a refined crowd. Kreisler played Bach's E Major Concerto, then Viotti's Twenty-second Concerto, and finished with Beethoven. I don't remember the conductor, but with Kreisler it didn't matter. Kreisler performed without paying much attention to the orchestra and conductor. With anyone else, this attitude would have seemed frivolous, but Kreisler was a genius and played so ravishingly! This time Horowitz was entranced, as was I.

The concert ended, the audience departed. But Volodya and I still sat in the box, alone. We were destroyed! An old usher tried to shake us up. "The concert is over, young gentlemen. Everyone's gone, they're all gone, go home." But we couldn't stand up from our seats. And we decided: We're going to stay in the West!

We had heard exceptional musicians before that, but Kreisler's performance that night was a gift from God. Later I heard Kreisler play not so brilliantly, especially when he hadn't been practicing. But even then, what would have been a catastrophe for others sounded charming from him.

In 1926 or 1927 Horowitz and I met Kreisler in Monte Carlo, where we were performing. I remember Kreisler asking Volodya and me, "Tell me, boys, do you gamble in the casino?" We simply didn't have the money to gamble, so we honestly replied, "No, we don't." Kreisler nodded approvingly. "Good, good, you're doing the right thing. I don't go there, either."

Some time later, Mr. Puttman, our manager in Monte Carlo, proposed, "Would you like to watch them play at the casino? You shouldn't bet, but just taking a look is all right. It's an amusing spectacle." And he gave us passes. And what did we see the moment we got in? Kreisler gambling away at roulette, putting stakes on different numbers, completely caught up in the game and utterly delighted! We left in a hurry before he noticed us. We didn't want to make him uncomfortable.

It couldn't have been good for Kreisler to play roulette, because he had a bad heart and gambling is exciting. He also had bad kidneys. But he lived by his own rules: he gambled, ate, and drank as much as he wanted.

Kreisler had no enemies; everyone adored him. He had that Viennese charm. Onstage he stood like a king, nobly facing the audience. You could see that he had a slight facial tic, but even that just added to his appeal.

Kreisler was very generous toward his colleagues, very approving and supportive. I never heard a disparaging word about anyone from him. Indeed, I don't think he ever thought badly of anyone. I remember I was doing Dvořák's concerto with Furtwängler in Berlin. Kreisler came backstage to compliment me on my performance. That's when our friendship began.

Once I came to Chicago to give a recital. Kreisler was in town playing with an orchestra. I got a call from his manager: "The maestro invites you to a rehearsal so that you can advise him which violin to use in the concert." I was delighted—the great Kreisler wants my advice! If I had known him better then, I wouldn't have felt so self-important. But at the time I was so proud, I even took a limousine from the hotel to the rehearsal.

I waited backstage for Kreisler. He came in but didn't even mention the violin. Instead, he inquired, "Nathan, do you know a good German restaurant around here?" We went to a big German place, where it was always dark. The walls were hung with sinister photographs of boxers, and the waiters in vests brought around enormous pitchers of beer. They flicked off the foam with wooden spatulas, and it flew into the customers' eyes.

Kreisler was happy! He went pink in splotches, the way young ladies did in the days of my youth when they were propositioned. I was rather dismayed that my idol could get so excited over beer and rathskeller food. We stayed in the restaurant until around five, even though Kreisler had to play that evening. To tell the truth, he was not at his best when he went out onstage.

I think Kreisler was rather proud of the fact that months went by without his picking up the violin. He insisted that too much practice is harmful (which I could agree with, sometimes). But not every concertizing musician can allow himself breaks in his work the way Kreisler did. At first, I admit I thought the stories of his disdain for regular training were exaggerated. But then I had the opportunity to see it for myself.

Jacques Thibaud was a good friend of mine. We shared an accompanist, Tasso Janopulo, and Thibaud and I would spend a lot of time playing bridge together. Once we were sitting in his Paris apartment when a telegram came from Kreisler in Corsica: he asked Thibaud to check on his Stradivarius, which he had left with a violin dealer three months earlier. You had to conclude that Kreisler hadn't held a violin in his hands in three months.

Thibaud didn't have time to see the dealer, and he asked me to do it. I was flattered to be asked to do a favor for Kreisler. When I went to the dealer, I discovered that Kreisler's Strad had only two strings; the others had broken. I asked the man to restring the violin and I played on it for a while, to keep the strings in tune. Kreisler was grateful for my help and asked for another favor: he would still not be back for a while, so could I rehearse Beethoven's *Kreutzer* Sonata with his pianist in his place? "I'd like the pianist to have a better understanding of the sonata." That was completely unexpected!

What I didn't know at the time was that Kreisler hated to rehearse. Even with Rachmaninoff, and they made several wonderful recordings. But Rachmaninoff was not going to let Kreisler get away with being lazy! When they were recording the Grieg sonata, they did it no fewer than five times, at Rachmaninoff's insistence. According to Rachmaninoff, Kreisler gushed each time that it was perfect and they didn't need to do another take. And each time Rachmaninoff maintained that they could play it even better.

If Kreisler didn't feel like working with Rachmaninoff, you can imagine how he felt about rehearsals with mere mortals. Generally speaking, you'd have to say Kreisler didn't care who his pianist was. His partner of many years was an imperturbable old man named Carl Lamson. Whenever Lamson played his *tutti*, Kreisler would tune up quite noisily. As Kreisler explained to me, "Lamson can't hear it anyway!" Mme Kreisler, who didn't think much of Lamson, considering him too phlegmatic, said, "Every soloist's accompanist gets sick from time to time! Some of them quite often! Only our Lamson never misses a concert! Isn't it horrible?'' She meant that if Lamson got sick, they could at long last get another pianist. But Lamson remained in good health, and Kreisler kept him, not wanting to hurt the old man's feelings.

Here I would like to say more about Kreisler's wife, Harriet. She was his companion for fifty years. Once in a conversation with me, she described herself this way: "People think I'm a bitch. Maybe I am. But without this bitch Fritz wouldn't be where he is today." You couldn't put it any better. Harriet was wife, friend, manager, strict teacher, and guardian angel for Fritz. But her abrasive behavior did take getting used to.

I was often a guest at the home of Charles Foley, Kreisler's and Rachmaninoff's manager. The Kreislers liked it there, since Foley was a hospitable man and a real gentleman. Nevertheless, I once saw Mme Kreisler spit out a sip of whiskey offered her by Foley.

Yet for all her unpolished manners, Mme Kreisler could be quite effective. I remember the big party in New York in honor of Kreisler's seventy-fifth birthday at the Ritz-Carlton Hotel. With his approval, the occasion was made a benefit for the Musicians' Emergency Fund. The fund's president then was Mrs. Helen Hull, and the vice-president was my wife, Thérèse.

The program had the brilliant Cuban pianist Jorge Bolet playing Liszt's "Funérailles"; I played the Pugnani-Kreisler Prelude and Allegro, and Kreisler's unaccompanied Recitativo and Scherzo-Caprice. On the podium, among others, were the Kreislers, Georges Enesco, Bruno Walter, Faye Emerson (who was married to former President Roosevelt's son Elliot), Cardinal Spellman, and Monsignor Fulton Sheen. At the party, heartfelt speeches were made in honor of the birthday boy. I remember that Sheen said to Kreisler, "When God decides that He wants to see you, you will be met by nine angels with violins. And they will say to you, 'Maestro, teach us to play the violin as divinely as you do!' "

In response, Mrs. Hull pleaded, "Wait a moment, Monsignor, we're not ready for that, let our Fritz stay with us a bit longer!"

The audience—rich ladies who had paid a hundred dollars for the concert and lunch—was very pleased. In conclusion, Mrs. Hull turned to them with an appeal. "Ladies"—there were no gentle-men—"when you get home, remember this marvelous party and the music that caressed your ears, and send a generous check to our Emergency Fund!" Mrs. Hull, from Kentucky, was a real aristocrat in appearance and manner. If there had been an election for queen of America, she would have been a candidate. Her appeal to the wealthy women was graceful and delicate.

At this point, Kreisler's wife stood up (she had been drinking a bit) and said, "Helen, you are too kind, you don't know how to talk to these people." Then she addressed the audience. "Why go home and wait so long, dear ladies? I'm sure you have your check-books with you. Look, I'm writing a check for two thousand dollars! I'm certain you'll do the same!"

Mme Kreisler had pushed the right button. The ladies pulled out their checkbooks. And since there were two or three hundred people there, we collected a substantial sum.

Of German extraction, Mme Kreisler regretted that "Fritz has Jewish blood." In fact, it was more than just "having blood"—the whole Kreisler family was 100 percent Jewish. But Harriet insisted that Kreisler was only part Jewish. Once she told the pianist Leo-pold Godowsky, "You understand, actually, Fritz has very little Jewish blood." To which Godowsky, who was never at a loss for words, replied, "I didn't realize Fritz was so anemic."

Harriet was a very practical woman, and under her supervision Kreisler became a rather wealthy man. He also developed an inter-est in stocks and other financial matters. Once, as I was strolling along Madison Avenue, I saw Kreisler limping along wearing a long coat that had once been gray but was turning green. I presumed he was headed for River House, 435 East Fifty-second Street—a fa-mous building with an impressive entrance and a marvelous back-yard—where the Kreislers had a large and elegant apartment.

I was about to hail him when I saw him turn in to the office of a well-known brokerage house on Madison. Apparently Kreisler wanted to get the latest stock quotes. It seemed so unlike him that I decided not to approach him: what if he were embarrassed to have his interest in the market exposed? I was later told that he was seen there quite often.

In 1941 Kreisler, then sixty-seven, was hit by a truck as he crossed a street in New York. He was brought unconscious to the hospital and was in a coma for a long time. Miraculously, he survived, but his hearing and sight were severely impaired.

Soon after the accident, Kreisler was at our house for lunch. I wanted to distract him, so I asked, "*Meister*, back in Russia I owned your recording of Cottenet's 'Meditation.' Who is that composer? I've never heard of him." Kreisler grew animated. "Oh, that's my old friend, an Englishman who lives in America. I haven't performed that piece in a long time." He asked for a violin. I gave him one, and I could see that it was hard for him to handle. He didn't know how to put his finger on F. "Is this F?" he asked me. But then he played a bit from the half-forgotten piece. Even in that condition he was the unique Kreisler, his musicianship full of charm and grace.

No one could play little pieces the way Kreisler did. People don't appreciate those salon bonbons anymore, because performers don't know how to put a finish and gloss on them, they only see notes— fast or slow. But when Kreisler took up those miniatures, every note spoke.

When it comes to Kreisler's own pieces for the violin, everyone remembers the scandal connected with his transcriptions of the classical composers. For over thirty years, the musical world believed that Kreisler was playing authentic works by Vivaldi, Couperin, Pugnani, and other old masters. When he revealed that they were his own compositions, some critics were shocked. But the public enjoyed the pieces as much as before. It didn't care about musical provenance.

I think that such works of Kreisler's in the old style are more pastiche than imitation. Take, for instance, his famous Prelude and Allegro in the style of Pugnani. I know six etudes for the violin written by Gaetano Pugnani himself—an eighteenth-century Italian composer—and without a doubt Kreisler borrowed from them. But clearly, he changed the rhythm. All these pastiches are smart work, but I think that sometimes Kreisler went overboard on modulations, not knowing when to stop. That's particularly evident in his arrangements of baroque music.

In general, Kreisler was a mystifier. In wasn't enough for him to radically change Schumann's Fantasy for violin and piano, he also wanted to prove that he had acted on the composer's personal authority! I remember his colorful and detailed story of how, when still a tiny child, he found himself in a café in Vienna frequented by musicians. He described the famous violinist Joseph Joachim, and then Brahms, "a pompous man with a beard." And then, Schumann entered the café!

Sitting down at the piano, Schumann showed Brahms his composition, the violin fantasy! Brahms didn't like something about it. They began arguing, with Schumann trying other possibilities: Maybe this? Or this? According to Kreisler, it was his memory of those variations that prompted his subsequent revisions of the Fantasy.

Kreisler told me about this remarkable encounter with such vividness and fervor that I was fully prepared to believe him. Why shouldn't Kreisler have met Joachim and Brahms? But Schumann? Alas, simple arithmetic showed that the composer had died almost twenty years before Kreisler's birth.

Kreisler also made major revisions in Tchaikovsky's concerto, which many musicians felt improved the composition. But naturally, there were defenders of Tchaikovsky, too. Kreisler insisted that the idea for reshaping the concerto had come to him in a conversation with the composer's friend Sergei Taneyev. Allegedly, Kreisler had met him before the revolution on one of his trips to Moscow, and Taneyev told him that Tchaikovsky had intended to redo his violin concerto but simply hadn't gotten around to it.

Another time the story was quite different: Kreisler had met the old composer César Cui, one of the "Mighty Five," in Petersburg, and Cui told him about Tchaikovsky's desire to revise his composition. Either way, the story wasn't very convincing, but I had no intention of arguing about it with the adorable maestro.

Kreisler's versions of the Tchaikovsky concerto and Schumann's fantasy did not catch on, and almost no one plays them now. But his smaller pastiches and his own compositions for the violin are another matter. And naturally, his cadenzas for Beethoven and Brahms concerti are tremendously popular.

In his last years, Kreisler performed less and less, until gradually he put an end to all concert activity. We met frequently at that time at various parties: the Kreislers were very social and liked going to the homes of the wealthy.

New York had several well-known hostesses then, among them Mrs. Robertson, Mrs. Hearst (wife of the newspaper tycoon), and Mrs. Donahue, who owned a major block of Woolworth's stock. Mrs. Donahue was a beautiful woman and an amateur singer. She used to complain to me that her boyfriend was interested only in her money, to which I responded cheerfully, "Why worry? What's the difference?"

Kreisler and I liked to tour Mrs. Robertson's house, which had a small room furnished with replicas of pieces in Marie Antoinette's boudoir. The room was roped off like something out-of-bounds at a museum. I didn't quite understand why a room like that was necessary in a private apartment, but I did admire a small chair of green wood with a footstool that had a mirror attached. While Marie Antoinette had her shoes put on, she could see what was happening behind her back.

Among the glamorous parties Kreisler liked to attend were those given by the syndicated columnist Elsa Maxwell. She had a big apartment at the Waldorf-Astoria, which cost her nothing: the management was happy enough with the publicity. Elsa Maxwell's society columns were influential then. (She was the type of woman who would say, "I was talking with Winnie yesterday. . . ." "Winnie who?" "Oh, Winnie Churchill. . . .") There was the time Kreisler and I met at Maxwell's for her birthday. Ever the social animal, Kreisler said to me, "It would be a good idea for you to play; our hostess would like that." Well, I lived nearby, so I went home for my violin. As soon as I returned, Kreisler asked to borrow it, and suddenly he started playing Tartini's "Devil Trills." He did it divinely, adding his improvised variations, and after that it was of course impossible for me to play.

No wonder Mme Kreisler liked to say, "Nathan! Of course, Fritz didn't have the technique of Heifetz or you, but he knew *how* to play! Isn't that so?"

Kreisler had an excellent collection of Italian violins, but *any* instrument in his hands, even the most mediocre, sounded like the best Italian-made. His wife used to say, "Everyone thinks that Fritz plays on a good violin when he performs. No, he leaves the good ones at home."

He used to call one of his violins the "Parker" Stradivarius. Intrigued, I asked him about the instrument's lineage, where it came from. Kreisler replied, "Oh, the violin is the work of Mr. Parker of London, an old and really not bad master."

"Why do you call it a Stradivarius, then?"

"It sounds so good!"

Kreisler also played the piano wonderfully. I remember one enchanting evening when we were invited to dinner in New York by Iolanda Irion, the Hungarian-born wife of the director of Steinway and herself a pianist. There were about twenty people; I remember the famous Polish tenor Jan Kiepura. My wife, Thérèse, was sitting next to Kreisler and diligently filling his plate. Suddenly Mme Kreisler, seated at the opposite end of the table, cried out, "Thérèse, stop killing my Fritz!" She watched everything like a hawk!

Later, to smooth over the outburst, Mme Kreisler turned to me. "Please take Fritz to the other room. Ask him to play the piano, he likes to do that." I took Kreisler to the room, which had a first-class Steinway. He sat down and played a waltz. Turning to me in delight, he said, "Nathan, this is my life. Here's what I love: good light music, the divine waltzes of Strauss, Lanner . . ." And suddenly he began improvising on the theme from the slow movement of Brahms's violin concerto. I had never heard a more astonishing improvisation in my life! It mixed different styles: Beethoven, and something from the Russian symphonies, and Biedermeier, all so cleverly crafted that you couldn't tell from where he took what. I listened in awe, holding my breath.

Clearly, the world of popular music was incredibly close to Kreisler. No wonder so many of his transcriptions are based on popular songs, like "My Wild Irish Rose" and "Londonderry Air." He also wrote an operetta in the Viennese style that was very popular. I liked that operetta of his, much more than I did the string quartet he composed "seriously."

The Kreislers liked coming to our triplex apartment in New

York, on Park Avenue and Fifty-Eighth Street. Madame told Thérèse, "You have divine dinner parties, no one ever annoys Fritz
with stupidities like 'Oh, maestro, it's such a pity you don't play
anymore.' Fritz can't stand that!"

One evening, when our guests were due at eight, the Kreislers
showed up at 7:15. It was a good thing I was dressed and ready. I
received them, and while Madame went to powder her nose, I took
Kreisler into the living room. The butler for the evening was a
young Frenchman, Eugène, who worked in all the fashionable salons and knew the drinking tastes of every celebrity. He turned to
Kreisler knowingly—"The usual, maestro?"—and brought a double martini, which Kreisler hurriedly downed. In three minutes
Kreisler put away four double martinis!

Harriet came back and sniffed the air suspiciously.

"Fritz, were you drinking?"

"No!"

"Fritz, open your mouth and breathe at me!"

"Don't be silly."

He got away with it that time; the usual storm didn't break, and
in a marvelous mood Kreisler settled down to listen to a friend of
ours, the former French consul in Los Angeles, sing and accompany
himself on the guitar. The man was very excited about playing for
Kreisler and asked the maestro what he would like to hear.

"Some nice gypsy music."

Our friend for some reason struck up a French song, but Kreisler
didn't understand at first that it was French and pulled out his hearing aid and blew into it. So the singer switched to the Russian
"Dark Eyes," a familiar melody with which Kreisler was happy
and even sang along. . . . And that's how I remember him, at peace
with himself, pleased with good food and wine, humming old gypsy
songs.

12. Three Musketeers: Piatigorsky, Horowitz, and I

Early in my story, I described how I became friends with Vladimir Horowitz in Kiev in 1921 and how he and I toured around Russia and then left for Europe. In Berlin we were joined by the cellist Gregor Piatigorsky, also a Russian émigré, and we became known as "the Three Musketeers."

Why did they call us that? Probably because we were young, energetic, cheerful, and successful. And we were great friends.

We helped one another, consoled one another, cheered one another up, amused one another. And criticized one another ruthlessly.

Volodya and I had had our success in Russia, and Piatigorsky, as I recall, was primarily an orchestra player in Russia. But in Europe we all had to start over.

Horowitz and I met Piatigorsky in Berlin in 1926, soon after our arrival from Russia. We were brought together by the promoter Alexander Merovitch, and immediately Volodya and I were addressing Piatigorsky by his nickname, Grisha. At the time, Grisha was first cello for Furtwängler's Berlin Philharmonic, but Merovitch persuaded him to give that up, promising to organize an immediate, incredible solo career for him, even though Merovitch was in no position to make such a promise just then. Luckily, Piatigorsky, like Horowitz and me, did not really need Merovitch's services. Grisha could handle his own career quite successfully, thank you, because he was a great talent with extraordinary charm.

Grisha was also a large man (six feet, four inches) who carried his cello as if it were nothing. His height made him the butt of endless jokes. But Grisha could put down any jokester. I remember his meeting the pianist Leopold Godowsky. Godowsky was a sweet man and a wit. So, when the short Godowsky met Piatigorsky, he said somewhat pugnaciously, "You're so tall! You should play the bass instead of the cello!" To which Piatigorsky responded immediately, "You're so short! You should play the piccolo instead of the piano!" It was, I'd say, a meeting of worthy opponents.

Piatigorsky deluged Horowitz and me with a cascade of incredible stories of his travels in Russia. For instance, he assured us that he had escaped from Russia by crossing the Dnieper River at night on his cello! We laughed so hard we had to hold on to our bellies.

Another incredible story involved Lenin. In Moscow in 1919, Grisha (then sixteen) became cellist in the respected string quartet headed by Lev Zeitlin. (This was the Zeitlin who founded Persimfans, the world's first "symphonic ensemble without a conductor," which I described earlier.) It was a revolutionary period, and Zeitlin's string ensemble was named the Lenin Quartet. As Piatigorsky told it, he was the only member of the group who spoke out against that honor; he demanded that the quartet be named after Beethoven. This unheard-of daring on the part of a young musician, in an era when "saboteurs and counterrevolutionaries" were shot without trial in the streets of Moscow, seemed farfetched to me. But, according to Piatigorsky, it was only a prelude. . . .

The Lenin Quartet was invited to the Kremlin to play for Lenin himself. According to Piatigorsky, when the musicians finished the performance, Lenin asked one of them to stay behind . . . none other than our Grisha! Lenin wanted to talk to him alone. "Why didn't you want to name the quartet after me? What do you have against me?" Lenin allegedly asked Piatigorsky. Can you imagine? The leader of an enormous country, known to have little interest in music, asking a boy cellist what he had against him! But Piatigorsky told this tale around Berlin with such fire and passion that many believed him. And the improbable story of crossing the Dnieper on his cello? It turned out to be a choice publicity gimmick, appearing regularly in the newspapers of the cities where Piatigorsky performed.

Piatigorsky was not a vulgar liar by any means. On the contrary, he was an honest and highly decent man. But he made things up, marvelously! Horowitz and I loved it when Grisha would start his storytelling. Eventually he published an amusing book entitled *Cellist*, a collection of his tales.

In the early thirties the three of us spent every summer in Switzerland. Contrary to a well-circulated legend, we did not play together. Each of us practiced at home, separately, though we usually got together for fun and relaxation. And Grisha's endless trove of adventures was an important part of our good times.

In turn, our Swiss summers became material for new Piatigorsky fantasies. I learned about that only much later. Once (this was after the war), Grisha and I were performing Brahms's double concerto in Denver, Colorado. There was a reception in our honor after the concert, with a lot of beautiful women present—a mighty catalyst for Piatigorsky's imagination. (They say that even Alexander Pushkin was bored in salons until a pretty woman appeared.)

Piatigorsky created his little oeuvres like a poet, improvising on the spot. And I have to give him his due, he included Horowitz and me in his stories; that is, he behaved like a good colleague. And so, lighting a cigarette, then taking long, nervous drags from time to time, Piatigorsky began unfolding his gripping tale for the rapt audience of Denver ladies. "It was in Switzerland. . . . Milstein, Horowitz, and I decided to ride horseback into the mountains. Beautiful sunny weather. . . . But suddenly, a storm. . . . Mountains, terrible roads. . . . The horses whinny. . . . We are in the middle of a hurricane. . . . The horses keep slipping, we almost plunge into an abyss. . . .'' And so on. In the end, of course, we were saved, but not before Grisha had happily tormented the imaginations of his charming listeners to their limit.

After that rendition, I quietly asked him, "Grisha, what were you talking about before? Nothing like that ever happened."

"Don't you remember?"

"Grisha, have some shame—I had just had my appendix out! How could I have gone horseback riding?"

But Piatigorsky insisted that it had been just the way he described, suggesting quite firmly that something was wrong with *my* memory. He was so persuasive, in fact, that I began to doubt my own recall and decided to check with Horowitz: what if I really had forgotten that exciting adventure? Horowitz laughed wildly. "Why, you were still recovering from your appendix operation! So Grisha and I took bicycles and had a quiet ride on a flat road. It wasn't high up at all there in Crans sur Sierre, remember? And on the way, there was some rain. That's all. . . ."

But how could you compare the actual event with Piatigorsky's marvelous tale? Grisha's version was incomparably more dramatic and entertaining. Just one thing worried me afterward. If Grisha could concoct such a horror story out of an ordinary bicycle ride, what had he told people about the time the three of us went to a Broadway burlesque show? I shudder at the thought. . . .

As I've said, Piatigorsky, Horowitz, and I met frequently, but we didn't perform together. I don't know how the idea came up— that we had to perform for the public as a trio. It must have been one of Merovitch's tricks. The concert was set for March 1932 at Carnegie Hall. We selected Beethoven's B-flat Major Trio and Brahms's C Major Trio. We also wanted to play a Russian work. But Tchaikovsky's trio seemed too long and we didn't dare make cuts in it. So we settled on Rachmaninoff's trio.

The composition has its divine moments, but it also has its longueurs. Rachmaninoff himself came to our rescue, cutting about twenty minutes of music. He was delighted that his trio would be on the same program with Beethoven and Brahms, and he attended our rehearsals regularly. (There is a picture of our trio rehearsing, but for some reason Rachmaninoff was not photographed with us.)

Listening to the Brahms at the rehearsals, Rachmaninoff would exclaim, "I don't like Brahms! Too bad!" and then would try to explain. "Brahms knew how to compose." This was not meant as great praise. It's true that Brahms could create music out of any material, but that music often sounds rather tired.

Rachmaninoff, of course, was not alone in his dislike of Brahms. And I'm not talking here about Wagner and his famous antipathy; many other composers—Tchaikovsky, Edouard Lalo, Hugo Wolf, Richard Strauss, and Prokofiev—criticized Brahms's music. Actually, Brahms's reputation was established only quite recently; even in the early part of the twentieth century he was not played widely in Russia, or for that matter in France, Italy, or Spain.

For me, Brahms is not in the same class as Mozart, Beethoven, or Schubert. When they composed, God was helping them. But Brahms composed his music, even if it is often quite marvelous, without any such divine inspiration. Sometimes he tried to make up for this lack with a kind of fake originality—what they call "scratching his left ear with his right hand."

Brahms's symphonies are good, but even they get convoluted. It's music that doesn't sing. The best of them, the most natural, is the First. Nor do I like his chamber works, though I suppose the violin sonatas are exceptional, and I particularly like the first movement of the G Major Sonata. I also find some of his intermezzi for the piano attractive.

I often get into arguments over Brahms's violin concerto. He borrowed the form of Beethoven's concerto and the result was one of his best compositions. But even here many of the wonderfully invented moments do not add up to an overall natural flow. Take the concerto's second movement. Why is the big solo given to the woodwinds here? The oboe starts and then the theme is taken up by the flute and clarinet, instruments that don't sound especially good together, and the result is an unnecessary fragmentation, the lack of a single line.

Another such example for me is the cello solo in the slow movement of Brahms's Second Piano Concerto. It's the most inspired moment of the concerto, but Brahms made an elementary psychological mistake in it. I realized this listening to the concerto with Arthur Rubinstein at the piano, in Montreux. He was playing with the Orchestre de Paris, which had an excellent young first cellist then, and I was looking forward to the cellist's solo, inspired by the presence of a musician like Rubinstein.

But what we heard was the bleating of a goat. And it was more Brahms's fault than the cellist's. The poor orchestral musician had gotten overexcited during the too long wait between the start of the concerto and the first appearance of the theme in the Andante.

I confess that I sometimes want to redo Brahms's concerti—the piano, and the double, and the violin. It's good music, but it's written down unsatisfactorily, to my taste. The best of them for me is the violin concerto. And though I'm not crazy about it, I did record the double concerto with Piatigorsky. But that was as a tribute to our friendship.

Pierre Fournier, the marvelous cellist (though I don't put him in the same league with Piatigorsky, even if he did marry Piatigorsky's ex, Lida Antik), once asked me to do a new recording of Brahms's double concerto. I explained that the violin is like a poor relation in that work: all it does is repeat the cello. And that's not interesting. (It's the same way with a joke: the first time, everyone laughs, but then if you repeat it immediately, no one even chuckles.)

To my mind, the violin part of the double concerto should be given away to the other instruments, leaving the cello as a solo. If I had the time, I'd redo it that way. The work would only gain by it. But I say that, I will admit, from a violinist's point of view. Cellists, as you can imagine, have much less to complain about. Grisha Piatigorsky floated in that concerto, completely in his element. (Nor did I mind it, but then it was always easy and pleasant making music with Grisha.)

One of our joint performances of Brahms's double concerto remains in my memory. It was at a 1949 festival in Aspen, Colorado, celebrating Goethe's two hundredth birthday. The orchestra was from Minneapolis, under the baton of Dmitri Mitropoulos.

A word about Mitropoulos. Here was a brilliant artist—a little neurotic perhaps, like Charles Munch, another famous conductor, but like Munch an enormous talent who knew and felt music. Besides which, Mitropoulos had an incredible memory. I remember a time we were rehearsing the Glazunov concerto. Mitropoulos stopped the orchestra, and without looking at the score he asked me, "Could you repeat measure one hundred and forty-seven after the last fermata?" I pleaded in response, "Forgive me, I don't remember what measure one hundred and forty-seven is! Hum it for me! I don't remember the measure numbers by heart, but I do know the music." Of course, the orchestra laughed, and as I've said, it's always good to break up the orchestra in rehearsal: they play better during the performance.

Many stars came to Aspen to honor Goethe, some from the intellectual world, like Albert Schweitzer, and others from the world of film, including Gary Cooper and Merle Oberon. Arthur Rubinstein played, and Ortega y Gasset gave a long lecture. (Piatigorsky and I went to hear Ortega, who spoke in Spanish, so of course no one understood a thing. But everyone shouted "bravo" loudly. He was a great success! As for Piatigorsky and me, all I remember is our perking up every time we heard Ortega juicily pronounce the word *mujeres*, which means "women." We took Ortega with a grain of salt.)

Piatigorsky always liked appearing in ensembles, and he very much wanted to continue to perform in a trio with Horowitz and me. In Chicago one time, all three "musketeers" had had great success appearing separately, and the local patrons insisted that we perform as a trio there, too. Piatigorsky grew excited. "It'll be sensational!" I disagreed. "Grisha, it'll be not so good, believe me." Horowitz sided with me. (Later, living in California, Piatigorsky fulfilled his interest in chamber playing by joining with Heifetz and Rubinstein.)

Grisha was always an epicure, but he was only able to indulge himself fully when he became an in-law of the Rothschilds'. Piatigorsky married Jacqueline, daughter of Edouard and Germaine Rothschild. Germaine loved music—she even wrote books about Boccherini and Locatelli—so you can imagine the Rothschilds' delight when their daughter married Gregor Piatigorsky. Grisha became the star of the family.

Germaine was a very charming lady. (I was touched by her coming to the ceremony in Paris making me an officer of the Légion d'Honneur.) I would visit her house in Paris. Everything was elegant, but not without a few surprises. Say, for lunch there would be a cold consommé with pressed caviar that looked rather like tar. It might have been a Rothschild lunch, but I was afraid to touch it.

In their dining room there were four Goyas on one wall and four portraits by Corot on the opposite wall. *Portraits* by Corot, not landscapes. Corot the portraitist has only recently become appreciated, so those four paintings indicated a highly cultivated taste. But the main thing was, all eight canvases were of the exact same size! Can you imagine the effort that went into achieving so symmetrical a collection?

During World War Two Edouard and Germaine Rothschild fled from the Germans to the U.S.A. Germaine told me that the Germans thereupon set up staff headquarters in their château. Yet, being German, they first made a detailed plan of how everything looked, where the paintings hung, how the furniture was placed, and so on. When the Americans liberated France, they found the German description at the Rothschild château, and so were able to set up all the furniture in its original places in time for the owners' return. It's good being a Rothschild. . . .

Jacqueline Rothschild was a rebellious woman. One time in Denver, I invited Jacqueline and Grisha to a good restaurant. We were ready to go, all dressed, when Jacqueline insisted on a trip to a local delicatessen, where she ordered herring and chopped liver. It made me sick just looking at it. At first I thought it was just eccentricity on her part, but I believe it was a form of protest. She was rebelling against her family, her upbringing, the establishment. (Of course, it's also possible that she just liked herring.)

In the meantime, Grisha Piatigorsky was enjoying life: he bought two Stradivarius cellos and started a collection of gold cigarette cases.

Grisha certainly liked a merry atmosphere, but he wasn't at all what could be called a court jester. He was a man with a rich imagination and serious ideas. Everything he did was substantial. Although he lacked a philosophical education, Grisha could discourse like a real philosopher. And write like one. I remember Piatigorsky reading me a work of fiction he wrote, *Comrade Blok*; it was impressive philosophical prose.

In Ecclesiastes it says, "In much wisdom there is much grief." If a man is no fool and also lives a sufficiently long time, he usually becomes disillusioned and cynical. But that didn't happen to Grisha. He stayed young to the end.

In a certain sense, he was lucky. When he was starting out, the cello was not considered a solo instrument. Its popularity began with the political acclaim around Pablo Casals. I remember Casals performing marvelously in the thirties in Paris: still the small hall was half empty. The situation changed drastically only when Casals was turned into the symbol of the struggle against fascism, particularly Franco. Casals's new fame helped other cellists. Piatigorsky finally got the attention he had deserved for a long time.

As a musician Piatigorsky wasn't always up to his own incredibly high standards, but there were many works he played like no one else. Universally consistent performers are very rare; even the greats have their hits and their misses. But we're afraid not only to criticize but even to analyze the work of the superstars, which is too bad. Say, take Casals's Bach: the slow movements, where he could sing, were unforgettable; but in the dancing parts he was sometimes heavy, almost crude. Or Dvořák's concerto. In Casals's performance it made a terrific impression, but that same Dvořák doesn't please me nearly as much in the hands of another great cellist, Rostropovich. He plays the concerto with a false cheerfulness, even though there's nothing particularly cheery about the music.

Some of Piatigorsky's performances are forever engraved in my memory. He used so much fantasy in his interpretation of Richard Strauss's *Don Quixote*—first with Furtwängler, then with Bruno Walter. Or the Schumann concerto with Walter again! I love that concerto, especially the second movement; when I hear it, I wish for the third movement never to start. I once listened to Piatigorsky's Schumann sitting in the same box with Fritz Kreisler and his wife, right next to the brilliant cellist Raya Garbuzova. Grisha's playing was incredibly emotional. Piatigorsky created an atmosphere, as if he were writing the music before our eyes. The orchestra under Walter's direction supported him softly. It was a reverie, a dream. . . .

After the performance was over, Kreisler sat a long time immobile. When he turned to me I saw his eyes were red, from tears. He was embarrassed. Like all of us, he had been terribly moved by the playing of Piatigorsky, a great and unique artist.

The other musketeer, Volodya Horowitz, stunned my imagination the first moment we met in wintery Kiev in 1921. We were both seventeen. Sitting at the piano, Horowitz was stormily playing the Wagner operas—by heart! And he looked incredibly romantic, like a pre-Raphaelite painting come to life.

About ten days after our meeting, Horowitz and I were already giving a joint concert in the hall of the Kiev Merchant Guild. We were so young we thought we could do anything! We didn't worry much about profound interpretations in those days. And so, for instance, Beethoven's *Spring* Sonata sounded horrible, as I now remember it. (We also played Saint-Saëns's D Minor Sonata and Grieg's C Minor Sonata.)

Formal dress was too expensive for us then, and in any case tails seemed "bourgeois." So at first we appeared onstage in the peasant belted shirts popularized by the writer Leo Tolstoy and nicknamed *"Tolstovkas."* In Soviet Russia then (as now), dressing well was a real problem. Once my trousers and jacket were stolen. I couldn't get another pair of trousers anywhere. Our manager gave me his pants, and since he was much larger than I, I had to go around holding them up.

Which reminds me of something that happened to Horowitz at the Odessa market. We wanted to buy some milk from a vendor who, plying her wares, insisted that her milk was very good and very creamy. She tried so hard that she accidentally spilled some on Horowitz's suit! Seeing Volodya's look of horror, she tried to console him. "Don't worry, sir! Don't worry, *panych*! The milk's not that rich, it's mostly water! When it dries, it won't leave a spot."

What money we made giving concerts in Russia we spent primarily on food. Understandably, what we loved best was pastry. Kiev had a marvelous pastry shop owned by Jean Fruzinsky, a remnant of the old prerevolutionary luxury with a smattering of its former clientele. We went to Fruzinsky's almost every day. His pastries were small and elegant in the Polish manner (he was Polish) and divinely delicious! Volodya and I would compete to see who could eat more. We would eat fifteen or twenty. Sometimes he won, sometimes I did.

It's paradoxical, but we started earning decent fees in Russia because People's Commissar of Education Lunacharsky proclaimed us "children of the Soviet revolution." Soon we had so much money we gave it away without counting. If a beggar came up to Horowitz and said, "Oh, *panych*, I'm starving, won't you help me out?," Volodya, young and generous, would pull a bill out of his pocket without hesitation, five rubles at least.

Alexander Merovitch brought Horowitz and me to the West. He proudly called himself an impresario, even though he knew absolutely nothing about his profession. In his letters to us, Merovitch compared himself to Napoleon and Mussolini! That's why I object to Glenn Plaskin using Merovitch's diaries as a "source" for his biography of Horowitz. Merovitch would tell Volodya, "Horowitz, you play—and you play marvelously! You also have many enemies! Don't be afraid, play bravely—I'll hypnotize all your enemies!" How can the diaries of a man like that give objective information about Horowitz, or anyone else?

Thanks to us "Three Musketeers," Merovitch was hired by Arthur Judson, the all-powerful boss of Columbia Artists Management. But Merovitch started making scenes and setting conditions, as if he were a big shot. In the end, the three of us—Horowitz, Piatigorsky, and I—left him. Merovitch was an unbalanced person and a lousy manager besides: he didn't plan anything, didn't foresee anything, and made loads of mistakes. Merovitch's influence on Horowitz in my opinion was very negative. He kept telling him, "Don't perform serious music! Let the Germans play it—Schnabel and Backhaus. You perform more Liszt."

Horowitz also left Judson eventually. This is how it happened: In the early forties, Horowitz wasn't feeling well and didn't perform for a while. When he decided to appear before an audience again, I suggested the following. "Volodya, you have a big name and your return will be a sensation. You used to get twelve hundred dollars a concert. Rachmaninoff gets up to twenty-five hundred. The difference is too great! Ask Judson for a raise. Besides, I know Judson—on his own, he'll give you two hundred and fifty. So you ask for a raise of a thousand!"

Horowitz was afraid to see Judson, a formidable figure. So I said, "If you don't want to go to Judson yourself, send Merovitch. Pay Merovitch a thousand dollars to give Judson an ultimatum: 'If you want Horowitz, pay him twenty-five hundred dollars a concert; if you won't, Horowitz will get another manager.' Merovitch has his own accounts to settle with Judson, he'll be delighted to bring him a message like that."

I was certain that the risk was worth taking. Volodya, convinced by my arguments, sent Merovitch to Judson, who heard him out and without a second thought said, "Take your Horowitz and go to hell!" So with Judson we lost. . . .

Horowitz was in a panic and blamed me and my adventuristic advice. I insisted, "Volodya, there are a million managers in New York. As soon as they know Judson no longer represents you, they'll rush to get you, because the public wants to hear you. I mean, I personally can arrange at least twenty-five concerts for you!" With those encouraging words, I left on a tour of the country.

When I got back to New York, Horowitz called me at night. "Nathan, you were right! I was called by Annie Friedberg, the sister of the pianist Karl Friedberg, and she guarantees me twenty concerts at three thousand dollars each!" And he went on. "Since you were such a help to me in this, Wandochka and I have decided to give you a present, a silver cigarette case."

I cried out, "Volodya, wake up! What do I need with a silver cigarette case? I have eight gold ones—from Tiffany, Bulgari, and Cartier. I don't keep silver ones. And then, if I get a present from you, I'll have to show it off. Can you imagine me saying, 'The famous Horowitz gave his best friend a silver cigarette case!' "

I could hear Volodya talk to his wife, Wanda Toscanini-Horowitz: "Wandochka, I think Nathan's right." The next day

Three Musketeers: Piatigorsky, Horowitz, and I

Volodya and I went to Cartier and he bought me a marvelous gold case, which he had engraved for me. I still have it in the safe, with my others. . . .

I don't need to prove that Horowitz was a pianist of genius, a phenomenon. I could name a few other musicians who perhaps were better artists than Horowitz, but they lacked Volodya's great talent. Genius is instinct. A real artist finds unique, truly new things by instinct. Horowitz made a multitude of such unprecedented discoveries.

Great artists create their own style, their own technique. You hear people talk about the "spirit of Picasso." That "spirit" is the direct result of Picasso's technique. And the revelations of van Gogh stem from his technique, too! The creator's individuality is made manifest through the new technique he develops. That holds for painters, and composers, and performers. It's why you can recognize the playing by Horowitz or Heifetz immediately, in the first few bars—and not only by their merits but by their mannerisms. (As is also true for painters.)

Horowitz created his own new style of piano playing. No one had ever played like that! This is not a qualitative assessment; I am speaking only of the manner of performance. Volodya's sound was incomparable. Sometimes it even seemed to me that he was in love with the sound of the piano more than with the music. Miraculously, Volodya could make the piano sound like an entire orchestra!

Horowitz invented his own special position for his hands when he played. Take a look at his flat fingers! Observing him play, I learned how to imitate his sound on the piano. Of course, I can only do a few notes à la Horowitz: separately with the left, separately with the right hand. His secret was this: after hitting the key hard (like the hammers in the piano itself), he immediately released it. That gave the "Horowitz resonance." If you continue to hold on to the key, it stifles the sound.

Horowitz was also a great master and innovator of pedaling. For many pianists the pedal is just camouflage. For Horowitz, it was color on a palette. And he had many colors, all different. With his "pedal palette," he created a beautiful musical canvas. Sometimes he used the whole palette even for the Viennese classics. That may not be the "right" approach, but the result was inevitably stunning.

And how marvelously Horowitz phrased! I'll never forget one of his appearances in Chicago, when he played a short song without words of Mendelssohn's called "Shepherd's Complaint." As soon as he began—just twelve measures!—my heart was in my throat, he played so naturally and with such feeling. Horowitz was a born poet of the piano.

Sometimes I wanted to compare Horowitz's playing with a volcanic eruption: the soil trembles underfoot, you can hear explosions, see flames and hot lava. Not every piece of music holds up to such interpretation. Fire can bring warmth but it can also burn everything down. Warmth is the result of steady burning, but such steadiness was not in Volodya's character.

From time to time Horowitz tried for self-control, but how do you control an eruption? All those explosions were strong and effective because they were spontaneous. That, by the way, is what strongly distinguished Horowitz from his countless epigones, who are capable only of a tortured imitation of a free and instinctive process.

Horowitz's development, as that of any genius, was natural to a great degree. The seeds were tossed into the ground back in Kiev: his mother began teaching him music, and then Sergei Tarnowsky took over and did a lot for him. Then, Volodya's work with Felix Blumenfeld played a major role in his development. Blumenfeld was the uncle of Heinrich Neuhaus, who taught both Sviatoslav Richter and Emil Gilels. Blumenfeld was present the first time I came for tea at the Horowitzes' in Kiev in 1921. He dragged his leg and had to sidle onto the piano bench—the aftermath of a stroke. It was on Blumenfeld's advice, passed along by Volodya's parents, that he and I decided to appear together for the first time.

Later, Rachmaninoff became an incredible authority for Horowitz. To a degree, Rachmaninoff and Horowitz were friends, but as I saw it, it was the friendship of colleagues, without much human warmth. I had the feeling that Rachmaninoff was slightly jealous of Horowitz as a pianist and did not want to acknowledge him fully.

But then, jealousy felt by one great musician toward another is not such an unusual thing.

The influence of a major musician like Blumenfeld is crucial in one's youth. Later, the seeds planted this way can grow on their own; the genius's gift blossoms, getting nourishment from its environment. That's what happened with Volodya.

Horowitz and I were friends for almost seventy years and I probably knew him better than most people did, but it still wasn't enough. The German Romantics liked to say that a real artist contains a whole nation in himself. And Horowitz was a real artist—he could be many people; he always surprised.

Sometimes he could appear uncertain of himself, and that uncertainty was often manifest in amusing trifles. For instance, Volodya was born in the Ukraine in a small town called Berdichev, but he insisted that he came from Kiev, a more important place. It's like being born in Kalamazoo or Sheboygan but maintaining that you come from Boston.

I don't know why Horowitz was embarrassed by his Berdichev background. What's wrong with it? It's the birthplace of Anton (not to be confused with Arthur!) Rubinstein, one of the great pianists of all time and the founder of the St. Petersburg Conservatory (and, incidentally, Horowitz's direct pianistic ancestor).

Generally speaking, it seems to me that critics devote too much attention to a performer's origins. They view Russians as better at interpreting Russian music; the French, French music; and so on. For instance, Virgil Thomson, who was music critic of the New York *Herald Tribune* for almost fifteen years, in reviewing Horowitz playing Debussy or Ravel, usually wrote something like, "Not bad, but I remember M. X—now he knew how to do it!"

That's the wrong approach. Horowitz had an aunt from Poland, but that didn't help him play Chopin. Rachmaninoff was Volodya's element not because he is a Russian composer, but because it's the type of music that Horowitz felt best: emotional, extroverted, virtuoso. That's also why he felt close to Liszt. I mean, what was Hungarian about Horowitz? Yet he played Liszt's B Minor Sonata better than anyone else. Why? Because the musical profiles of the composer and the interpreter coincided. I regret that Volodya never performed publicly or recorded Liszt's transcriptions of the Beethoven symphonies. Horowitz played those transcriptions for friends so beautifully, better than any symphony orchestra ever dreamed.

Virgil Thomson was no admirer of Horowitz, or of his father-in-law, Toscanini, or for that matter of Jascha Heifetz. Thomson once wrote that with his talent and prodigious technical gifts, Heifetz playing trifles was like taking the *Queen Elizabeth* to get from New York to Hoboken. He probably just didn't like that type of virtuosity.

The feud between Thomson and the Toscanini family culminated in a famous incident. Thomson fell asleep once during a concert of Toscanini's. Volodya's wife, Wanda, saw him, came over, woke him with a smack of the program, and said, "I am Wanda Toscanini-Horowitz, and I observed you sleeping from the first note to the last. And yet tomorrow you'll probably write a bad review!" And that's exactly what happened.

Speaking of Thomson, I was friends with Geoffrey Parsons, his publisher at the *Herald Tribune*, and I recall one time when Parsons invited Thérèse and me to lunch at his Paris house. There were many musicians, including Ralph Kirkpatrick, the harpsichordist, and Thomson, who spent a lot of time in France, was also there. He and Mrs. Parsons (a young American who had been in the French Resistance) started an animated discussion about wine. In France, if you talk about wine a lot—even if you don't understand anything about it—you are considered refined. That's why all American Francophiles devote a great deal of their attention to wine. But the Frenchman pays for his knowledge of wine with a bad liver, whereas the American wants to be both healthy and a connoisseur. Even an American Francophile.

After lunch, Parsons's guests moved to a small room with a harpsichord. We all sat down, but Thomson had to be conspicuous—he sat on the floor in the corner, leaning against the wall. Now as everyone knows, the harpsichord is not loud, and when Kirkpatrick started playing, as if imparting a great secret right in your ear, everyone strained to hear. In that atmosphere, even breathing can sound like heavy artillery.

And suddenly we heard horrible snoring! It came from Thomson, who, having tasted various wines, had fallen asleep. The noise he made must have wakened him and he got up and pretended that nothing had happened. (Personally, I see nothing wrong in a man falling asleep to classical music after a good meal with wine. It shows excellent health.)

I met Thomson many times, and he always spoke about wine or food, never about music. Nevertheless, he wrote prose about music as no other American critic did. I didn't read his articles about me— I was afraid of his sharp pen and preferred to remain in ignorance— but I was told that Thomson's views on me were kinder than they were about Heifetz. I think that his Francophilia played a part here, too. I performed a lot in Europe, particularly in France, where I was quite popular, and so could be regarded as a "European product." But Heifetz was an American violinist as far as Thomson was concerned.

Horowitz's reactions to critics and criticism were as complex and contradictory as his personality. On the one hand, Volodya sometimes displayed considerable edginess toward criticism. He would publicly disagree with Virgil Thomson, for instance, something I probably wouldn't have done. On the other hand, I know that Horowitz could be criticized severely and not take offense at all.

Earlier, recalling my friendship with Rachmaninoff, I wrote how I called his attention to the rhythmic exaggerations in Horowitz's interpretation of the Tchaikovsky concerto. And how I dared to express to Toscanini himself my not very favorable opinion of Horowitz's recording of the same concerto with the maestro. But those were public occasions, so to speak. When we were alone I sometimes expressed my objections to Volodya in much more categorical form. And Horowitz didn't mind.

I remember in the early thirties we were living in a pension in Carlsbad. Horowitz often played Mozart for me, among other music, and I began telling him not very pleasant things. "Volodya, how can you play Mozart like that? It's not Romantic music! You have to keep the rhythm in Mozart, and in general keep it simpler, simpler!" Almost anyone else would have been hurt, or angry, but Horowitz actually agreed with me.

I might not be believed about this, but Horowitz sometimes *wanted* to hear criticism of his playing! The elevator operator in my New York building was a colorful Italian with a broken nose, a former boxer named Joe. Horowitz always gave him tickets to his concerts, and afterward he would ask, "Joe, tell me, what didn't you like?" How many other celebrities would be capable of something like that?

Horowitz was always listening attentively to himself, trying to understand what's going on inside. In his concern over his health, Volodya could persuade himself that he was not well—with the most disastrous results. For instance, when he got stomach pains in Europe in 1936, he decided it was appendicitis. He went to the Berlin sanatorium of Professor Bergmann, who told him, "You don't have appendicitis, it is nervous spastic colitis. If you remove the appendix, it will make things worse." But someone else told him that there was a brilliant surgeon in Paris who would remove his appendix just like that! And Horowitz went to Paris for the operation.

Nowadays the removal of an appendix is nothing; in New York they throw you out of the hospital the next day. But back then the operation was a major affair. Horowitz spent six days on his back and as a result developed a dangerous case of thrombophlebitis. The recuperation was long and boring. Volodya had to see the doctor regularly, take pills, and his usual schedule was shot to hell, not to mention his practicing and performing. And, as Bergmann had predicted, his colitis got worse after the operation.

In the summer of 1934 Horowitz was staying with me in Gstaad, Switzerland. By then the events in Germany had taken an unexpected turn. Hitler had plotted the murder of General von Schleicher and, at the same time, had ordered the killing of scores of his former supporters, the storm troopers, including the notorious Captain Ernst Röhm.

It was July. Through the day Volodya practiced and I composed cadenzas for the violin concerti of Beethoven and Brahms. In the evenings we sat by the radio, tensely listening to the latest news on the station Suisse Romande. First the announcers talked about Röhm's execution and speculated on the possible consequences of this unexpected change for the Nazi Party and for Germany. Then the Orchestre de la Suisse Romande under Ernest Ansermet played something. I remember that day well because right after the first selection came the announcement "Now you will hear music in memory of the pianist Vladimir Horowitz. News of his untimely demise just came in from Paris." Upon hearing this, Horowitz went pale and burst out: "That's not true!" Then he thought a bit and added, "But what good publicity!"

I think the main pleasure in a situation like that is the unique opportunity to read your own obituary. Especially if it has nice things to say about you. They say that a man whose death has been announced prematurely will live a long and fruitful life. In Volodya's case, at least, the omen held true, for another fifty-five years.

The public grieves when it learns about the death of a favorite in the newspapers. But the same public loves to have performers "die" onstage. In imperial Rome, gladiators shed real blood in the arena and did so to save their lives. Now the performer thinks not of life, but the box office. Yet when you hear real virtuosi, like Horowitz, you are aware of that figurative "drop of fresh-spilled blood," which, according to Arthur Rubinstein, every artist should leave onstage after a concert. That's why Horowitz unfailingly astonished his public.

Volodya was a very impulsive, involved person who sometimes got carried away. At one time he had a passion for collecting paintings. I remember how it started. Back in 1942 or 1943, when I returned to New York from a tour of the country, Volodya called me. "Come over and see the paintings I bought."

Horowitz knew that I've been drawn to art since childhood. I loved going to the Hermitage museum in Petersburg when I was a boy. The Russian tsars had a marvelous collection of paintings—they had Raphaels, Titians, Velázquezes, one better than the next. I was particularly struck by the Hermitage's Rembrandts. At the

Alexander III Museum, I delighted in the Russian painters—
Levitan, Repin, Serov.

When I later moved to Western Europe, I literally devoured
art—I spent whole days in museums, especially in Italy and Spain.
I knew the exact place of every Goya portrait. At the Prado in
Madrid I used to stare transfixed at his painting depicting the execution of the rebels. I came almost to hate that work—it reminded
me of the horrors of the civil war back in Russia.

I fell in love with Delacroix, who was also a brilliant musician
and did the best portraits of Chopin. Delacroix's Chopin is untra-
ditional—he is strongly dynamic, almost authoritarian, and at the
same time you feel the great poetry hidden in the man, as it is in
his music.

I also came to appreciate the modern palette of Courbet: some
of his works are vivid and colorful as symphonies, and others as
stale as old tobacco. Step by step I began to understand something
in painting. It's like wine—you drink and compare, drink and compare. And finally you learn how to tell which wine is good and which
is not. And that's enough for the nonspecialist. If you go on to
understand the comparative value of each variety—then you are a
specialist!

When I came to Horowitz's house to look at his newly acquired
paintings, Volodya exclaimed, "Aren't these good? They're by contemporary American artists." I wasn't too enthusiastic about his
purchases and suggested, "Why don't you buy yourself something
really first-class? You can afford it."

A while later, Horowitz invited me again and said, "Look,
Nathan, I bought a Picasso for fifty-four thousand dollars and a
Cézanne for eight." The Cézanne was an unsightly sketch for a portrait of his wife; the kind of thing most painters used to throw away.
My advice to Horowitz was to return the Cézanne to the dealer,
even if he lost money on it. But I stopped in my tracks before the Picasso—it was a grand work depicting an acrobat in red. Nevertheless,
I had some doubts about its price. At the time one of my friends
was the conductor Vladimir Golschmann, who had a good collection
of Picasso and Bracque. We often went to art dealers together, so

I was aware of current prices. I told Volodya, "I think you were cheated on the Picasso. The most expensive Picassos nowadays go for around twenty-five thousand."

Volodya was pleased! He said to his wife, "Wandochka, Nathan knows prices!" And then he explained to me that actually he had paid only twenty-four thousand for the Picasso. He had just wanted to impress me.

Gradually Horowitz put together a marvelous art collection, which included a charming painting of a garden by Edouard Manet (whose pianist wife, incidentally, was a student of Liszt's), an exquisite Rouault, and a brilliant small Picasso of the blue period: a doctor at the bedside of a woman patient. Horowitz tried to learn as much as he could about art, and would go on reading binges about painting. And then, quite suddenly, he sold all his paintings. He must not have been so deeply involved with collecting after all; otherwise he couldn't have parted so easily with such wonderful masterpieces. Many years later I saw his Manet painting gracing the wall of the American embassy in London.

Several times in his life, Volodya curtailed his appearances on the concert stage, and sometimes these hiatuses lasted many years. Everything to do with Horowitz is legendary, so these breaks became legendary too. I think, if you can help it, you should avoid sabbaticals. I remember a conversation on that topic with Jascha Heifetz, which took place at the house of mutual friends in Beverly Hills. He said that he wanted to take a sabbatical and not perform for a year. I was surprised, because at the time Jascha was already appearing infrequently.

Heifetz tried to explain his decision. "I want to think. . . ."

I attempted to talk him out of it. "What does it mean to take a sabbatical to think? A person is always thinking, even when he goes, excuse the expression, to the toilet." Heifetz laughed. But he did what he planned.

Why did Horowitz stop playing? Perhaps his health was not at its best, which is an important consideration for a concertizing artist.

But another, more likely, reason is Volodya's incredible sensitivity vis-à-vis his audiences. When Horowitz performed, it wasn't just a concert, it was a natural phenomenon of gigantic magnitude. And Volodya wanted the public to sense that.

When pianists from the Soviet Union—Richter, Gilels, and others—first appeared in the U.S., they created a sensation, even though they played, in my opinion, less interestingly than Horowitz. But it was a novelty—partly political—while Horowitz was a familiar name. So maybe people began to underestimate the elemental nature of his genius.

Then Van Cliburn returned triumphantly from Russia. That was yet another kind of political sensation. Appearing after the Soviet performers and Van Cliburn meant entering into some kind of competition. Besides, Horowitz rightly felt that he was indisputably more significant than these other pianists. And he was disappointed that the public did not, at least in this instance, base its opinion on an artist's value.

But I think that after some tribulations Horowitz overcame all these psychological difficulties. He showed that he had incredible willpower. Because only an artist with iron will is capable of returning victorious to the stage after a long interruption.

Among those who had a real understanding of Horowitz's gift and power, both as a personality and as an artist, was Arthur Rubinstein. I often observed the two of them together and can testify that they were real friends. It's important to underscore this, because some would imagine otherwise, relying on certain episodes from Rubinstein's memoirs. But things must be read in context. Rubinstein understood that while Horowitz could be moody, capricious, and sometimes self-centered, these characteristics also added a special feeling and color to Volodya's playing. I remember Rubinstein once said to me, "When Horowitz plays Liszt's sonata, it's Volodya, his self-portrait."

Rubinstein appreciated Horowitz's spontaneity and unpredictability. He told me once that being *comme il faut* was not the same as having a personality. Rubinstein forgave Horowitz a lot, and Volodya was grateful for that. They admired each other.

Later Rubinstein created an apocryphal story that became popular: allegedly, upon hearing Horowitz in concert, he quit playing for a while, he was so stunned by Volodya's virtuosity. I'm convinced that the story is 99 percent baloney, invented to impress people with Arthur's modesty. Rubinstein certainly knew his own worth. Rachmaninoff once told me that Rubinstein was probably the greatest talent among the new crop of pianists. And you can believe Rachmaninoff.

Everyone knows how subtly Rubinstein interpreted Chopin, but I was also a fan of his Beethoven. Rubinstein didn't need to think long in order to play profoundly: he was one more proof that the instinct is more important than the intellect.

Rubinstein continued to perform marvelously until the age of ninety. One can easily think of other pianists who have played extraordinarily into their advanced years: Horowitz, Claudio Arrau, Rudolf Serkin. (It is harder for a violinist to remain in top form than for a pianist, so there are fewer such examples in our craft.) An artist in his old age is free of excess. Verdi composed his best operas when he was old—in *Otello* and *Falstaff* he got rid of all the decorative stuff. And think of the astonishing works the old Picasso created!

A performer who wants to continue in old age must find new opportunities and new paths. Working on difficult passages is not enough. You have to find a comfortable approach to the virtuosic passages, and you try to express their musical content in a more natural way. I don't practice much now, not even every day. You can come up with some new and interesting musical idea without necessarily holding the instrument in your hands. Nowadays my improvements and interpretive changes come mostly from the mind, not the fingers. The mind finds a better understanding of a work's form, adds new colors, new touches, as well as ways to incorporate them.

I'm eighty-six years old, but I don't feel my age. Time goes very quickly; two or three years feel like two or three months. But you can't do anything about that.

I recall a conversation I had with Marc Chagall, who used to attend my concerts with his wife, Vava. He invited me back to his hotel and started complaining. "I've had a hernia for twenty-five years, look how big it is! But I'm afraid of having surgery."

I asked why. He replied, "Maybe it's dangerous?"

"Ask your doctor. As far as I know, a hernia operation isn't all that serious."

"But I'm afraid of dying!"

"Why? How old are you?"

Chagall replied, "Ninety-two."

"Are you planning to live another ninety-two?"

Chagall grew pensive. "I'm afraid even to think about death!"

I responded, "Our death is obviously unavoidable. There's nothing terrible about it, it's only gotten bad publicity: all those skeletons and skulls. We've only rented our lives—the time comes to return the loan. If we always remember that, we can avoid so many wrong decisions."

I think that comforted Chagall a bit. He was a good artist, though for my taste too mannered and sometimes saccharine. It's not hard to imitate Chagall. But try to do it with Picasso!

Not so long ago, I was sitting with an old friend, who started whining, "Nathan, we're getting old. . . ." And I said, "First of all, we've lived enough. Secondly, it's quite probable that we will live still longer." It's imperative not to be afraid of death, otherwise you start degenerating. I've seen people in old age try to seem younger, to make up lost time. But when you try to race time, you strain yourself. It's what the Germans call *übertreiben*. And that's when a catastrophe can happen.

The public, which is always fascinated by a great artist's personality, wanted to know everything: Horowitz's character traits, his habits, his seclusions, the reasons why he so often canceled his concerts. Voices were heard alleging that Horowitz sometimes used illness as a pretext and that in fact he canceled concerts in order to heighten interest in them, especially when they weren't sold out. There were also complaints about the high cost of tickets to his concerts.

I reply to those charges simply: an artist of Volodya's level is a supersensitive being. The Russians have a saying: "What's good for Russians is death for Germans." You know, "One man's meat is another man's poison." A circumstance that an ordinary person might not notice at all can disable an artist completely. I feel it is a musician's absolute right not to perform if he feels that he cannot give the audience his best.

The same goes for ticket prices. Yes, Horowitz got high fees, but his expenses were also enormous. Everyone knows that Horowitz took his own piano wherever he played. His secretary traveled with him, and often his cook. When Horowitz checked into a hotel he reserved the adjoining rooms as well—so that he could practice. And, of course, he paid for all that out of his pocket.

I think that every true artist knows his own worth, including the commercial value of what he does. Many of the great creators I have known were not excessively generous. In the West that's called being a good businessman. Picasso was like that, and he wasn't ashamed of it. But Chagall, for one, behaved quite differently.

Frederick Mann, a music patron of Philadelphia, told me this story. Mann had an auditorium in Jerusalem named after him and was a big Jewish patriot and philanthropist. Naturally he had to have paintings by a Jewish artist. He decided to buy something from Chagall, so he went to see the artist in the south of France, where Chagall lived. Chagall tried to talk him out of it. "Why do you have to buy from me?" Mann insisted Chagall show him his works. "They're all bad," Chagall said coyly. But finally he relented.

Mann selected a canvas with flowers, which Chagall always depicted beautifully. But then Chagall suddenly refused to sell! So Mann turned to Vava Chagall, and as they started talking about prices Mann saw Chagall in the mirror signaling his wife sums on his fingers with great animation!

It's interesting that in art everyone recognizes that painters like Claude Monet and Alfred Sisley are masters, even though they were not great philosophers. But in music, for some reason, you have to be "profound." When I say that Saint-Saëns's *Rondo capriccioso* is a masterpiece, no one agrees with me because it is not "profound." What nonsense! Great mastery does not necessarily presume great depth. For instance, I adore the Russian satirist Mikhail Zoshchenko and consider him a master, even though he is not as deep as Chekhov. Zoshchenko has a different, lighter form.

Everyone approves of the way Rudolf Serkin plays Beethoven. But when Horowitz played Beethoven, people picked on him. Every performer has his repertoire, just as a painter or writer has his genre. Serkin does not play Beethoven as brilliantly as Horowitz did, but he interprets the *Emperor* Concerto as freely as if he had composed it himself. Horowitz lacked that freedom in Beethoven, although he felt absolutely free in, say, Tchaikovsky or Rachmaninoff. Serkin couldn't play those composers at all; his is a different genre.

Horowitz once told me, "Beethoven wrote for the piano as if he were composing especially for bad pianists!" I may not agree with that, but I must admit that for my taste Beethoven did not know how to compose for the violin. (In his violin concerto all the passages are crafted as if written for the piano.) That's why I don't like all of Beethoven's violin sonatas, only three or four of them. The violin part in the others is not interesting or rewarding. And usually the pianists play too loud.

My favorite sonatas are the Fifth (*Spring*), Seventh, Eighth, and Ninth (*Kreutzer*). Three of them (excepting the Seventh) I recorded with my longtime partner, Arthur Balsam. I planned to record the Seventh with Horowitz (plus the *Kreutzer* and Franck sonatas, so that Volodya would have something loud and brilliant to play); but Horowitz suggested other composers—Grieg, Saint-Saëns, maybe Medtner. I pleaded, "Volodya, we're not so young, let's make a substantive statement." We never did agree. . . . So our only joint recording is the one we did a long time ago: Brahms's Third Sonata.

Sometimes I wonder, Would Liszt and Anton Rubinstein have been as successful today as they were in their time? Probably yes, because they were real showmen who understood their audience. If you're a stage designer, you don't work with the refinement of a van Gogh. You paint in broad strokes so you can be seen from every seat in the house. On the stage you have to play for the hall, and Horowitz understood that. In that respect, as in many others, he was a worthy successor of Liszt and Anton Rubinstein.

For one of Volodya's recent birthdays, a New York critic called me in Lausanne for a quote. He began questioning me. "Don't you think that Horowitz sometimes exaggerates in his interpretations? And isn't there too much of this and too much of that in his playing?"

I told the carping critic, "Forget your petty complaints! Horowitz isn't simply a great pianist, he's a wonder of nature. Are you ready to criticize Niagara Falls for having too much water?"

13. Music and Politics II: David Oistrakh and Other Soviets

When I came to the West, I encountered many misperceptions about Russia and its history, especially among liberals. One such, widely held, was that the tsar had been overthrown by Lenin and the Bolsheviks. Actually, Lenin got rid of the liberal provisional government, which came to power after a popular antitsarist revolution. The Bolsheviks broke up the popularly elected constituent assembly and established a dictatorship that was in many ways more cruel than any reign of the Russian tsars.

I remember a public discussion in Paris in the late 1940s. I had been invited to the press club on rue St-Honoré (under the auspices of the Circle Inter-Allie) to discuss the proposition that there was more freedom in Russia then than under the tsar. Louis Aragon was there, a robust, self-confident fellow, hardly the pale, thin, spir-

itual poet I had expected. With him was Jean-Paul Sartre—all
crooked and cross-eyed. I remember also Raymond Aron and Walter Lippmann; and included among the musicians, the conductor
Roger Desormier.

One after another, the speakers hailed the freedom of contemporary (Stalinist!) Russia as compared with tsarist times. Finally, I
couldn't take it anymore. "Nothing of the sort. You don't know the
facts! There was more political freedom under the tsar!" I tried to
explain that in prerevolutionary Russia there was the duma, an
elected council where monarchists, socialists, even Bolsheviks pre-
sided together.

They knew all about it, referring to it as "Parliament . . .
parliament."

"No," I said. "Parliament is when you talk (*parla*). The duma
is where you think, from the Russian word meaning 'thought.' "

That was their first surprise. I went on. "Of course, the Socialists weren't allowed to rule under the tsar, but at least they got to
speak up. Now in Russia no one dares open his mouth!"

In fact, the Stalinist regime was so repressive that compared with
it even Hitler could be considered more liberal. The notable exception would be the Jewish question; but as we are now learning,
Stalin was planning to deport the Jewish population of the Soviet
Union in the early fifties. So only his death prevented another geno-
cide.

Hitler was kinder to Germans than Stalin was to his people.
After all, the Germans at least could amuse themselves, go to cab-
arets, listen to jazz, travel. For me communism is the same as fascism, only badly organized, with inefficient industry and ruined
agriculture.

Western leftists deny this parallel. One time I got a telegram
from conductor Claudio Abbado and pianist Maurizio Pollini. They
were inviting me to participate in a benefit concert for the families
of victims of fascism. I answered that I would gladly play for the
benefit of victims of fascism if we would also do a concert for the
victims of communism. I never got a reply from Abbado or Pollini.

Both Abbado and Pollini are talented musicians. I really like Pollini, who lives in London near us, on Chester Square, in a house

207

that we used to rent. (The house once belonged to Matthew Arnold.) As for Abbado, his conducting does not overly enchant me.
It's a matter of taste: some people like cauliflower and some don't.

The leftists are still certain that except for a "few mistakes" the
Russian revolution benefited the country. What nonsense! I was
there during the revolution, and I saw everything with my own eyes.
My father was robbed by the revolution, as was the family of my
friend Vladimir Horowitz. True, Horowitz and I lived comparatively well—I described our adventures in Russia in previous chap-
ters—but we traveled a lot around the country and saw how the
Russian people as a whole suffered under the Soviet regime.

It's my nature to avoid trouble, to push it away. In Russia we
saw nothing but trouble. The experience of the Russian revolution
for me is altogether negative. I like Russia's customs—its songs,
dances, and its people's instinctive love of music. But how could
such a talented people put up with Soviet tyranny all these years?

At the turn of the century Russians were highly esteemed in
Europe—both in art and in technology. Not only has the Soviet
regime failed to use the genius of its people, it has done everything
it could to stifle it. The Communist leaders of the country, one after
another, have hardly been creative personalities. In fact, they have
suppressed creativity in all its manifestations. They destroyed the
Russian avant garde and Russian ingenuity. They even executed
their most talented military men, like Marshal Tukhachevsky and
Uborevich.

How many Kremlin bosses have there been in all these years?
Just a few. And those few men ruined the lives of more than two
hundred million people! Any system that allows that has no justifi-
cation. That's why I'm anti-Soviet.

Before the revolution, when I was a youth, Russia exported
grain. I remember huge grain elevators brimming over in the port
of Odessa, and all those colorful foreign ships that were transporting
the grain to Europe. And now, so many years later, Russia is one
of the greatest *importers* of grain! Without annual shipments from
America, Russia would not be able to feed its population. How
could that have happened?

After every crop failure the Soviets keep saying, "bad weather," "frost," "drought." Nonsense again! In the U.S.A., in wheat-growing states like Kansas and Nebraska, there are droughts that burn everything down to the roots, but American farmers still feed the world. Now even Gorbachev admits that the inefficiency of the Soviets is due to the fact that their economic system does not work. I'm interested in that question, so I never miss an opportunity to discuss it with people who know.

I remember in Lucerne, when I played with Karajan, I was visited by a German who intended to arrange a tour for me in Turkey. This man represented Turkey's interests in various commercial enterprises, particularly in negotiations with the Soviet Union. I didn't want to go to Turkey, but I was curious to find out how the Soviets did business.

"We buy tractors from them," the man told me. "One or two hundred a year. The tractors are low-quality, ugly to look at, and break down quickly, and to make it worse, when you order spare parts, you learn there aren't any. But we still buy those damned tractors because Russia is a mighty neighbor, and Turkey wants to keep its border quiet. We'd be better off buying American tractors, of course: they look better and last longer. And the Americans send spare parts immediately, and for free!"

I had another telling conversation on this subject, with the UN representative from the Congo (now Zaire), which was ruled at the time by the notorious Patrice Lumumba. Lumumba was a radical socialist, but his New York emissary was not crazy about his premier's ideas. He came one night to hear me play Bach at the Metropolitan Museum (I used to play Bach there annually), and afterward we met at the marvelous restaurant at the Stanhope Hotel, where I was staying. I remember the Congo diplomat saying ironically, "Yes, Russia helps us. The Soviets send us sheepskin jackets. . . ." Just think, some Soviet bureaucrat had decided that Africans needed warm jackets!

That's how Russia loses potential allies. Yet the Soviet Union could have many friends. When Third World countries won their independence, the majority of the new leaders were disillusioned by capitalism and were seeking alternatives. Russia could have been an example for them. But it didn't happen, and now the developing countries are turning to free enterprise as their only salvation from economic chaos.

I had an uncle who left Russia in 1905 and settled in America. He didn't like Stalin, but he nevertheless insisted that "Russia is the future!" To which I always replied, "What's the future in politics? There is only the present. What future does an African country have where one dictator replaces another? All those dictators promise freedom and enlightenment, but it always ends with yet another bloodbath followed by famine. It's the same thing with Russia. . . ."

Gorbachev began the democratization of Russia by concentrating power in his hands, and of course Western liberals were delighted. They were just as delighted by Stalin, by Khrushchev, and by every new Soviet leader. Every time, they thought, here's one we'll be able to talk to.

I remember a disappointing conversation on that subject with Walter Lippmann. We used to see each other at parties given by the young, handsome publisher of *The New York Times*, Arthur Sulzberger. Lippmann once gave a cocktail party at his house in Washington, D.C., after my concert. He was a pleasant, learned gentleman, but I still didn't like his desire to seek a "reasonable compromise" in every international situation.

This desire to achieve compromise at any price is one of the reasons why liberals, for all their good intentions, almost always lose. I think that if you abhor something, you should take a firm position. Otherwise all negotiations will inevitably be reduced to another scrap of paper, a new Munich.

Sure, we should come to terms with Russia, but only if the people there have the right to vote. Otherwise, yesterday with Brezhnev you have one policy, today with Gorbachev another. Tomorrow there will be a new boss, and the policies will change again. And not because there are shifts in popular perceptions or in the country's needs, but out of the whims of a single person who can do whatever he wants.

Kremlinologists are looking under a microscope for changes in Soviet ideology. But Marxism suffered its fiasco long ago. That's why the sudden shifts in Russian politics are not caused by ideological changes but by the wishes and whims of one man—the one in power at any given moment.

I remember how glad everyone was to have Khrushchev, how they sought and found a rational basis for his policies. In my opinion, he was simply an eccentric demagogue. A *New York Times* correspondent, a friend of mine, came to Vienna for a meeting with Khrushchev and his wife, Nina Petrovna. He told me that Khrushchev announced to him, "Soviet people don't need cars because they are harmful to their health." Of course, Khrushchev traveled around in a car, and it didn't seem to harm his health. Probably black caviar isn't good for the stomachs of the masses either, but it's all right for the leaders—their stomachs are cast-iron.

The Soviet Party bosses have treated their writers, artists, and musicians all with the same demagoguery, eccentricity, and hypocrisy. Under Stalin many talented people died without having done anything wrong. (Vladimir Horowitz's father, a decent man and a good engineer, died in a Stalinist camp.) The "liberal" Khrushchev persecuted Boris Pasternak, whom I remember fondly, and Yevgeny Yevtushenko. Brezhnev threw Alexander Solzhenitsyn and Joseph Brodsky, a current and a future Nobel Prize–winner, out of the country.

The obvious became "clear" under Gorbachev: all these barbarities were the results of the tantrums of uncontrolled dictators. It turns out that Solzhenitsyn's exile was "illegal": surprise, surprise! (I have great respect for Solzhenitsyn. Even though his political statements are sometimes too radical for my taste, I agree with many of his positions.)

The poet Yevtushenko, who was once considered a dissident, is now an official spokesman for the Soviet regime. I met him many years ago on a French ship headed for the U.S.A. I was with the French violinist Zino Francescatti; I looked up and saw not far away a tall, good-looking, not very well-dressed blond, whom I recognized as Yevtushenko. I said, "Zino, there's a Soviet poet. Shall we offer him a drink?"

But when I went over to Yevtushenko with our invitation, he looked at me with incredible suspicion and roared, "What for?" As if we were planning to pry Soviet state secrets out of him! Maybe he had been made wary by my Russian? (In those years Soviet tourists abroad were not supposed to mix with émigrés.) But later, Yevtushenko joined us. He drank little but boasted a lot, and for some reason he started to explain that he liked gangsters, and other fashionable nonsense of that sort. I was sorry I had invited him.

Yevtushenko behaved like a man who had been caged up a long time and was suddenly allowed his freedom. Perhaps that was not his fault but the fault of the government that established the Iron Curtain and for many years blocked contact between Russians and the rest of the world.

Such absence of contact most affects creative people. It leads to provincialism in the arts. The Soviet musicians I have known became the victims of a stupid and cruel political experiment. I felt particular empathy for my friend David Oistrakh, a marvelous violinist, a charming and sweet man, and, like me, a native of Odessa.

When Oistrakh arrived in New York for the first time in 1955, he called me. I was living in a hotel, since my apartment across the street from the Metropolitan Museum on Fifth Avenue was being painted and refurbished. I invited Oistrakh to dinner, and we reminisced about old Odessa. Oistrakh reminded me that we had appeared together in Odessa over forty years earlier, in the spring of 1914—he had opened the student matinee, and I was last on the bill, as a graduate of the school run by our professor, Stolyarsky.

But I couldn't remember, beyond a vague recollection of Oistrakh. Yes, there had been a boy with a round face (a round, smiling, boyish face that Oistrakh kept to the end of his days) who played Bach's Allegro Assai and Paganini's "Perpetuum mobile" in unison with the rest of us.

Most likely Oistrakh was not particularly outstanding in those days. The student of Stolyarsky I vividly remember was a child genius named Misha Fainget. We called him the "miniature Kreisler." He played with such inspiration and feeling that tears rolled down the cheeks of the audience. I used to ask many musicians from Odessa who visited the U.S.A. in later years about Fainget: no one had ever heard of him. He had vanished. . . . How could a talent like that disappear without a trace? Of course, the times were harsh. Fainget could have perished during the civil war, or later. . . .

Oistrakh said that back in 1914 he was a little over five years old. It seems to me that he should have been considerably older then. He recalled how we played Borodin's Second Quartet at Stolyarsky's apartment, with me as the cellist. That's true. By then I had learned to handle the cello. When it came to playing in string quartets, I was the "dummy"—as in bridge, when three players seek a fourth partner. There are usually enough violinists, but cellists are hard to come by. So I took up the cello gladly. And I adored the Borodin quartet, especially the Nocturne, the divine slow movement.)

Oistrakh recalled that once in Stolyarsky's office in Odessa he heard me play Dobrowen's charming "Fairy Tale." He liked the piece so much he decided to learn it in one day. And he did, really impressing his Odessa comrades.

In our conversation Oistrakh kept expressing amazement that I, despite my decades as an émigré, still could speak good literary Russian without a foreign accent. Yes, I love Russian, so precise and rich, and I love Russian literature—Pushkin, Lermontov, Gogol.

I'm almost afraid to say this, but I feel no affinity for Leo Tolstoy. His novels give me the sense of enormous frameworks, but the pictures, compared with those frames, are small. Also, Tolstoy writes about the *haut monde* (which is why he is so popular in the West). Nor do I like his personal habit of attacking classical music. Tolstoy once even pounced on Rachmaninoff, who came to visit at his estate, Yasnaya Polyana. Rachmaninoff would never forget it.

For me Chekhov is greater than Tolstoy. Greater than Dostoyevsky, too. Dostoyevsky presents his characters in an intentionally deforming way, while there is such wisdom and warmth in Chekhov. Reading him is like being in a hospitable Russian house, where you are given soothing, fragrant tea and the conversation is gentle and wise. Yet for all that, Chekhov is an extremely sophisticated writer.

During Oistrakh's first visit to New York, three violinists were scheduled for concerts on the same day in Carnegie Hall. Mischa Elman played at two o'clock, Oistrakh made his debut at five, and

I played that evening. It was a sensation! Oistrakh later recalled how he worried and trembled. I didn't tremble, but suddenly my legs were hurting so much that Oistrakh helped me out onstage. He literally pushed me out! It's not for me to judge who won this unusual competition. I tried to present a program that would be interesting, and the reviewers noted that.

People say Oistrakh suffered such nerves when he came out to play the violin, that's why he took up conducting. But when I listened to Oistrakh play I never sensed that he was afraid. True, he was a self-conscious violinist, and perhaps he did worry—I recall that whenever he performed with an orchestra, he was always trying something on the violin during the *tutti*—but at every solo entrance, he played effortlessly and confidently, apparently calm and controlled.

I've heard only good things about Oistrakh as a conductor. I saw him once, in Vienna, conducting a Schubert symphony. And he was very successful—with Schubert in Vienna, quite a feat. His Brahms symphonies got positive notices, too. I have heard it suggested that musicians playing under Oistrakh tried harder because he advised them on more practical bowing. Perhaps. But inspired performance is not a matter of correct bowing, believe me.

I remember how Stokowski kept experimenting with bowing. In an attempt to achieve an uninterrupted flow of sound, he changed the bowing so that the musicians weren't bowing in unison. But it didn't work. I tried to persuade him that he was making a mistake. Playing so that you can't hear the change in bows is like singing without taking a breath. There cannot be such a thing as uninterrupted singing; a person has to take a breath. So the results of Stokowski's manipulations sounded quite unnatural. However, even Arturo Toscanini told me once, "Stokowski is a good conductor!"

I always listened to Oistrakh the violinist with enormous pleasure. I liked his attractive, typically Russian style. Now such Russian style is disappearing. . . .

But I wasn't fully satisfied with Oistrakh's Tchaikovsky. The Russian soul is good up to a point, but Tchaikovsky, especially, can suffer from an excess of emotion. You end up with Russian kitsch.

Tchaikovsky's instrumental concerti and even his symphonies

are organized less than ideally. When playing them you must forget "soul" and watch form. That's why the first truly great performers of Tchaikovsky were Westerners: Hans von Bülow, Adolf Brodsky, and Arthur Nikisch. A good painting needs a good frame!

People sometimes disagree with me. They ask, "Does that mean that you are against feeling in playing?" Not at all. I am against excessive sentimentality; it is dangerous to one's music making. You can smear your porridge around the plate when you're still young, but an adult musician must understand that he has means in his arsenal to impress the audience other than waxing sentimental.

And then, Oistrakh played the Tchaikovsky concerto without cuts. That's a mistake! Auer made certain very reasonable cuts. The main one was twelve measures in the third movement. Tchaikovsky has a short refrain repeated seven times there. If you're listening to a recording, you might think it was stuck.

I remember asking Oistrakh, "Why do you play the Tchaikov-sky without cuts?" He responded with some patriotic remark—an example, to me, of the pressure of the totalitarian state on artists. In the Soviet Union in those days Tchaikovsky, whose music Stalin liked, was being proclaimed a "realistic" composer for the masses, while Auer's revision was considered "bourgeois," a hostile at-tempt to deform the great classic. Oistrakh must have felt he had no choice. And apparently he did not wish to discuss the topic with me.

Oistrakh also had certain problems with Bach, problems of a political as well as a musical nature. After the revolution Bach was played rarely in Russia—his music was considered religious propa-ganda, and why propagandize religion, the "opiate of the masses"? (For me, Bach's cantatas, his *St. Matthew Passion*, and Mass in B Minor are the best music ever written.)

So that's why Soviet violinists have not been particularly in-volved with Bach. Also, Russian audiences like their music and per-formances to be charged with emotion; there is little interest in the music per se. That's why, for instance, ensembles playing baroque music sprang up so much later in Russia than in the West.

I remember one of the first visits to New York by Soviet pianist Emil Gilels. Horowitz invited both of us to tea, and we spoke of

Domenico Scarlatti, whom Horowitz adored. Gilels acknowledged that Horowitz's interest in Scarlatti was completely incomprehensible to him. "Why are you striving to get into the stratosphere, where there is no air, nothing to breathe? I like it here on earth!"

In Russia at that time, they played perhaps one of Scarlatti's 550 sonatas. Subsequently, I believe, Gilels did master some Scarlatti, but with or without Scarlatti, his playing never made much of an impression on me. In my opinion, Gilels lacked real culture and musical erudition, which is a general weak point of Soviet musicians—alas, not their own fault in most cases. Soviet Russia's self-imposed isolation, banning the free flow of cultural information from the West, exercised a hugely negative influence.

On his first American visit Oistrakh and I talked a lot about Bach. He would come to my hotel, and I would play Bach for him and try to persuade him that the old Russian editions of the Bach sonatas and partitas for solo violin were wrong.

I recorded all of Bach's sonatas and partitas twice. The first time was in the mid-fifties, and the second in the mid-seventies. I think, perhaps immodestly, that those recordings—especially the second—will hold up for a long time. The slow movements worked better in the first recording and the fast ones in the second. Oistrakh, I remember, said that he brought two copies of my first Bach album back to Russia, and I said jokingly, "Do you want your commission right now?"

Oistrakh later recorded the F Minor Sonata by Bach, with a piano instead of a clavichord. But it was very good, especially the slow movements. The pianist was Lev Oborin, an excellent musician whom I met at Horowitz's house. (All the Soviet pianists came to pay their respects to Horowitz. It was like visiting the pope in the Vatican.)

Oistrakh wanted to buy a good violin in New York. His own instrument wasn't bad, but it belonged to the Soviet government. He had been "lent" a Stradivarius from the state collection. That violin, and many other instruments, had been confiscated from private collectors and music lovers right after the revolution.

In the twenties, when I was still in Russia, the cellist Victor Kubatsky was in charge of this unique collection, and on his orders

I was given the Guadagnini violin that I played for a while. When I left Soviet Russia, I returned the violin to Kubatsky.

I took Oistrakh to the famous violin dealer Rembert Wurlitzer. Good violins were expensive then, though not as much as nowadays. Oistrakh wanted everything at Wurlitzer's. Unfortunately, his dollars were very limited.

Not everyone knows that the Soviet government cheated its artists for decades. Until recently, whenever they appeared in the West they could keep only 10 percent of their actual fees. The rest had to be turned over to the local Soviet embassy.

And God forbid you should make an inadvertent "mistake" in your financial report: the government agency Goskontsert fined artists fivefold for such mistakes. It was a kind of serfdom, humiliating for major artists like Oistrakh. Now the Soviet authorities admit that they acted greedily and stupidly.

At the New York Wurlitzer shop Oistrakh compared his state-owned Stradivarius with the instruments the dealer was offering. It was interesting for me to observe Oistrakh checking out the capabilities of a violin new to him. He tried to squeeze out as loud a sound as possible, eventually reaching a screech. Onstage Oistrakh never took his instrument to such extremes; he never squeaked.

When the examination was over, Oistrakh wrapped his violin in a piece of canvas. He didn't even have a decent bag. So I asked Wurlitzer to bring him one. The dealer brought out dozens in different fabrics and colors: silk, flannel . . . He tossed them on the table: pick one! Oistrakh was stunned. Wurlitzer, seeing the Soviet violinist's bewilderment, graciously offered one as his gift. I said, "Look, David, your case is lined with green velvet; if you pick a bag in contrasting material, say dark brown, that would look nice."

Still flabbergasted, Oistrakh stared at me as if I had just arrived from another planet! I laughed. "You can get anything you want in New York, so long as you can pay for it. Maybe you'd like to pick out a cover for your son's violin, or for a favorite student? Even a mediocre violin looks a lot better in a beautiful silk bag."

(By the way, his son, Igor Oistrakh, grew up to be a first-rate violinist. Sometimes when he appears in the West, managers print his first name in tiny letters and his surname in big ones on the posters, so the ignorant public thinks it's the "famous" Oistrakh. Of course, this cheap trick can hardly be blamed on Igor, who is a master in his own right.)

Oistrakh didn't buy a violin at Wurlitzer's that time, but he continued his search. Afraid of making a mistake, he asked for my advice. He said there was a Russian living in Boston who had offered him a Stradivarius, but he couldn't make up his mind.

I told him, "Listen, David, I'm no specialist. Of course, experience and intuition mean something; if you study violin long enough, you begin to understand what 'works' and what doesn't. But when you get down to it, buying a violin is like marriage—it's subjective."

After giving it some thought, Oistrakh bought the Boston Stradivarius. It was almost totally without the original varnish, but at least he had to pay comparatively little for it, I think only nine thousand dollars. (This was already in the days when good Italian instruments cost fifty thousand dollars and more!)

I asked Oistrakh why he would buy a defective instrument. He was frank. "As you can guess, I have little hard currency. If I bring back the dollars I earn here, they will be exchanged for rubles at the official rate. So I will be robbed completely. But I can always sell the Stradivarius for a decent amount."

I heard Oistrakh perform on that violin and it sounded marvelous. My friend Fernando Sacconi, a New York violin dealer, told me that apparently this Strad was crafted especially well: without its original varnish it still sounded terrific.

To me, the most important factor was that it was now Oistrakh's personal violin. You always try to squeeze the best out of your own violin. It's like a peasant who gets his own land. Private ownership is efficient not only in agriculture but in violin playing too.

For many years the rulers of Soviet Russia tried to eradicate their subjects' capacity for independent thought. And not only on big, important state issues, but in daily life as well. And I think they succeeded. Soviet artists even today—talented, creative people—seem strangely constrained when it comes to the simplest decisions.

I remember other telling episodes with Oistrakh. We met in June 1961 in Vienna. It was during the famous Vienna summit between

Monte Carlo, 1927: (FROM LEFT) Milstein, Vladimir Horowitz, Choura Danilova, and Alexander Merovitch.

Karlsbad, 1932: Relaxing with Horowitz between tours.

Igor Stravinsky: "A tragic figure." *(Volkov Archive)*

1925 portrait by Konstantin Somov of Sergei Rachmaninoff, whom Milstein met in 1931.

Wilhelm Furtwängler: Milstein declined to sign the proclamation against him.

On the SS *Rex*, 1933: (FROM LEFT) Horowitz, Milstein, Piatigorsky, Toscanini, and the conductor Bernardino Molinari.

Arriving with Toscanini in Paris, 1935.

"The Three Musketeers" arrive in
New York, 1932.

Rehearsing for their first and only joint concert appearance: Carnegie Hall, 1932.

inting, a favorite hobby.

Milstein in Hollywood, 1932, with his
cousin, the movie director Lewis
Milestone.

With his wife, Thérèse; step-daughter, Jill (LEFT); and daughter, Maria.

Giving a master class in Siena, Italy, with Queen Elisabeth of Belgium (FIRST ROW, SECOND FROM RIGHT) among the guests.

h Fritz Kreisler and Elsa Maxwell, the hostess and syndicated society columnist.

id Oistrakh inscribed this photograph in
5: "To a fantastic artist and the nicest of
:agues, dear Nathan Milstein, with
iration."

This photograph of George Balanchine was
inscribed in 1979: "To sweet and dear
friend Nathan, from Murka the Cat and
George."

Washington, 1987: Nathan Milstein is congratulated by President Reagan after receiving the Kennedy Center Award, with Nancy Reagan looking on.

New York, 1987: Before appearing at a benefit concert with the New York Philharmonic. *(Photograph by Marianna Volkov)*

Nikita Khrushchev and John Kennedy, when Khrushchev decided that Kennedy was a weakling, one result being the Cuban crisis the following year.

Khrushchev came to Vienna with his wife, Nina. Oistrakh was sent as a Soviet cultural export. The two world leaders were busy, but Nina Khrushchev was free. She came to Oistrakh's concert with the Vienna Philharmonic under Karajan. Karajan conducted a Brahms symphony, then a work by Webern. Now, if a Viennese audience doesn't like something, it's not shy. This one hissed and booed the Webern. Mrs. Khrushchev was horrified. She was afraid it was the start of a revolution! After all, in Russia audiences were thoroughly disciplined.

The next day, when I performed, she and Oistrakh came to the concert. Later I invited Oistrakh to dine with me at the Sacher Hotel. His sweet and loyal wife, Tamara, was with him. (Always modestly dressed, she accompanied her husband everywhere. After Oistrakh's death in Amsterdam of a heart attack, she fell into a deep depression and committed suicide.)

There in Vienna, Oistrakh was cheerful and animated. He plowed through dinner with an excellent appetite, even though he had announced that he was on a diet. But there was a small incident. Oistrakh had ordered a chateaubriand, which is usually grilled on the outside and raw on the inside. When Oistrakh cut into it, blood gushed out. He didn't know what to do. Clearly he was confused: he hadn't wanted rare meat but he didn't dare mention it to the waiter.

I made a suggestion: "Do you want it well-done? Tell the waiter, he'll change it." Oistrakh hesitated. "We don't do that at home. In Russia we take what we're given." I had to ask the maître d' to have the meat cut in half and then grilled, which was done without ado.

We took up the conversation. "Where are you going now?" Oistrakh asked.

"I don't know," I replied. "Maybe Paris, maybe Zurich. . . . And maybe back to London. I haven't decided yet."

Hearing this, Oistrakh broke into a smile. "See! You have to make a choice, you can't make up your mind, and that's why you have a poor appetite! I have a good appetite because others make decisions for me and I don't have to worry. I know where I'm going, because I'm told where I must go. Isn't that an easier way to live?''

I'm afraid that this habit of living without having to make independent decisions is one reason why few Soviet musicians flee to the West. Another is the relative value of material comfort. Living in the West, you can dress well, but then many people dress well here. It's another thing to appear in fashionable Western clothes in Moscow or Leningrad. Also, in Russia fresh vegetables and fruits on the table are a sign of belonging to the elite, while in the West they are available to the majority of people. The same goes for cars. Soviet violinist Leonid Kogan once bragged to me, "In my Renault, I'm the king of Moscow! When I get in my car, traffic stops!" But who would be impressed by a Renault in London or New York?

Oistrakh was a loyal Soviet citizen, even if he didn't agree with everything that happened in the Soviet Union. He wasn't a dissident, even in his thoughts. And, naturally, dealing with Russian émigrés, he was even more careful.

But in his last years Oistrakh became more self-confident. Sometimes when we met we even touched on political topics.

Once he and I were dining in Paris with some local Russians. It was a grand meal with lots of vodka. Oistrakh had vodka, I drank whiskey. After dinner he had to go to the Soviet embassy, and I walked him there. It was getting late, and we were alone on the street, so I felt I could start a more frank discussion.

I asked him why the Soviet government robbed him so shamelessly. He countered that the money went to support conservatories, for the education of young musicians.

"But you played well before the revolution," I said. "The state didn't spend a kopeck on your education, your parents paid for it."

Oistrakh sighed. "That's the law, we all obey."

Then we got into an argument over a story that was in all the papers in London and Paris at the time. Bolshoi Ballet dancers touring England had taken advantage of an opportunity and all had had their teeth fixed—about eighty dancers in all!—at the British government's expense. It had become something of a state scandal in England. The newspapers wrote that this naturally demonstrated the superiority of British health care, but on the other hand, why should the British pay the dental bills for Soviet dancers?

I said to Oistrakh, "But here is a ballet company supported in part by your money! Why couldn't they have their teeth fixed in the Soviet Union? Why do cultural representatives of one of the greatest countries in the world have to behave like beggars?"

I could tell that the conversation did not please Oistrakh. He couldn't answer frankly, even though he felt uncomfortable toeing the party line. He tried to evade an answer, and I was sorry that I had brought it up.

As for the Bolshoi companies, our paths crossed in Milan in 1964 when the Bolshoi Opera arrived. It was their first appearance in the West. The soloists were staying at the same hotel I was in, the Continental—since torn down, alas—and I was sick in bed. In the next room the famous Russian bass Ivan Petrov was clearing his throat incessantly and singing loudly.

The Bolshoi soloists paraded around proudly: they had been given Russian sheepskin coats for the trip. But apparently the craft of leather tanning had been forgotten in the Soviet Union and the jackets stank! That Sunday I had guests. I came out to meet them, and the hallway reeked as if ten thousand dead rats were decomposing. The manager was hysterical: all his usual clients had run off, leaving only Soviets!

In Milan the Bolshoi did the Russian classics: *Boris Godunov, Eugene Onegin.* The press raved about the chorus but was more critical of the soloists. Russian vocalists—even the best, like Irina Arkhipova and Galina Vishnevskaya—have a "wavering" voice; they sing with a wide vibrato. (Whenever I hear them, I recall a joke told by conductor Sir Thomas Beecham. He was rehearsing with violinist Jacques Thibaud. At the start of rehearsal the oboist, as usual, sounded an A so that orchestra and soloist could tune up. But he was nervous and his A wavered, over quite a range. Sir Thomas turned to Thibaud with a broad gesture. "Jacques, take your choice!")

The appearance in the West of musicians from the Soviet Union almost always creates high interest. Russia is a mysterious country. For decades it was closed to foreigners, so comparatively little is known about it. Sometimes it seemed to me that the Soviet Ministry of Culture, which ultimately controlled the Western tours of Soviet musicians, deliberately limited their trips abroad, the idea being that if they went often, they wouldn't draw such big crowds.

When Oistrakh came to America for the first time, it was a sensation. Tickets were impossible to get. But there were plenty of tickets for his subsequent appearances. The same thing happened to pianist Sviatoslav Richter. His first concert in New York was covered like the landing of a Martian! These days, the arrival of a Soviet artist in the West doesn't create such a sensation. Some are not even invited back: there is no interest in them.

Soviet pianists are good but not better than others. There is nothing especially mysterious about them, not even Richter. I remember Richter playing the Tchaikovsky First Concerto and Liszt's Second in New York with Bernstein conducting. As far as technique was concerned, Richter's performance was enviable, but from a musical point of view it was a clash of diametrically opposed individuals. Richter is not at all a passionate pianist, so he tried to keep everything under control, while Bernstein indulged in such gymnastics he almost fell off the podium.

There is something too rational about Richter's personality, even though he is a major artist. I remember an amusing exchange about Richter with Arthur Rubinstein. We were at the Paris Ritz, after a lunch given by a wealthy lady. I was with Thérèse, and I remember that Greta Garbo was also at the restaurant.

The company of beautiful women always inspired Rubinstein, and he began showing off and making up stories. (Gregor Piatigorsky was considered champion in this area, though I'm not sure who was better, Piatigorsky or Rubinstein. Piatigorsky's pluses were his height and handsomeness, while Rubinstein got points for temperament.)

We began arguing about Richter. I said that Richter was certainly a marvelous pianist but not as impeccable as he was reputed to be. His music making was too dry for me. In Richter's interpretation of Ravel's "Jeux d'eau," instead of flowing water you hear frozen icicles. Rubinstein, playing the true and noble knight, countered: "I have a great admiration for Richter."

But as soon as Thérèse went off to talk to Greta Garbo, Rubinstein leaned over to me and whispered, "Nathan, I didn't want to say it earlier, but I agree with you a hundred percent!" Now he was worried that his praise a moment ago had raised my opinion of Richter!

In the Soviet Union, too much stress is placed on technique. They make sure that musicians play loud and fast, and problems of individuality and style are not that important for them. "Sprinter" performers like Lazar Berman are the result—phenomenal technicians but second-rate musicians.

That's why Bach and Mozart can be a disappointment in the hands of Soviet musicians. Even such a marvelous violinist as Leonid Kogan was not very successful with Bach.

I heard Kogan many times, and we often met and talked. I was aware that many people did not like him. Once there was even a protest demonstration against him, because of rumors that he was involved with the KGB.

I don't quite understand why Kogan was singled out. I've read the memoirs of Soviet intelligence officer Colonel Oleg Penkovsky, who wrote that all members of Soviet delegations to the West, whether scientists, musicians, or ballerinas, are obligated to report to the government on everything they see and hear. For instance, they're asked, "Well, you met with Rothschild, what did he say, what does he think?" And so on. Leonid Kogan was not an exception in that regard.

I always wondered why the Soviets make their artists report on their contacts with the West. I mean, what useful information could a Kogan bring back? I once asked that marvelous violinist and dear man Isaac Stern whether the CIA or FBI invited him in for a chat after his trip to the Soviet Union. He said no. And it would never occur to Stern to go to a government agency with any information, even though he is a patriot. There are professionals for spying. But under the Soviet system, every citizen is made to engage in espionage, to humiliating and inefficient effect.

Kogan, like Oistrakh, was a private man. But I liked Oistrakh better, because he was more honest: he made no pretense. Kogan, on the other hand, wanted to appear franker than he was. But I could sense his constant wariness, even though I never tried to pry state secrets out of him. We talked only about music.

I don't think Kogan was as important a musician as Oistrakh. Oistrakh was a true master; Kogan was a phenomenal violinist, no more, though that's plenty. From a musical point of view, Kogan's ideas were never as interesting as Oistrakh's. Also, in Kogan's last years you could feel that he was playing with some difficulty, while Oistrakh's remarkable qualities as a violinist were sustained to his last day. Oistrakh could have played into advanced old age if he had not died prematurely.

Oistrakh's real fame began with his appearance at the violin competition in Warsaw in 1935, where he took second place to fifteen-year-old Ginette Neveu from France. (Neveu was a good violinist but uneven. She was killed in a plane crash when she was only thirty.) A year later Oistrakh came to Brussels for the Ysaÿe competition with a whole squad of Soviet violinists. They all took prizes, with Oistrakh the top winner.

Stalin used the sensation for propaganda, and after that the Soviet Union approached this business of international music competitions with utter seriousness. Victory at such events became important political acts for Soviet authorities. They were planned and prepared for, sometimes years in advance.

In 1953, when I was in Paris, Jacques Thibaud invited me to be on the jury of the Marguerite Long–Jacques Thibaud Competition. I tried to joke my way out of it: you can't smoke during the competition and I wouldn't be able to last. Thibaud insisted. Then I told him the truth: I wasn't a big fan of Soviet violin playing, and I might be less than objective. (To tell the truth, I'm not very objective on the whole. When I like a person, I praise him more, perhaps, than he deserves. And vice versa.)

I also recounted for Thibaud a pointed tale about a music competition. When I came to Berlin in 1925, I became friendly with the pianist Mitya Nikisch, son of the great conductor. And Mitya told me this story.

One of the first international competitions for musicians, held in Petersburg in 1890, was the idea of the legendary pianist Anton Rubinstein. Rubinstein had dreamed up a beautiful thing, but it ended in embarrassment. He had funded the competition out of his own money and established two prizes—one for pianists and one for composers, each five thousand francs. Ferruccio Busoni came to Petersburg for the competition, and he entered both as pianist and composer. And he got only the composer's prize! He was beaten in the piano competition by a certain Nikolai Dubasov, who would never become a great soloist but took up teaching.

The most piquant detail, as Mitya Nikisch informed me, was that it was Rubinstein himself who insisted that Dubasov, not Busoni, get the prize. Everyone was astonished. Busoni was so much better! But Rubinstein explained that Busoni didn't need the prize, he'd become famous anyway, while Dubasov needed encouragement and support. So much for the ideal of musical competition.

After hearing me out, Thibaud gave up but said, "Well, if you won't be a judge, I'd still like you to see how my competition goes. Come to my box."

Oistrakh, representing the Soviet Union, was on the jury. He complained to me about it. "I don't like it. You sit as if in a cage, and there's no real musical discussion. And I do enjoy talking about music!"

Nevertheless, Oistrakh obeyed his government's dictates dutifully and worked hard to get prizes for the Soviet contestants.

The first prize went to Nelli Shkolnikova, who played somewhat more accurately—that is, hit fewer wrong notes—than the other participants. And there was a talented Japanese girl who didn't get anything at all. Soon afterward, I was at a reception at the Japanese embassy in Paris, where I tried to explain the situation to my hosts.

"Listen," I said. "You see how the Soviets treat these competitions. If you want the Japanese to win prizes, you have to approach this business just as seriously. Your cultural attaché has to work on it, since he has the contacts. He knows important people. And the Japanese government must provide your young violinists with good instruments and comfortable lodgings when they come to Paris." And so forth. Just what the Japanese are doing now. . . .

Music, unfortunately, has turned into a big political game. But if you are going to play the game, then at least do it professionally. That was the motto of the great master of international cultural politics, my close friend Nicholas Nabokov. After World War Two, Nabokov supervised the process of denazification of German musical life, and it was probably then that he met with Willy Brandt, who had worked for American intelligence during the war. Later, when Brandt became mayor of West Berlin, he asked Nabokov to organize a permanent international music festival for the city.

This was right after the erection of the horrible Wall, which, happily, has at last come down. Brandt wanted West Berlin to remain an important international cultural center. Nabokov, as head of the Berlin Festival, tried to attract as many stars as possible. I know that he regularly invited Stravinsky, whom he considered the greatest composer of the twentieth century.

In 1966 Nabokov asked me to perform in Berlin. I had not played in Germany since 1933 and was reluctant to go, but Nika persisted. At the time, I was performing a lot in Europe—in France, Austria, Switzerland. The reviews of the European critics were not bad at all, so even though I hadn't appeared in Germany for over thirty years, my name was well known there. Nika persuaded me that it was necessary to come to Berlin to play then. "It will be an important symbolic political gesture!"

I had just spent several weeks in bed with a horrible case of sciatica (and getting injections from Sergei Tolstoy, grandson of the great Leo, who would have been the perfect copy of his grandfather if he'd grown a thick white beard). So I was in terrible shape. But it's impossible to resist Nika Nabokov for long! When I arrived in West Berlin, I was mobbed by the press and TV people, and all I could think was, How will I stand this, what do I need this for?

I was supposed to play the Brahms concerto with Karajan and the Berlin Philharmonic. At the first rehearsal, Karajan put on airs. "You know, I'll just go off in the back to hear how the orchestra sounds from there!" He didn't need to walk back. Karajan knew how his orchestra sounded; it was just a mannerism of his. Well, he went off, he heard the orchestra play well without him, and he ran right back.

Despite his little tricks, I admired Karajan—he was a greatly talented man who simply was used to being the constant center of the universe. But at the time, I wasn't so kindly disposed. My illness was killing me, my whole body ached, and I thought, I played the Brahms with Richard Strauss, with Furtwängler, and neither one felt compelled to play the fool. Why do I have to put up with this now, in West Berlin?

So I decided to escape from Berlin and headed for the train station. And there was Nabokov! He rushed toward me. "What are you doing here? You have a rehearsal tomorrow with Karajan!" And I asked Nabokov, "What are *you* doing here?"

"I'm meeting Rostropovich, the cellist from the Soviet Union."

"Back in Russia I used to know a cellist named Rostropovich."

"That's his father!"

That was how I first learned of Mstislav Rostropovich.

In the end, Nabokov talked me into going back to the hotel. I called Thérèse and asked her what I should do. She said, "Definitely play! Even if it's a catastrophe, you have to do it. Otherwise you'll be creating problems for yourself." Just as I was about to fall into bed, Nabokov called. "Nathan, are you dressed? You've been given a suite for the price of a single room. Move your things!"

The reason for the change became evident a while later, when Mayor Willy Brandt and his lovely Scandinavian wife came to call on me in my new and larger hotel room. They came to "visit the patient" and brought me so many flowers there was hardly room to move. Brandt was courteous and kind, and he gave me his photo, with a warm inscription: "How wonderful that you have come to Berlin at this glorious time of its history." Et cetera, et cetera.

It was all to emphasize the significance Brandt attributed to the festival. And from that point of view, Rostropovich's arrival was a great coup, for both the festival and Nabokov. In agreeing to send a Soviet musician, the Russians were acknowledging—at least in the realm of culture—that West Berlin had a certain sovereignty. Afterward, Nabokov was so delighted that everything went well, he invited us all to the grill at the Kempinski Restaurant.

Rostropovich is a marvelous cellist, but for my taste he works too hard at being affable. He tries to give everyone within reach a bear hug, and while he's at it he kisses and addresses you as *golubchik*, which translates roughly as "honey" or "sweetie." Auer used to call everyone *golubchik* too, but that was because he was old and couldn't remember names. Why does so young and gifted a man need that kind of come-on? Rostropovich is popular enough as it is.

When a musician moves to the West from Russia, the public's fascination with him gradually fades. Of the new generation of émigré performers only a few have kept their glamour: Rostropovich, the pianist Vladimir Ashkenazy, the violinist Gidon Kremer.

As for my performance with Karajan, my sciatic pain vanished as soon as I stepped out on the stage—vanished from stage fright. My knees were shaking! One critic wrote, "It's interesting to see the famous Milstein so humble." Luckily, he didn't see my trembling legs, he was too far back. But then even Karajan was nervous: in one place he cued the orchestra to come in too early.

When he conducted, Karajan used to close his eyes. After our joint performance, he complained to an interviewer, "I open my eyes, and Milstein is playing with his eyes shut! After that I couldn't let myself close my eyes!"

So after thirty-three years I was playing in Germany again. So many horrible events had taken place over those years. But in a certain sense this was now a different country, with solid democratic institutions. That's why I finally agreed to play for Germans once again. Yet I have never had a similar desire to go back to Russia, which has remained basically the same despotic one-party state I fled when I was twenty-one. And Russia is still a one-party state.

People say to me: "But you have Russian roots, why don't you want to return to Russia?" What are Russian roots? I have international roots! Russia gave me a lot, but really, in the final analysis, how many years did I spend there, years when I was truly conscious of myself? Actually, I only remember myself clearly from age six, from the time when Mama began manipulating things so that I could start the violin.

So who am I? A Jew from Russia, a citizen of the U.S.A.; my house is in London and I spend extended periods in Switzerland, in Lausanne. Many Russians I admire lived in Switzerland: Tchaikovsky (who composed his violin concerto in Clarens), Rachmaninoff, Diaghilev, Stravinsky (who wrote several brilliant opuses also in Clarens).

In America I feel comfortable but not warm. Only in Russia did

I know that feeling of warmth. Superficially you can say I was un-
lucky, for there is no one country I can consider fully, unequivocally
mine. But ultimately, that makes me rather glad.

For several years David Oistrakh and I shared a manager: the famous Sol Hurok, legendary as a super-impresario who created rep-
utations and nurtured artists. Even the legendary Hurok could not
persuade me to return to Russia. And Hurok was more enterprising
and persuasive than other managers. He was the first to start im-
porting Soviet artists to the U.S.A.: the Bolshoi Ballet, the Moiseyev
Dancers, and so on.

As opposed to many of his colleagues, Hurok worked hard and
believed firmly in the infallibility of his own taste. Sporting a black
ascot, a hat à la Léon Blum, and a silver-tipped walking stick, he
rarely lost money, because he knew that what he liked, the majority
would like.

Hurok's energy was impressive but not inexhaustible. I remember how he once appeared unexpectedly in my dressing room, after
a concert in Brooklyn, exclaiming in agitation, "I can't stand it, I
can't stand it!" It turned out he was having a lot of problems with
the New York appearances of the Bolshoi: one of the ballerinas had
twisted her leg and he was looking for a substitute. He was no longer
young, he was tired of the glamour, and was looking for some peace
and quiet. We went off to have some hamburgers.

Hurok negotiated twice with the Soviets about my appearance
in Moscow, but both times, at the last moment, I decided not to go.
Once, an important bureaucrat from Goskontsert by the name of
Zhukov was trying to persuade me in front of Hurok. "Come to
Russia; everyone lives well there now, just like under capitalism!"
I retorted: "Then why did you need to have a revolution?"

Zhukov turned purple. So did Hurok. "Milstein, you're crazy!"
was all the great impresario could say.

I spent one Christmas with Oistrakh at the rooftop restaurant of
the St. Regis in New York. It was a beautiful, festive night. In a
sentimental mood, Oistrakh said, "Come to Russia! You'll be
treated so well!"

"David, I left Russia because I didn't like it. If I were to come back now—even for a few concerts—it would mean admitting that everything is fine there now. And as you know, that's not the case!"

If I had decided to give a concert in the Soviet Union, I'd have been arrested before the second half. Why? Because, after playing the first half, I would have addressed the audience. I would have said, "How can such talented and hardworking people put up with this cruel and stupid government?"

Of course, there would have been repercussions: arrest, expulsion, they might even have confiscated my violin. And then there would have been a scandal, bad publicity for the Soviets. Yet if all the artists visiting at that time, or just some of them, had behaved this way, it could have had a positive effect.

But no one did it! (With one possible exception. I think Menuhin, giving a speech at some musical congress in Moscow, dared to mention the then banned Solzhenitsyn.) Instead Western musicians rushed off to Moscow unconditionally at the first opportunity, in order to boast later of a conversation with Khrushchev. Or even today with Gorbachev. And they repeat like parrots: "In Russia the audiences are so marvelous, they love serious music like no one else!"

That's not true! The Russians don't love classical music more than the Germans, Italians, or Americans. It's just that there are fewer opportunities to hear it in the Soviet Union. And more is made of those few occasions because there are almost no other forms of amusement—no tourism, no restaurants. . . .

I remember Oistrakh bragging, "In Russia our audiences are so extraordinary, they don't want to go home after a concert!"

I countered, "That's because thanks to bad living conditions, they have to sit at home five to a room."

Another myth is that Soviet leaders like classical music and culture in general more than Western leaders do. The tale is repeated endlessly of Lenin listening attentively to Beethoven's *Appasssionata* as played by my friend Dobrowen. Also, as mentioned, the story of Grisha Piatigorsky playing in a string quartet for Lenin became popular.

Musicians recall such emotional occasions (whether or not they're true) for two reasons. First of all, it's always harder to get access to a dictator than to a democratically elected leader. The British prime minister Edward Heath (an amateur conductor, by the way) regularly attended my concerts in London, but it made no great impression either on me or the audience. Western politicians are always in the spotlight, everyone knows everything about them, there is no mystery to them.

By the same token, I remember playing in the late twenties at a private party at the house of French socialist Léon Blum, later premier of France. He and his family were charming and pleasant—they served a lovely tea and paid me well for my performance—but it didn't leave a profound impression. (Later I became friends with another important French socialist, Pierre Mendès-France. I often had discussions with that wise politician in Gstaad, where he rented a villa.)

The other reason why performing for a tyrant thrills musicians more than playing for a democratic leader is that an artist's life and death depend on the tyrant's mercy, not to mention such minor perquisites as food, decent clothing and housing, and so on. That's why Soviet violinists like Oistrakh and Busya Goldstein remembered forever how they played for Stalin.

In the West performing for a politician, even a mighty one, cannot have that kind of significance. An influential manager plays a much more important role in a musician's life than does any president. (In general people in the West do not overly respect their politicians and tend to forget them quickly. But I've noticed a strange thing: major airports in Western democracies are named in honor of politicians and not aviators. This may be justified somewhat in the case of de Gaulle, but what was the reason for naming the New York airport for John F. Kennedy? I feel that he did little for the country and still less for the development of aviation. Why not honor some of the great American aviators, the Wright brothers or Charles Lindbergh, who made his famous transatlantic crossing in 1927, instead?)

Nevertheless, meeting politicians can be amusing and memorable. In the early thirties in Switzerland I met Louis Barthou, noted French politician. He was staying in a hotel not far from the stone chalet I was renting in Bürgenstock. I was practicing, and from the window I saw Barthou in a beret strolling by and engrossed in lively conversation with General Ewald von Kleist, a typical Prussian with a monocle in his eye. I had read von Kleist's article on Kutuzov, the great Russian field marshal who fought Napoleon, in *Die Wehr*, the German military magazine.

Suddenly Barthou and von Kleist vanished. I knew that there was a bench not far from my house and guessed that they were sitting and listening to me practice. This made me feel uncomfortable, because I was doing rough work and was squeaking terribly. So I stopped playing; Barthou and von Kleist waited a bit and then resumed their walk.

The next day, when I dropped by the hotel for tea, I was introduced to Barthou and von Kleist. Both were courteous gentlemen, but their knowing I was staying nearby created a problem for me, since now they started coming by every morning to listen to me practice. So instead of working purposefully, I found myself trying to please my notable listeners.

Both Barthou and von Kleist suffered dramatic fates. Barthou, who devoted all his efforts to create a European anti-Hitler coalition, was murdered in 1934 by a terrorist in Marseilles while together with King Alexander of Yugoslavia. Von Kleist, a descendant of the great poet and at one time adviser to the Kuomintang army in China, was also anti-Hitler. In 1938, on orders from Admiral Wilhelm Canaris, he went on a secret mission to London to persuade the British to oppose Hitler decisively on the question of Czechoslovakia. Alas, no one listened, and fateful Munich lay ahead. Subsequently, von Kleist participated in the unsuccessful conspiracy of the German generals against Hitler and was hideously executed.

Among the politicians I came to know, the first prime minister of Israel, David Ben-Gurion, made a memorable impression on me. When I appeared in Israel, I was invited to a party to which Ben-Gurion came late. I remember how he spoke with humor about Israel becoming a real state at last: "We even have our own gangsters, and I'm almost happy about it!" His words reminded me of the famous dictum by my former Odessa neighbor Jabotinsky (the spiritual father of Israel's Likud party): "Allow us to have our own scoundrels!"

I believe that only young musicians should be invited for command performances. It's important for them psychologically and as a boost to their careers. For Vladimir Horowitz, performing for President Hoover in 1931 meant more than playing for Jimmy Carter in 1978. I was at the White House on that first occasion, when Horowitz was receiving congratulations after his recital for President and Mrs. Hoover, and I will never forget how he nervously mixed up the phrase he had been practicing. "I am delightful, I am delightful!" he repeated.

People nowadays do not know that having musicians at the White House is an old tradition. Some think it began with Kennedy, who supposedly nurtured and publicized the arts. Actually, it wasn't culture he was publicizing, it was himself. As far as I know, Kennedy never invited any young musicians to the White House. He invited Pablo Casals when the cellist was of an advanced age and could no longer play with his vaunted brio.

A huge publicity campaign was mounted over this with a cynicism strident enough to offend even Stravinsky, who was a professional used to that sort of thing. Thus, when Kennedy invited Stravinsky to celebrate his eightieth birthday at the White House, the composer refused at first. It was arranged only after complicated diplomatic maneuvering on both sides.

I played for President Roosevelt, whose foreign policies I always found catastrophic. Think about Yalta! Roosevelt trusted Stalin more than Churchill; he was suspicious of England as a colonial power. In his negotiations with Stalin, Roosevelt could have gotten many more democratic rights for the Russian people, who would have been so grateful to him. After all, the Russians have a tradition of respect for Americans. I remember back in prerevolutionary Odessa how *chansonniers* sang popular songs praising American ingenuity.

I came to the White House with my pianist, whose name was Rabinovich. He was a marvelous musician, and Chaliapin used to joke, "There's only one Jew I like and that's Rabinovich." (Well, thanks for that at least!)

Before the recital, Eleanor Roosevelt, who clearly ran the show, said to me, "The audience at our concerts is very musical, but still I would ask you not to play for more than forty-five minutes. If they ask for encores, then go right ahead." I liked her directness and businesslike manner. She was almost charming.

When I finished playing, the audience, consisting mostly of refined diplomats, applauded wildly. Having come out for bows, I was thinking about what to play for an encore, when Roosevelt, who must not have been the greatest fan of classical music, gave a sign with his cigarette holder from his wheelchair, and the military band blasted out Sousa's "Stars and Stripes Forever." I was a bit taken aback, but at least I had the pleasure of hearing the band: they were terrific!

I liked President Reagan. I met him in December 1987, when I was one of the honorees at the Kennedy Center. It was a memorable occasion. Thérèse and I came to Washington from New York and were put up at the Ritz-Carlton, in a wonderful suite. We had a limousine at our disposal, waiting outside, and a special escort.

On that trip I also met Secretary of State George Schultz. The awards were handed out during lunch at the Department of State. First Leontyne Price sang "America the Beautiful," after which Schultz remarked about the words of the song: "As we look to next week, that is the message." (He was referring to Reagan's summit meeting with Gorbachev, which was going to start in Washington two days later.) Then Schultz said he hoped that in the future "nations will be more recognized for their art than for the force of their weapons." Those are nice words, and of course one would like to see it happen, though in my opinion there is little hope that it will.

Schultz and I chatted the next day at the White House. There were a lot of people, and I had found an armchair away from the crowd and had sat down to rest. Schultz asked if he could join me. He was very polite. We touched on the Gorbachev visit once more and he sighed. "Today is a lovely and nice day. Tomorrow with Gorbachev coming, it will not be so nice. Today we enjoy ourselves, but tomorrow will be a different story. Very complicated work lies ahead of us."

The newspapers were full of reports on the coming summit meeting. I, for one, didn't think that it would be an important meeting at all. And that's how it turned out. Gorbachev's visit was more symbolic, with almost no practical results.

Starting with that visit, the American media began making a folk hero of Gorbachev. Today they write that he is changing the course of Russia, that he is starting a new economic policy.

I am reminded of Lenin's NEP! I recall being at a rally in Moscow in the early twenties when Lenin announced the "New Economic Policy." In his speech he defended this surprising turn. It was a fortunate moment for Russia. I remember that literally ten days later everything appeared in hungry Moscow—food, clothing, entertainment. But then Stalin did away with NEP. He wanted absolute rule, and NEP created an economic alternative.

So I am rather skeptical now. Whatever Gorbachev says and does, the political system has not changed in the Soviet Union. And that means that any economic changes can be repealed overnight. Also, clever decisions must be implemented by clever people. And most people are not clever, they just want power. The Soviet political system must undergo such an extent of *perestroika* that power does indeed move into the hands of the people.

In 1987 I told everyone who would listen in Washington, "Be happy that there is a politburo, which fears to make bold economic reforms. Otherwise, Russia would be even more powerful, not only militarily but also economically. Under clever leadership that could happen in twenty years." Secretary Schultz nodded sympathetically.

President Reagan collects Soviet jokes. So I told him the latest one, a commentary on Gorbachev's economic experiments. "What is socialism? The longest and most painful road to capitalism." Reagan was very pleased and laughed heartily. He was so gay, so sincere. (Rather, he *behaved* sincerely. *Being* sincere is something else.)

This was the tenth ceremony of the Kennedy Center honors; honored with me were Bette Davis, Sammy Davis, Jr., Perry Como, and choreographer Alwin Nikolais. In a special little speech Reagan said a few warm and thoughtful words about each of us. He spoke, by the way, without a prepared text, without peeking at notes; yet they say that he couldn't memorize anything!

Reagan was particularly attentive to his former Hollywood colleagues, also a nice trait. He seemed to feel more comfortable with
them and liked to joke about his own Hollywood past. For example,
he told Bette Davis that if he had acted as well as she does, he would
never have left Hollywood for politics. In his remarks, Reagan singled out Bette Davis's latest film, *The Whales of August*, and said, "I
found out just how hard it is to get good reviews from *The New York
Times*."

Bette Davis looked thin and tired. She offered me her trembling
hand—it was cold. I recalled sadly how I had met her in Vermont,
where I had an estate. This was forty-five years ago, when she was
young and striking. She was a top-notch character actress, a real
professional who was not afraid to look ugly in her parts.

Sammy Davis, Jr., told me that he was about to have hip surgery. Still, he was cheerful and active. I always liked his movies: he
has a good voice, he's a marvelous dancer, and he even plays the
trumpet well.

Perry Como, whose singing I first heard many years ago at Radio City Music Hall, was still handsome. He had started out as a
small-town barber. In the concert they gave in our honor at the
Kennedy Center, he was greeted by a chorus of barbers—first a
barbershop quartet, then ten singers, then a hundred! Como was
very touched; he practically wept.

I was pleased to hear words from Pinchas Zukerman addressed
to me during the performance. Pinky, as his friends call him, spoke
beautifully, almost like a poet. He is a charming and social man.
I've known Pinky for many years and often attended his performances. I have high regard for his great mastery of the violin, as I
do for that of his friend, Itzhak Perlman.

Pinky introduced Thérèse and me to his beautiful wife, the actress Tuesday Weld. A surprise for me was Mozart's duet for violin
and viola played by Zukerman and one of his pupils, the wunderkind Midori. Midori is an amazing talent who could grow into a
real artist.

I predict a great future for another participant of that concert at
the Kennedy Center: dancer Irek Mukhamedov, who flew especially
from Moscow with his partner, Ludmila Semenyaka. How he

jumped! He made a greater impression on me than young Nureyev had. My wife, who also liked the pair from the Bolshoi very much, expressed her raptures to Alwin Nikolais. Alas, that was a faux pas! Nikolais made a face. Understandably, as a modern choreographer, Nikolais would not find traditional Russian ballet to his taste.

At the Kennedy Center, dancers from the Nikolais theater performed a spectacular number choreographed by Nikolais. And Nikolais himself is a nice fellow. But my friend Balanchine had good reason for not fully liking modern dance. There is almost always more spectacle than dance substance to it.

I returned from the Kennedy Center with pleasant memories and an incredibly heavy medal on colored ribbons. The medal was so heavy that Bette Davis couldn't wear hers and immediately took it off and put it in its case. I was told that it was gold. I hope not, at least for the sake of the taxpayers who subsidized our trip to Washington, the luxurious lunches for three hundred (alas, my health did not permit me to taste all that food), and the festivities themselves.

14. My Friend George Balanchine

I am not optimistic about the fate of serious music in this century and into the next. If there are any composers today writing masterpieces that will last a hundred years, I haven't heard about them. Besides, the world is engulfed by pop and rock. Radio and television are feeding the public, especially young people, musical fast food that is so trashy and heavily spiced that it kills their taste for the spiritual in art. In that ocean of intoxicating and corrupting sounds a small island of classical music can barely survive.

But understanding that, I am still not a proponent of any artificial democratization of serious music. A proper appreciation of a masterpiece is a difficult thing. And for many, alas, it remains out of reach. Of course, in some European countries classical music took roots in a natural way. In Italy Verdi's operas are folk music. You could say the same about Schubert's symphonies in Vienna.

Wherever there are no such natural roots, attempts are made to force classical music on the masses through propaganda. Often it's done in a crude and tasteless way by which music is turned into a commodity that has to be sold no matter what. This demeans both the music and the audience. And in the final analysis, it corrupts the artists.

Composers and performers remind me more and more of bazaar hawkers or clowns. They try to lure the public and sell off their wares. They make faces and contort their bodies. When someone tells me that so-and-so may not be a great musician but he does have "personality," I know that a new successful traveling salesman of music has been born. He'll do any trick, try any gimmick, in order to attract paying customers. And the public doesn't even suspect that these antics have only a tangential relationship to real art.

I rarely despair, but sometimes in the middle of this vanity fair I just feel like giving up: Have all standards been changed irrevocably? Is there no one left as an example for young artists? Could the cynics who proclaim "After us, the deluge" be right?

And then I think of George Balanchine, my old friend George.

I met him in 1926, soon after Vladimir Horowitz and I came to Western Europe from Russia. It was in Monte Carlo. We quickly became friends: we had so much in common.

Balanchine had also recently emigrated from Russia. Except that when he left Petrograd in 1924 (just before it was renamed Leningrad) he knew he would not return, while Vladimir Horowitz and I still assumed that we were in Europe temporarily "for the purpose of artistic refinement and cultural propaganda" (as it said in our official mandate from the Revolutionary Military Council of the Soviet Republic).

Monte Carlo was a marvelous place for such refinement—for me, for Horowitz, and for Balanchine. He was with Diaghilev's ballet company then. In Monte Carlo, under the auspices of the countess of Monaco, Diaghilev found himself a refuge. His troupe occupied a small but beautiful local opera theater. On that stage he presented ballets featuring his current favorites: first Léonide Massine, then Serge Lifar.

Initially Diaghilev needed Balanchine to do fast choreography for the opera season—in Delibes's *Lakmé*, Offenbach's *Tales of Hoffmann*, and *Boris Godunov*. Georges (as we called him then, using the soft French pronunciation) also did some dancing.

I was engaged for several concerts in Monte Carlo, as was Horowitz. We went there for two or three weeks and stayed at the Palace Hotel. It was an inexpensive place but we thought it incredibly luxurious, especially after Russia. The comforts and food were incomparable! We were amazed and amused by everything—by the toy kingdom of Monaco, by the prince's guard (his miniature army parading around importantly in colorful uniforms), by the famous roulette wheels.

The musical director of the theater was then someone named Puttman. He was a severe gentleman and everyone feared him. No one had ever heard of unions in opera companies in those days, and Puttman bossed everyone around. He instructed Horowitz and me: "Don't play in the casino! If you want to watch others play, ask me, I'll give you passes. But no gambling!" We agreed readily, since we had no money to spare anyway. I walked around Monte Carlo. It was in January, and I remember wearing a coat. Monte Carlo isn't Nice.

It was easy to meet people at the Palace. All you had to do was reminisce out loud in Russian about the famous pirozhki of Petersburg: "Oh, how wonderful those pirozhki at Filippov's were!"

"I loved them too!" a voice would respond, and there you'd have a new friend.

Pretty ballerinas flitted through the hotel lobby. You could bump into Diaghilev himself, somewhat heavy but still with elegant bearing, or the businesslike Stravinsky (the composer lived not far away, in Nice). Huffy Lifar appeared frequently, and everyone bowed before Lubov Tchernicheva, Diaghilev's star. What a place it was, filled with life and glamour. And not because it was a deluxe establishment like the De Paris, but because of its clientele—young, talented, beautiful, brash. (I visited Monte Carlo recently and passed the Palace. It was empty, the windows boarded up.)

My Friend George Balanchine

In our free time (and we had more than enough of it in Monte Carlo), Balanchine and I would sit in a café, observing the passersby and chatting about whatever came to mind, especially music. Balanchine made many subtle and original remarks. It turned out that we had much in common musically as well—we both had attended the same conservatory in Petersburg! People forget it now, but Balanchine studied piano at the conservatory. I can attest that he played not badly at all.

Of course, Georges was no virtuoso—he couldn't have given recitals—and I doubt that he could even have been a professional accompanist. When he sat down at the piano, he didn't play so much as "noodle," blurring over the hard parts. But, really, that didn't matter. Balanchine sight-read freely. And you could see immediately that he was a refined and responsive musician. I felt that quality instantly in his first ballets.

Yet Balanchine was far from a purist in music. For instance, he liked a popular *chansonnier* from Odessa, Leonid Utyosov, whom I also liked (it turned out we had both gone to his concerts in Russia). Balanchine retained that catholicity of musical taste. He not only wrote little songs himself, he freely used popular music in his staging—in particular, arrangements of songs by our mutual friend George Gershwin in the ballet *Who Cares?*.

Animated and witty when the conversation was about music, Balanchine usually became much more reserved when the topic changed to women. Handsome and elegant, definitely a ladies' man, he gracefully avoided bragging about his conquests. When we met, his companion was Alexandra ("Choura") Danilova, soloist in Diaghilev's ballet company, a merry woman as cocky as a bantam rooster. No one ever knew whether Georges and Choura were married. The four of us used to get together: Balanchine, Danilova, Horowitz, and I. Horowitz tried courting Danilova, and she flirted with him charmingly.

Everyone around us fell in love, came together, broke up. There must have been something in the air of Monte Carlo! For some reason this amorous atmosphere didn't affect me, and I didn't even try to follow the example of most every other man there, courting the ballerinas. I played the role of an observer. Monte Carlo is a small town, and the world of the Palace Hotel was even smaller. All the love dramas took place right in front of me. The beautiful Tamara Zheverzheyeva had tear-stained eyes. She had married Georges in Russia, but here in Monte Carlo, Georges obviously preferred Danilova. (It seems to me that he also had an affair with the glamorous Tchernicheva, but that was just an "aside" for him.)

Diaghilev—always the professional impresario—disliked long Russian names, which the paying European public found hard to pronounce or remember. He changed Georges's Georgian surname, Balanchivadze, to Balanchine. He shortened Tamara Zheverzheyeva even more severely: she became Geva. After a lonely time in Monte Carlo, Tamara decided the town had nothing more to offer her and went off with Nikita Balieff's group, Chauve Souris, to New York, where I believe she later starred in musicals and variety shows.

By then Balanchine had begun his famous collaboration with Igor Stravinsky. He used Stravinsky's music for a ballet that was then called *Apollon musagète*, now shortened simply to *Apollo*. On Diaghilev's orders, the Greek god was danced by Serge Lifar. To tell the truth, I did not like him. Lifar came from Kiev, and I called him the "fake Ukrainian," because everything about Lifar was fake and affected. Later he attended my concerts, and it was always a major production—Lifar carrying himself into the dressing room with widespread arms and exaggerated delight that began with his shrieking "Nathan!"

Lifar always had to be the center of attention, always in the spotlight. And that, alas, led him to collaborate with the Nazis during World War Two. One doesn't like to judge others. The whole business with Hitler's arrival in occupied Paris with Lifar showing him around the Grand Opéra was, after all, Lifar's personal affair. But then he shouldn't have felt insulted later when some people refused to shake his hand.

During subsequent years I saw many of Balanchine's ballets set to Stravinsky's music: *Jeu des cartes*, *Le Baiser de la fée*, *Orpheus* (which I particularly liked), *Firebird*, *Agon*. But I find it interesting that Stravinsky wrote two ballets that are true works of genius—*Petrouchka* and *Sacre du printemps*—and Balanchine never choreographed them! There's something mysterious about that. . . .

My Friend George Balanchine

One thing is clear to me. I don't think that anyone except for a small circle of specialists would ever have known Stravinsky's late works if it had not been for Balanchine. Georges believed in that music passionately and championed it with the consistency and conviction that was typical of him. Balanchine, it seems, liked almost all of Stravinsky's music. He adjusted many of his nonballetic compositions for the stage: for instance, *Symphony of Psalms* and the violin concerto. And Balanchine was interested not only in Stravinsky's major works, he also staged Stravinsky's *Polka for Circus Elephants*—a masterful and very witty piece of music—with dancing elephants!

Ballet, in my view, just doesn't compare with music. Nothing compares with music, no art at all. You study for fifteen years first, and only then you discover that, alas, you are a bad musician. Music is 75 percent science. You have to toil! But if you want to be a bad painter—go ahead, you can be one right away, without any special training. I have lots and lots of friends who are bad painters.

You might argue that in order to dance ballet, you also have to spend a lot of time and effort on training. That's so. But the ballet depends on purely physical abilities much more than music does. People say: how graceful that ballerina is! Excuse me, but a beautiful, young woman who is graceful in everyday life will be graceful on the stage as well. Being "graceful" is not an artistic quality. That's why I say that physiology is a greater component of dance than it is of music.

And that's why I feel that the most important thing in ballet is a talented choreographer. And precision in embodying his ideas. That's why Balanchine always demanded precision from his dancers. He was obsessed with precision. And he was right: carelessness in performance destroys any art, but ballet most of all. Balanchine often spoke of this.

They say that for Balanchine ballet was woman. I feel that ballet for him was music. That's why his significance for me goes beyond the realm of ballet per se. He was the only true choreographer-musician.

When I met Balanchine in Monte Carlo, I was not particularly interested in ballet. I simply liked some dancers more than others. I remember being excited by Pierre Vladimirov, the premier dancer of Diaghilev's troupe. He was so heavy that when he leaped, I froze: I was afraid he would smash the scenery and cause a catastrophe. (Much later Balanchine invited Vladimirov to teach at his New York ballet school.)

Balanchine stood out from other ballet people. I loved being in his company. His presence, his tales and opinions made no less an impression on me than did his ballets. He told me that his father was a Georgian composer, and I liked that too. We agreed on everything; sometimes it seemed to me that we thought like the same person. That's what you call real friendship. Things reached the point where people started to confuse us. Rita, my first wife, told me she sometimes called out "Nathan!" when it was Georges. And Balanchine, amused, recalled that people would try to get his attention by calling him Milstein!

Balanchine was only spreading his wings in Monte Carlo in 1926, as were Horowitz and I. We were glad to have left Russia behind us and we were trying on our new "European life." We were all earning very little, including Balanchine. (In those days dancers made pennies.) Lifar lived better than the rest, but that was because he was Diaghilev's lover. (People used to wonder if Balanchine hadn't become one of Diaghilev's favorites, too. We just laughed, Georges's interest in women was so obvious.) Now dancers are paid significantly more. That's fair, and much of it is due, of course, to Rudolf Nureyev. His defection in 1961 attracted worldwide media attention, and with it a broad audience. Ballet suddenly became a profitable commercial venture.

By the way, Diaghilev's last favorite was the quite heterosexual youth Igor Markevitch, who subsequently became a famous conductor. He married Nijinsky's daughter, Kyra. Markevitch was a talented man, but I didn't like him much. There was something hidden and wary about him.

Balanchine was lucky to work for Diaghilev right out of Russia. Georges went through a real European schooling with him. We all learned a lot in Russia, but we lacked European polish. Diaghilev was the ultimate "Russian European." His sophistication was an invaluable example for Balanchine.

But Diaghilev's snobbish tastes were not all-encompassing, and in some directions his influence limited Georges's horizons. That happened with Rachmaninoff's music, which Diaghilev despised. For him it was too emotional.

While in Russia, Georges—like Horowitz and me—adored Rachmaninoff's music. As soon as he found himself in Europe, Balanchine went to see Rachmaninoff, who had left Russia a few years earlier. Balanchine asked for permission to do a ballet to "Vocalise," one of Rachmaninoff's most beautiful works. It seems especially created for dancing—it has so much fluidity! (I'll never forget playing it with my friend Piatigorsky, for the composer himself.) Typical of the man, Rachmaninoff brushed Balanchine off. He must have thought that the young, still unknown choreographer would slap together a terrible burlesque out of his "Vocalise."

Rachmaninoff was wrong, of course. Balanchine would have made a gorgeous ballet out of it! But at that moment the possibility of their collaboration collapsed. And later, Diaghilev's distaste for Rachmaninoff rubbed off on Balanchine. And Georges never did do a single ballet to the music of that great composer. It's a pity.

When Diaghilev died suddenly in 1929, it was a terrible blow for ballet, and for Balanchine. As for many others, Diaghilev's death struck like a catastrophe. Yet I think that once he became independent, Balanchine developed into a much more interesting choreographer. It would have been harder for him to create an individual style in Diaghilev's shadow.

After Diaghilev's death and later, in the early thirties, Balanchine and I often met in Paris, continuing our animated discussions on musical problems. I loved wandering around Paris with Nicholas Nabokov, Balanchine, and Pavlik Tchelitchew. We were inseparable. By then we had some money and were able to patronize the best and most expensive Russian restaurant in Paris, Chez Korniloff.

One of the restaurant's habitués was Feodor Chaliapin himself. His striking photographs in operatic roles hung on the walls. Famous Pavel Milyukov—the former minister of foreign affairs for the provisional government, now political leader of the Russian émigré community and publisher of the émigré newspaper *Poslednie novosti*—was often there. Prince Felix Yousoupov and his wife, a beautiful blonde, had their own table. Rich American tourists came specially to get a glimpse of Yousoupov, asking, "Where's the prince who killed Rasputin?"

The owner himself was famous—former chef to the tsar. Imposing, gray-haired, in a snow-white apron, Korniloff shook hands with guests and traded a joke or a bit of political news. It was very important to have Korniloff come to your table. Otherwise you were a nobody.

You could have icy vodka and excellent black caviar at Chez Korniloff. They also made the best chicken Kiev in the world. As everybody today knows, it's chicken breast filled with hot butter, but back then the cutlet posed a danger for novices; inexperienced American tourists would jab a fork into the cutlet and hot butter would spurt all over their fancy evening dress. So, for Americans the maître d' would make the first cut. But habitués of Chez Korniloff were left to look inside the cutlet on their own: that was a sign of Korniloff's trust.

Chez Korniloff flourished for many years. And then, literally overnight, it disappeared. The Russian celebrities vanished—they either died or moved to America—and with them vanished the tourists, who had no one to stare at anymore.

Balanchine had always appreciated good food, but in Paris he became a real gourmet. The same with music. He had learned to dig into music back in Russia, but Paris honed his taste, made Georges a real musical connoisseur.

His next European teacher after Diaghilev was Igor Stravinsky, before whose authority Balanchine bowed. Yet his artistic intuition was such that he could even argue a musical point with Stravinsky, and win! That's how exquisite a musician Georges had become.

Georges had always loved Tchaikovsky, and Stravinsky, happily, reaffirmed that love in him. For Stravinsky, Tchaikovsky was a Russian composer who crafted his work in a European manner. For Balanchine he was the foremost creator of great ballet music. The famous St. Petersburg choreographer Marius Petipa made a path for Tchaikovsky's ballets to the stage. Balanchine adored Petipa and, I think, wanted, like a new Petipa, to create a world of Stravinsky ballets.

My Friend George Balanchine

From a professional viewpoint Stravinsky and Balanchine had a lot in common: great talent, mastery, the ability to work fast. But it's hard to imagine two people more different! Balanchine was a loyal friend, faithful to the end, especially if the friendship began in his youth. I don't think Stravinsky had any real friendships.

Their attitude toward financial matters also differed radically. Money per se meant nothing to Balanchine; he was able to get by on a bare minimum as long as he had something to eat and a roof over his head. Never once in his life did he sacrifice friendship or principle for money.

In the late thirties the famous film mogul Samuel Goldwyn invited Balanchine to Hollywood to choreograph dance numbers for two films. The autocratic Goldwyn spared no expense, and paid Balanchine up to fifteen hundred dollars a week. An enormous salary in those days! I was in Los Angeles then, giving concerts. In fact, Balanchine flew to California early to spend some time with me.

We appeared everywhere together, we even went to buy suits together. Literally every suit fit Balanchine perfectly, one more elegantly than the last. He ended up buying a marvelous ready-made gray suit for twelve dollars. Not a single one suited me! I'm not meant to buy off the rack. . . .

I introduced Balanchine to my cousin Lewis Milestone. Lewis and I were not only cousins but friends. When I first came to America late in 1929, I visited Hollywood. Milestone's secretary came to see me and asked, "Where are you from?"

"Odessa."

"And where is your father from?"

"Kishinev."

"What's his name?"

"Miron."

This man told me that there was a film director in Hollywood named Milestone, who came from Kishinev and remembered that when he was leaving Russia he was told about a small cousin who played the violin.

Lewis invited me to the set, where they were filming a scene from his movie *All Quiet on the Western Front*, which was destined to become a classic. In this particular scene the German soldiers had to cross a bridge while being fired upon. A squad of firemen brought in for the occasion was busily hosing down the ground, trying to re-create the mud through which the soldiers had to slog. But the hot California sun dried the earth quickly, and the film crew was having a hard time.

Milestone used to give huge parties. At one, I remember, there were three bands, and you could hear waltzes, tangos, and jazz from different parts of the house. People there enjoyed life, dancing and flirting wildly, and playing baccarat and blackjack for large stakes.

Lewis belonged to a charmed circle of celebrities that included Charlie Chaplin and Mary Pickford. It was a merry group, but politically they leaned toward Soviet Russia, which would not have suited Balanchine at all.

In Hollywood, Balanchine had a lot of free time because the production on the film kept being postponed. But Goldwyn paid his salary anyway. It was marvelous, we had a great time, until I was supposed to leave. Balanchine grew sad and went to Goldwyn to find out how much longer he had to wait until filming began. He was told it would be a minimum of four or five weeks. Balanchine said to me, "I can't go on like this. In New York I have old friends, Kopeikin is waiting for me, I miss eating pirozhki. New York is much more interesting than Hollywood. I don't want to sit around waiting and doing nothing." He packed his bags and left without a thought for the money he would lose. Friendship, old pals, talking about music were more important to him.

I should say a few words about Nikolai Kopeikin, a friend of Georges's and mine since the Diaghilev days. A Russian émigré, he was a rehearsal pianist for Diaghilev and then, in New York, at Balanchine's theater. Stravinsky liked him. Plump, sweet, not very interested in the opposite sex, he was a good accompanist—like Georges, that is, more a musician than a solid professional. Kopeikin and I played a few concerts together, but mostly we met in Georges's company.

A lot of people took advantage of Balanchine's generosity. He was an easy touch for a loan, and crooked impresarios regularly made money on him. I remember, in the post-Diaghilev period, Balanchine worked for such a crook, who pompously called himself Colonel de Basil. That scoundrel was no colonel. And no de Basil, either. In Paris he'd gotten a third-rate job in Prince Alexis Zereteli's émigré opera enterprise, and suddenly he surfaced, pretending to be a Russian aristocrat, and a rich one at that!

Getting the "de" and a false military rank was not hard in those days. But where did that character get his money? I think I've figured out his little secret: the money didn't belong to de Basil or even to Zereteli, his backer. The star soprano in Zereteli's opera enterprise was Galina Kuznetsova, and all the money came from her. Or rather, from her incredibly rich patron.

De Basil used Balanchine and then threw him out. Luckily, Georges met a young visionary, the wealthy American Lincoln Kirstein. Kirstein brought Balanchine to the U.S.A. and helped him create a ballet school and theater there. Already a famous choreographer in Paris, Balanchine in New York became a legend. He also became George (instead of Georges): that was the last transformation of his name.

In New York Balanchine remained as indifferent to money as he had been in Monte Carlo. He didn't like talking about it. As soon as conversation turned to financial matters, he got up and left. Kirstein tried in vain to force him to pay attention to the financial details of coming productions, for they were always short of money. Kirstein would tell Balanchine, "You'd better do something!" Balanchine would shrug him off. And, of course, Kirstein would have to deal with the problems himself.

The turning point came in 1963, when the Ford Foundation gave the Balanchine school and theater an enormous grant for those days, several million dollars. Before that Balanchine hadn't even gotten a salary, either as director of the ballet or as director of the school; he'd made do with royalties from his ballets. But the foundation people made a condition that Balanchine be given a steady salary. After all, they couldn't give a grant to an organization whose director worked for free! So for the first time, Balanchine was making real money.

Kirstein played an important role in obtaining that grant—like everything else, it was done through him. Kirstein is an extraordinary, original man of impressive stature who resembles the stern principal of an old St. Petersburg *Gymnasium*. As far as I know, in the fifty years of working together Balanchine and Kirstein never had a single moment of animosity.

In 1939, with the start of the war, I moved from Europe to America and settled in New York. George and I renewed our tradition of evening walks. We rarely looked into elegant restaurants, seeking instead a cozy spot that would be more like what we were used to. Gradually the Russian Tea Room became our favorite meeting place. This restaurant next to Carnegie Hall later became quite famous, but back then it was still a purely Russian establishment, with Russian owners and primarily Russian customers, including Mikhail Fokine and Rachmaninoff. George and I met there to exchange the latest political news, to gossip, to talk about art. And, of course, to enjoy delicious Russian food!

We two were demanding clients because of what we knew about gastronomy. Balanchine would personally go to the kitchen and help them prepare chicken Kiev the right way. And he was permitted to do that! It was a sign of great respect on the part of Tolya, the maître d'hôtel of the Russian Tea Room.

Whenever George and I showed up, Tolya would come out to greet us. We had a permanent "loge" reserved for us until late in the evening, by which time we'd have made up our minds whether to go to the ballet or to the Russian Tea Room. Our group included my first wife, Rita, Kopeikin, and Valentin Pavlovsky—a sturdy Siberian and obliging pianist, with whom I performed often in those years. Pavlovsky was an open and friendly man whom even the aloof Rachmaninoff liked.

We would spend hours over our Russian borsch, pirozhki, and chicken Kiev, debating the political developments. I remember Balanchine's gloomy mood after the collapse of France. He couldn't understand why so many Frenchmen welcomed the Nazis. And we recalled how the French foreign minister had foolishly congratulated Hitler on the occasion of Austria's *Anschluss*.

Gradually the restaurant would empty, leaving only Balanchine and me and patient Tolya, who also joined the political discussions.

My Friend George Balanchine

We could stay till morning at the Russian Tea Room—no one chased us out—because we were such good customers.

This is all in the realm of memories now, including the legendary chicken Kiev. It's a catastrophe now—like eating at Howard Johnson's. (Just imagine the chicken Kiev you would get at Howard Johnson's.) For a while the only good Russian food in Manhattan—real, rough borsch, pirozhki, and herring—was at the Russian Bear, but I believe it has closed. . . .

I often visited Balanchine at his ballet school on Madison Avenue. Girls flitted all over the place, with Balanchine watching them like a hawk and sniffling all the while (a habit developed from having a lung removed when he was young after contracting tuberculosis). Balanchine's remarks to his pupils were always precise and businesslike. He was a model pedagogue, because, as I've stressed, he knew exactly what he wanted. (I also know exactly what I want both in my craft and in my teaching. That's another thing we had in common.)

Exactness of intention produces elegance of style. That's why the dance movements Balanchine invented look so incredibly elegant.

Balanchine also liked elegant things and clothing. But of course he didn't concentrate on that, being first of all a very busy man: he had two major organizations to run—the school and the theater. And then, he wasn't a narcissist. But since elegance was in his nature, he always looked like a dandy. As I've said, everything fit him perfectly, even when he allowed himself a touch of eccentricity, like a shoestring tie in the Texas manner.

George exuded refinement. (Which is not the privilege of the upper classes; simple people can often be *raffiné*—just recall the spiritual type of Russian peasant in Leo Tolstoy's writing.) He was also enormously charming. It was impossible to take offense at George, even though he was a direct man who never avoided giving his opinion. He could be sharp, yet even when he criticized someone's art he did not try to cut the person down.

Balanchine, even though he adored music, rarely attended concerts. He would come to my house, I'd put on a record, and he would quietly enjoy it. If he didn't like it, he would say, "Nathan, enough." That was it, without any demeaning tirades.

251

But his opinions on ballet were another matter. Here George could be ruthless: "That's just a bluff, that's shit." Balanchine didn't care a whit for modern dance. On the other hand, he considered Fred Astaire the greatest dancer and choreographer. And he adored the Fred Astaire–Ginger Rogers movies; he would watch them time and again, enchanted especially by her beauty. No, dance was not a highfalutin art for Balanchine. Virtuoso Astaire twirled fast, leaped agilely, and looked elegant, and that was enough to get Balanchine's highest marks. George did not look for particular depth in Fred Astaire's art. His attitude was sober but without demagoguery.

It was the same way George shrugged off critical articles that analyzed his ballets from a metaphysical point of view. He paid no attention to the critics, saying, "First they criticized me stupidly, and now they praise me stupidly." People forget that New York ballet critics first met Balanchine with bayonets; only after he became an acknowledged master did they fly into raptures over any of his works.

Balanchine made his debut in the U.S.A. with a choreographic interpretation of Tchaikovsky's "Sérénade." And, as has happened since with other of his ballets, the American critics first roundly denounced it, only to praise it to the skies years later. As for me, I love all Balanchine's ballets to music by Tchaikovsky. His *Serenade* I liked from the first time I saw it! It reminds me of Ivan Turgenev's love stories. *Serenade*, of course, depicts romantic love—but with restraint and wisdom, so typical of George. He was a very sensual man but ever controlled, even secretive. I was his friend for many years, but I always sensed a mystery about him . . . a mystery he managed to hide in his ballets.

His *Ballet impériale* to Tchaikovsky's Second Piano Concerto is a fantastic thing: a real imperial work—majestic, lofty, and very Russian. And his *Allegro brillante* set to the Third Piano Concerto delights me too. George had a wonderful sense of Tchaikovsky, whether interpreting the cheerful works or the tragic ones.

He and I often discussed Tchaikovsky's music and fate. I remember Balanchine being amused by my story of how we played "Sérénade" in Stolyarsky's class in prerevolutionary Odessa: our group of boys included David Oistrakh and the little virtuoso Misha Fainget, the "miniature Kreisler." Balanchine told me how much Stravinsky loved Tchaikovsky. True, Stravinsky never did say anything nasty about Tchaikovsky. His homage to Tchaikovsky—the ballet *Le Baiser de la fée*, marvelously choreographed by Balanchine—is a pastiche of Tchaikovsky's works redone with Stravinsky's brilliant but rather cold mastery.

Balanchine and I agreed that Tchaikovsky had been a likable man. How he had loved Glinka and Mozart! He once wrote to his patron Mme von Meck describing how he had listened to Mozart's G Minor Quintet at a concert. Tears rolled down his cheeks, and he had to leave his seat so that people wouldn't notice. He stood for the rest of the concert, hidden behind a column. I've read Tchaikovsky on music: no composer has ever written so clearly, intelligently, and elegantly.

Was Tchaikovsky a homosexual? Balanchine, like Stravinsky, tended to think so. It's hard to say definitely now, since in old Russia such things were hardly advertised. Probably the young musicians who formed Tchaikovsky's retinue were attracted to him, but I believe as a master, a teacher. He was a kindly, amiable man who helped many people.

There is no doubt that Tchaikovsky suffered; that's why his music so often expresses some kind of struggle with fate. We all remember the finale of the Sixth (*Pathétique*) Symphony. (By the way, it's typical of Balanchine not to have used any of Tchaikovsky's symphonies in their entirety for ballet. As he once said, "Why ornament music that speaks for itself?")

Tchaikovsky was an introvert, like Balanchine. Maybe that's why Balanchine could intuit so much about Tchaikovsky's character. He did not believe that Tchaikovsky died of cholera, but rather that his death was a suicide. Various such theories have been proposed in recent years. Some maintain that Tchaikovsky poisoned himself. Probably we will never know the truth.

We can't judge Tchaikovsky. He was a profoundly Russian man. Yet somehow we want him to have behaved like Immanuel Kant, who was so precise and punctual that the people of Königsberg set their clocks by him.

I've heard that in his later years Balanchine would sometimes show up at rehearsal and announce, "I talked with Tchaikovsky on the telephone last night, and he told me to do this and that." Some of his dancers actually believed it (many of them probably didn't even know that Tchaikovsky was dead); others thought it the eccentricity of an old choreographer. I think it was a smart idea, referring to Tchaikovsky's "authority." Balanchine no longer had the energy to argue, and it must have been hard for him to convince skeptically inclined young people. But here he didn't have to try: "Tchaikovsky said," and that's that.

Balanchine's most popular ballet is *The Nutcracker*, which in New York is as much a part of Christmas as the tree and Santa Claus. People who saw *The Nutcracker* as children at Balanchine's theater now bring their grandchildren to enjoy the Christmas fairy tale. I am delighted every time by his production and Tchaikovsky's music. Balanchine and I talked about *The Nutcracker* a lot. Now that's first-rate Tchaikovsky! It is full of marvelous compositional inventions. And it's truly modern, sounding as fresh as if it had been written today. In orchestrating *The Nutcracker*, Tchaikovsky was looking a hundred years ahead. (Richard Strauss, who adored Tchaikovsky, told me that he didn't know any better orchestration than Tchaikovsky's. And Strauss knew his orchestration.)

The music of *The Nutcracker* is imbued with an incredible nostalgia, as are some of the best Russian poems. And its waltzes are so unmistakably poetic! Tchaikovsky appreciated the spirit of the waltz better than anyone, you can recognize his waltzes from the first notes. Next to Tchaikovsky Ravel is just a craftsman, mechanically transcribing Viennese waltzes. (Ravel was one of the very rare cases where Balanchine and I didn't agree on music. George adored Ravel and set several ballets to his compositions. I can't understand that enthusiasm, except as a case of sentimentality. Balanchine was the first to choreograph Ravel's opera *L'Enfant et les sortilèges*. The composer was still alive then. A tiny Chekhovian character. . . . That's how I remember Ravel.)

It gives me pleasure that one of Balanchine's ballets with Tchaikovsky's music was choreographed at my suggestion. Here's how it happened: I had recorded Tchaikovsky's Waltz-Scherzo with an orchestra—I recall that Robert Irving, longtime musical director of Balanchine's theater, conducted—and it was a very successful record. I played it for Balanchine, he liked it, and I began persuading him that it could be a marvelous ballet. Balanchine nodded. But the surprise lay ahead.

Some time later Balanchine said, "Come to the theater! You'll see something interesting!" It was the ballet *Waltz-Scherzo*! Tchaikovsky's piece is a brilliant concert number, and Balanchine's ballet was just like it—a soaring bravura work. I was thrilled that I had suggested the composition to George. During the intermission Balanchine came over to me and said, "Well? Did you like it?" And he sniffed, the way he did when he was excited. . . .

I remember that Balanchine's *Four Temperaments*, set to Paul Hindemith's music, was on the same program. I was involved with that composition too.

Before the war, Balanchine rented an apartment on the corner of East Fifty-second Street and Fifth Avenue, next door to Cartier's. He held regular musical soirées, in which I participated. Now as I understand it, a rich Frenchwoman helped Balanchine commission a piano sextet from Hindemith for one of these soirées. I remember the musicians gathered at Balanchine's apartment—in addition to myself, there was Kopeikin, the violinist Samuel Dushkin, the marvelous cellist from Russia Raya Garbuzova, and the wonderful violist Leon Barzin, a Belgian. (Barzin later married a Kellogg heiress, gave up the viola, and took up conducting. A real musician, Barzin conducted at Balanchine's theater, even though he apparently didn't need the money. We recorded Max Bruch's First Violin Concerto and the Mendelssohn concerto together.)

We all played through Hindemith's piece, and I found myself (as first violinist) not liking it much: it seemed rather dry and uninteresting music. So as I played, I didn't try very hard. (On that occasion I should have been second violin instead of first!)

They say Hindemith was paid five hundred dollars for that work, so even though *The Four Temperaments* isn't great music, it still was a bargain for Balanchine and his financier: Hindemith's name was widely known by then. (For the sake of comparison, Louis Krasner paid, as I remember it, fifteen hundred dollars each for the violin concertos he commissioned from Berg and Schoenberg much earlier.)

I don't care much for Hindemith, but for Balanchine *The Four Temperaments* became a great success. It is one of his most daring works, even radical. I feel in it the revolutionary spirit of the Russian avant-garde theater of our youth.

I had something to do with a few other of Balanchine's ballets, too. I suggested he do something with Johann Sebastian Bach's D Minor Concerto for two violins, and partly as a result we have the famous ballet *Concerto barocco*. For me it's one of George's greatest creations: inspired, with sculptural terraces of movement similar to Bach's own musical terraces.

Balanchine had a subtle sense of Bach's music, which is not very typical of people from Russia, since Bach was not popular over there. But Balanchine and I listened to many recordings of Bach. I remember him saying that he was attracted by two things in Bach: the mathematical basis of his music and, at the same time, its purely emotional and unfeigned striving for God.

Bach's faith in God was total, all-encompassing. Almost anyone today, however sincerely devout, couldn't believe with such unquestioning completeness. That's why Stravinsky's religious music sounds to me so theatrical and, therefore, suspect.

As I understand it, Balanchine faced the same problem. His choreography of Bach's *St. Matthew Passion* in New York during the war is characteristic of his approach. It was an attempt to recreate a miracle play on the stage of the Metropolitan Opera. Leopold Stokowski conducted. Balanchine set his students—depicting Pilate, Peter, Judas, and so on—in beautiful groups. Bach's music steadily prepared anticipation of Christ's appearance. But in Balanchine's production there was no Christ onstage. Instead, there was a glow. . . .

I think that Balanchine found the perfect, subtle way out. In Bach's day miracle plays were an integral part of people's lives. Relying on such naiveté was an impossible alternative for Balanchine. Modern man couldn't accept Christ being impersonated by a ballet school student.

I was midwife, if I can call it that, for yet another famous Balanchine ballet. George often came to our Park Avenue apartment. We had lots of guests, with Balanchine usually sitting at the piano, noodling. The jeweler Claude Arpels was a guest one time. Balanchine and Arpels got to talking, liked each other, and became friends. Arpels showed Balanchine his collection of precious stones. Balanchine was thrilled. Not covetously, but purely aesthetically. After all, he was from the Caucasus, and anyone from the Caucasus loves jewelry! Balanchine kept repeating, "What marvelous stones!"

And so Thérèse and I started to tease him. "Why don't you choreograph a ballet on jewels? You've never done anything like it." To tell the truth, I didn't expect him to do it. The notion seemed a bit representational, while Balanchine preferred abstract ideas.

Suddenly Balanchine did a ballet on jewels! It was a huge hit. There were three parts: "Emeralds," "Rubies," and "Diamonds," with music by Gabriel Fauré, Stravinsky, and Tchaikovsky—sort of an homage to three countries: France, America, and Imperial Russia. The Russian part was all in white, to music from Tchaikovsky's Third Symphony, and made you think of St. Petersburg and the Maryinsky Theater. That's "Diamonds." "Emeralds," in green tones, set to Fauré, is a reminiscence of France. The red "Rubies" is Stravinsky, in jazz rhythms. It was impossible to get tickets to *Jewels*. Arpels was so proud! And grateful to us for introducing him to Balanchine. . . .

George's fame kept growing. It made little difference in his personality or manner; he was still the same Georges of our youth— honest, unpretentious, simple in his tastes. He moved to Central Park South, not far from the Hampshire House Hotel. It was a stone's throw from his ballet school, and he walked there every morning—that was his stroll. (I can't remember Balanchine ever in a car! Though, of course, he had one . . . and I know that he adored all kinds of gadgets and enjoyed them like a child.)

One thing did change in the behavior of the "new" Balanchine. At work he was still surrounded by ballerinas, of course, but outside work . . . it became more and more unusual to see him with women. With his wife (whoever she was at the time), yes, but girlfriends would disappear as soon as friends came over. It hadn't always been like that, he hadn't particularly paid attention to the rules of etiquette before. But he hadn't been so famous before, either, so there had been no need to be *comme il faut*.

I don't think Balanchine ever married Choura Danilova. After Tamara Geva, his next wife was Vera Zorina. Her real name was Brigitta Hartwig—her mother was Norwegian, her father German—but the point was that Zorina was starting out as a ballerina, and in those years ballet was considered so much a Russian profession that potential stars took Russian-sounding stage names. That's how British ballerinas named Sokolova and Markova surfaced.

By the way, it wasn't only in ballet, but in music, too, that a Russian aura—or at least a Slavic one—seemed glamorous. I've mentioned the conductor Leopold Stokowski, and my American debut took place in 1929 with the Philadelphia Orchestra under him. "Stoki," as people called him, was an extremely eccentric personality. One of his peculiarities was turning himself into an ultra-Slav. Meeting me, he insisted on speaking French with a thick Russian accent. (I was on a ship with Ray Milland, the actor, once. He turned out to be a neighbor of Stokowski's, lived in the same building. When I mentioned the conductor's strange pseudo-Russian accent, Milland laughed and said, "His real name is Stokes! He is pure Welsh!")

During the war I was appearing with Stokowski. The concert was a benefit, and after the rehearsal we were photographed for publicity. I listened in astonishment as Stokowski ordered the photographer around in broken Russian-English. Whatever for?

In contrast with such eccentricity, Balanchine's absolute naturalness was endearing. Balanchine also spoke English with an accent, but his accent never grated—after all, his native tongue was Russian. And here, in America, the majority of his friends were Russian. That's probably why Balanchine's English was serviceable, no more.

I know how important the native tongue is for immigrants. They don't want to forget it, to break away from their native culture, and so they don't submerge themselves totally into the foreign language. Another example of this ambivalent attitude toward foreign languages was Stravinsky: only after the death or estrangement of all his old Russian friends, and then the close relationship with Robert Craft, who had moved into his house, did the composer come to master English. However, he continued speaking Russian with his wife, Vera.

Once upon a time, in the eighteenth and nineteenth centuries, the Russian nobility spoke at least two languages: French as well as Russian. Just think of Pushkin's letters written in French. Or Tolstoy's novels, with pages of dialogue in French. That's realistic: the Russian court preferred to speak French; it set them apart from the ordinary people. But then, gradually, this bilingualism disappeared. Now, as a rule, a person lives in the milieu of one language, and all the others are more or less foreign to him.

I think that Balanchine understood instinctively that a Russian choreographer who spoke perfect English would seem and sound unnatural. His mistakes in English merely added to his charm.

Balanchine spoke English with Vera Zorina, even though she knew some Russian. I knew Zorina quite well—we all called her Brigitta. Of all of Balanchine's wives, she was, I think, the most sophisticated.

I met her first in Chicago, where I was performing in concert. Balanchine was producing something there. We met, and he introduced her to me as "Brigitta, my wife." This was, if I'm not mistaken, in 1943, at The Pump Room, during some reception where the famous Dolores Del Rio was present. I remember that evening also because the owner of the restaurant promised George and me hamburgers that we wouldn't forget for a long time. "From the best steaks!" Alas, George and I were disappointed. Apparently the best steaks don't guarantee the best hamburgers.

Now they tell stories about how madly Balanchine was in love with Zorina. Supposedly he stood under her window, wept, and generally behaved like a fool. I'm sure that these stories are nonsense. I can't even picture Balanchine weeping.

In my opinion their marriage was more or less accidental. Without a doubt, Brigitta was Balanchine's most beautiful wife. An unbelievable beauty! Yet there was something Germanic in her looks, and as a ballerina, she also looked very German, quite masculine. It seemed strange: not Balanchine's balletic ideal at all. On the other hand, Brigitta was more than ten years younger than George. . . .

Zorina learned a lot from George. He contributed to making her a real star, on stage and in films. Her best-known role was in the Broadway musical *I Married an Angel*. But she never developed into a major dancer or actress. (I have to note her honesty. I don't think that Zorina had any pretensions to being a great actress or ballerina. She simply wanted to be a star.)

Brigitta and George moved into his house on Long Island. It was actually a not very glamorous Russian dacha, best left undescribed. Brigitta's Norwegian mother, who spoke German, lived with them. The mother was bored at the dacha, since there was nothing to do there. So, she planted potatoes. When it was time to harvest the potatoes and they needed extra hands, they called on me. In true Russian fashion, I responded; otherwise the potatoes would rot. And so I spent quite a few weekends at the Balanchine-Zorina dacha.

Brigitta, like George, was an introvert. But Balanchine had spontaneity, while Zorina lacked it totally. Both were hardheaded. It was curious to observe their conversations—they were laconic, not at all intellectual. Still, it wasn't the words so much. Tension hung in the air. . . .

It was clear to me that their marriage was falling apart. Balanchine spent less and less time on Long Island, staying instead at his Manhattan apartment. After the war, they divorced. She got the dacha. I introduced Zorina to Goddard Lieberson, who was my music producer at Columbia Records. Lieberson was handsome and pleasant, Zorina, lovely and wise; the romance began almost immediately and was quickly climaxed in marriage.

I think that Lieberson and Zorina complemented each other marvelously. He understood music fairly well and loved to be taken for a musical intellectual. But scratch the surface and you'd find a businessman. His genius at keeping a balance between music and commerce took Lieberson to the top of Columbia Records. There he produced many recordings of Stravinsky's works, which may be his real claim to fame.

My Friend George Balanchine

To distract himself after the divorce, Balanchine went to Paris, having been invited after Serge Lifar was fired as choreographer of the Grand Opéra because of his collaboration with the Nazis. Balanchine used an early Bizet symphony to create for the French one of his best ballets, *Palais de cristal*, now called *Symphony in C*.

The Paris audience went wild! Thérèse and I were in Paris at the time, and naturally we came, together with Nika Nabokov and Pavlik Tchelitchew, to the Grand Opéra to cheer for Balanchine. We adored *Palais de cristal*. It's a masterpiece. Tchelitchew was particularly excited.

Pavel Tchelitchew was one of Balanchine's closest friends. Pavlik was incredibly charming and refined, and was constantly producing new art theories. Once, Tchelitchew told me that he was going to paint the human face in its totality, from all sides simultaneously—including from inside! I asked, "Are you going to depict the brains too, Pavlik?" With contagious enthusiasm, radiant Pavlik replied, "But of course!" I am not sure if Tchelitchew ever carried out the idea—like so many of his inspirations. (In general I don't understand artists who give you theories instead of paintings. Did Picasso create theories? Yet I would be glad to hang any of his one-eyed or four-eyed women on my wall—and would enjoy it. Picasso's complete artistic statement is in his works. No theorizing was necessary.)

Pavlik Tchelitchew did take Thérèse and me to meet the notorious Leonor Fini, the designer of *Palais de cristal*. Fini turned out to be a tall, handsome woman, naked except for a robe and a slew of cats literally hanging from her. She had ten or twelve cats on her! They were all of different colors, all mewing and leaping off and back onto her. And they stank terribly. Thérèse got sick. I don't blame her: it was very weird, with those cats peering into your eyes like evil spirits. But Pavlik adored Fini, even though he wasn't particularly involved with females. I think he saw a kindred eccentric spirit in her.

Balanchine also adored cats. But luckily he had only one cat at home, called Murka, which he taught many fancy tricks. In 1979 Balanchine gave me a photo of himself with the cat, inscribed in Russian: "To sweet and dear friend Nathan, from Murka the Cat and George."

My friend Vladimir Horowitz was a big cat lover, too. At one time he had five cats at home. Five! Taking care of that many must be a full-time occupation. And then you probably have to sit by the TV and watch commercials: which kind of food to buy for the cats, what time to feed them, how to medicate them, and so on. People get attached to cats. I remember Horowitz crying when one of his cats died.

Balanchine liked to say that he could make a prima ballerina even out of a cat, not to speak of a normal, young, fluid woman. He usually added, "Of course, the material makes a difference. One ballerina may have a better complexion than another. One may be more graceful, another faster. But a beautiful woman onstage is not yet art, only material. Ballet begins when the choreographer comes! Dancers themselves don't know what they can achieve, what they're capable of. Only the choreographer knows that."

As Balanchine matured, his relations with women became more those of a Pygmalion with a procession of Galateas. Interestingly, Balanchine's Pygmalion influence applied only to dance. His women did not speak like him or think like him; they had their own tastes in food and dress. And they entertained and amused themselves differently than did George. But in ballet, they were his creations totally.

Almost immediately after his divorce from Zorina, Balanchine married Maria Tallchief, a striking-looking half Indian (from the Osage tribe). I don't think that George was madly in love with Tallchief, but he was in an emotional vacuum just then, and she filled it. Balanchine liked the fact that his new wife was Indian. It seemed exotic to him and, at the same time, made him feel *echt* American. It was then that Balanchine began dressing like a cowboy, with those ubiquitous Texan string ties (although he'd begun watching westerns before that).

Balanchine didn't spend much time with his wives outside the theater and ballet classes. Ballerinas generally have to work long hours—even more than musicians—so it was always the same story: instead of joining us to eat a bowl of borsch and a pirozhok, Balanchine's girlfriends had to go to class. "I have to go stretch my legs" was the refrain. And Balanchine and we would sit and eat to our delight (and perhaps to the detriment of our health).

All this talk of Balanchine's taste in food may make it seem that he was some sort of Gargantua. Not at all! Balanchine was a gourmet, but he rarely overindulged. He ate sparingly (as was evident in his lean figure), but the food was always of the best quality. In that area, as in ballet, he was a perfectionist. He loved to cook. And in the kitchen, just as in the ballet, he knew exactly what he wanted to achieve.

Once Thérèse and I were giving a party in our New York apartment. We invited quite a few people, around forty. Balanchine announced, "I'll make the kulebiaka. But no one must interfere. I will be alone in the kitchen, and even Thérèse can't come in."

Kulebiaka is a marvelous Russian dish—like a big pie, with fish or meat baked in pastry. It is usually stuffed with all sorts of things—mushrooms, rice, eggs—and served with a sauce. It requires great virtuosity to prepare. Thérèse bought all the ingredients, and then the kitchen was turned over to Balanchine, who proceeded to make an unforgettable kulebiaka.

I entered into a culinary bout with George for that evening, selecting a lighter-weight category for myself—borschok. It's the same old Russian borsch but with a fancy name and Polish overtones. The recipe was my own proud invention: a simple, even primitive base—Manischewitz store-bought borsch—but then I did variations on the old theme, adding spices. (You need a little artistic imagination in these things.) For my Polish borschok I used tomato paste, sugar, vinegar, and lemon. Adding this and that, I tasted and added again. The hardest part, the biggest secret, is in knowing how to use the lemon, which is very potent; it can kill even the vinegar.

The dinner began with Russian zakuski, then the main program opened with Balanchine's fantastic kulebiaka, followed by my borschok. We ended with a great kissel, the traditional Russian fruit pudding. The guests were ecstatic, but for me the greatest kudo of the evening was Balanchine's admission that my borschok was even better than his!

Because Balanchine had so many wives, people sometimes talk about him as if he were a Don Juan. Balanchine was a womanizer, of course—as I've already noted, he was very sensual—but he always sought permanent relations with women, not quick liaisons. George was prepared to get married every time, and what kind of a Don Juan is that?

Besides which, women cursed Don Juan after he'd jilted them; they pursued him and swore revenge. There was nothing of the kind with George. Even after he'd broken with them, his wives and girlfriends continued to adore him. For them, he remained teacher and master. One possible explanation would be the age difference. When Maria Tallchief married Balanchine, she was half his age. The gap in age between his next wife, Tanaquil Le Clercq, and Balanchine was even greater.

Tanaquil Le Clercq was a tall, thin woman, delicate as a figurine, and rather fragile. Her long legs seemed too long, like a gazelle's. Le Clercq was of French origin, but she looked more the British refined type. In 1956, when Balanchine was fifty-two and Le Clercq twenty-seven, a tragedy befell them. During the ballet's tour in Copenhagen, Tanaquil became paralyzed. It was poliomyelitis.

Balanchine was in despair. The most horrible part was that ten years earlier, George had choreographed a small ballet for the students of his school in which he'd danced a figure in black, symbolizing polio. In the course of the story, he touched the very young Tanaquil and left her paralyzed. Everything ended happily in the ballet—the heroine got better—but in life, alas, it was not so. Tanaquil remains paralyzed from the waist down.

George did everything possible for her—and more. He was husband, father, physician, nursemaid. He cooked for her, he invented special exercises. I visited frequently at their Central Park South apartment, and I was touched watching George taking care of Tanaquil.

Their marriage lasted quite a long time, longer than the others. If not for Balanchine's obsession with Suzanne Farrell, perhaps Tanaquil would have remained his wife. After all, Balanchine was by then a public figure, and as they say, *noblesse oblige*; Balanchine would not have permitted himself to divorce again over a momentary fling.

My Friend George Balanchine

So he and Tanaquil, though living in separate apartments, were still considered man and wife. But then Farrell became more than an infatuation, she became Balanchine's passion.

George was totally immersed in his new love. Farrell was very young, more than forty years younger than Balanchine. She could have been his granddaughter. She was incredibly lovely and extremely talented. For George she was marvelous material, an ideal.

Even though Farrell bowed to him as a choreographer, she did not defer to him otherwise. She had her own life. This was upsetting for Balanchine. In order to marry Farrell, he had divorced Le Clercq. But then Farrell didn't marry him. Instead her husband became Paul Mejia, a dancer from Balanchine's troupe. So, Balanchine and Farrell didn't consummate their relationship. It remained platonic forever, and Balanchine was very disturbed by this.

I remember he would come to my house after a performance with Farrell and Paul Mejia. He would be sad. To distract himself, he would start cooking. That would help a little.

(Balanchine especially loved to make kissel. He usually ate the whole thing himself, without giving anyone else a taste. That's a little like my friend Volodya Horowitz. Volodya didn't know how to cook except for one dish—plum soufflé with cream. He made a wonderful soufflé. But it was very rare for someone to get a taste of it: Horowitz made it, Horowitz ate it. . . . But I'm not complaining; I don't like desserts anyway.)

In order to cheer up the depressed Balanchine after Farrell and Mejia had left, I would start conversations with him on his future plans. "I'll leave the theater," George would say. And I would chime in, "And I'll stop touring." Balanchine would laugh. "Then let's open a small restaurant in New York! I'll put on a small ballet there once in a while and you'll circulate among the tables and play gypsy music . . . or something from Tchaikovsky. . . . Only don't play Bach, they won't appreciate it."

Can you imagine a restaurant like that? The hamburgers would go for fifty or a hundred dollars, no less! In New York a place like that could be successful—people there like expensive and extravagant things.

The situation with Farrell in the theater was growing tense.

When Balanchine offered his hand to a ballerina, it wasn't simply a whim. He pictured her in his future ballets, he began imagining movements for her. Balanchine always married potential stars, not girls from the corps de ballet, some ingenues. But by the same token, when Farrell refused him it became hard for him to work with her, even though he valued her talent highly. Then Farrell and her husband went to Europe, to dance with Maurice Béjart.

This was a tragic period for Balanchine. His friends helped him in everything, and most selfless was his assistant, the sweet Barbara Horgan, whom we all loved. Still, at least in conversations with me, Balanchine kept talking about Farrell; he was very regretful. But then Farrell didn't settle at Béjart's. She decided to return to Balanchine, and when she approached him, she was generously accepted back. I feel that in this unusual situation Balanchine proved the strength of his character. His unrequited love for Farrell turned into high drama for him, but he didn't break. After she returned to the troupe, their relations were no longer even platonic, they were simply professional.

Toward the end Balanchine proclaimed that women had become more important to him than art, because while he understood art somewhat, women were still a complete mystery. It would be extremely naive to believe that. I think Balanchine was winking at us. He could afford to say it, knowing that smart people wouldn't take it at face value. Balanchine knew his own worth, even though he was modest about it.

At school or in rehearsal at the theater, he behaved like the owner, the boss, and many complained about his being a dictator. Nonsense! Dictatorship in art is not at all the same as political dictatorship. Art's essence, its meaning, lies in the dictatorship of genius. And Balanchine didn't put his dancers in jail! He didn't force anything on anyone.

Americans mistakenly transfer their democratic political principles to art. They would like a genius to make artistic decisions only after the majority have voted for them. Balanchine didn't need to discuss his ballets with the people. He knew exactly what he liked, what he wanted to achieve, and how to embody his ideas. So he always spoke softly and didn't even carry a big stick. They complained that he discouraged his ballerinas from marrying. I think he was right! For a music student, male or female, marriage and family are often the end of real practice, the end of artistic development. It happens all the time. . . .

Balanchine and I loved talking politics. He was a very conservatively oriented man but with a broad view, not dogmatic at all. He believed that the state should help the poor and should sponsor culture. And he was extremely pro-American, proud of being an American citizen. He was also pro-Russian (like me) and anti-Soviet (like me).

Some people don't understand that Soviet communism is a degradation of Russia. Balanchine and I were convinced that without Soviet rule Russia would have achieved far greater triumphs both in culture and in science. It is such a talented and potentially wealthy country! The whole world knows the names of the great Russian scientists of the prerevolutionary period—Mendeleev, Mechnikov, Timiriazev, Pavlov. And look what the Soviets did to their academician Sakharov.

Balanchine constantly talked about Russia, he was always immersed in its news. And he missed Russia, perhaps more than I did. But he had made his choice a long time ago, and forever. Balanchine did take his theater to the Soviet Union twice—in 1962 and in 1972—but I know that he didn't want to go there. Yet his theater was always in need of subsidies, and the State Department put pressure on him to travel to the USSR—they considered it an important symbolic act of détente. So he had to agree.

Balanchine's first trip to the Soviet Union almost coincided with Stravinsky's. That was a study in contrasts. For Stravinsky the Soviet trip was largely a question of publicity and, consequently, more money. You might ask, Why would the world-famous and rich Stravinsky care? But Stravinsky was like that—he needed all the publicity he could get, and more. So he behaved himself in the Soviet Union, trying not to criticize or offend the cultural bureaucrats. Perhaps that's why Premier Khrushchev granted him a private audience.

Khrushchev didn't talk to George. But at least the tour of the Balanchine company shook up Soviet concepts of ballet! In Russia during the Stalin years they grew accustomed to ballet performances of one kind only: long and grand and with traditional or patriotic plots. But Balanchine brought plotless works, in which the important thing was the beauty of dance itself. Almost no scenery, the most modest costumes. "Formalism," as the Soviets used to call it.

By the way, Balanchine had been criticized in New York for his stage designs and, even more, the costumes of his ballets. His favorite costume designer was Karinska, who bore the brunt of the New York critics' wrath. But George remained loyal to Karinska and paid no attention to the press. As always, friendship was more important to him than public opinion.

Besides, he had his own concept of stage designs and costumes in ballet. Diaghilev had created a revolution in decor—brightness, a feast of color, an exotic palette—that shook up jaded European theatergoers. Balanchine represented a kind of counterrevolution. He believed that nothing should distract from what was most important on the ballet stage—the dancing. Which is why he felt that in some ballets, especially chamber works, he could let his dancers out onstage in their rehearsal clothes.

(Tellingly, Diaghilev was interested only in the costumes for his male dancers. The ballerinas' outfits were the domain of Diaghilev's female consultants, like the all-powerful Coco Chanel. With Balanchine, it was the opposite: he gave priority to the women's appearance.)

Balanchine's spartan approach to staging worked, particularly in ballets with music by Stravinsky; it gave them a modern look. And so often, as I sat in the audience, I recalled similarly designed revolutionary plays I had attended in the twenties in Moscow.

When Balanchine came to Moscow in 1962, they had already forgotten their own avant-garde ideas. Soviet ballet was strong in technique, but it was musty and provincial. The Balanchine troupe's arrival was like a thunderstorm that cleared the air. George told me how he was surrounded by young Soviet dancers—they came dreaming of something new; they wanted to experiment, the way Balanchine did.

While in the Soviet Union—in contrast to Stravinsky—George was quite outspoken. He saw what his life would have been like if he had stayed in Russia, even if he'd managed to avoid arrest and the camps in Stalin's day. He would have suffocated there, like Prokofiev, Shostakovich, and many other gifted people. After his trips to the Soviet Union, he became even more anti-Soviet.

I'm sometimes asked if Balanchine was a monarchist. Well, yes and no. First of all, he was a democrat, but one does not preclude the other. Balanchine's monarchism was nostalgic. I had only one friend who was a true monarchist, the pianist Alexander Brailowski. A marvelous virtuoso and a sweet man, he would practically faint at the sight of a portrait of the last Russian emperor, Nicholas II. The mere mention of the late monarch's name made him jump up, as if he were at a performance of the imperial anthem "God Save the Tsar" in old Petersburg.

Another question I'm asked about Balanchine is whether he was anti-Semitic. The answer is an emphatic no. He didn't even like Jewish jokes, what's called the "Jewish genre" (neither do I, by the way). Generally, in my relations with Russian friends, I have almost never come across anti-Semitism. Perhaps Stravinsky was a crypto-anti-Semite, but it never surfaced, at least not with me. The same for Rachmaninoff.

I remember a conversation I had with Balanchine. Discussing Tchaikovsky's violin concerto, we agreed that its performers (many of them Russian Jews) present this music in a Jewish manner. Playing the second movement, the Canzonetta, they "weep," figuratively speaking. But the Canzonetta is not Jewish music at all—rather Italian, in fact; a type of barcarole performed by a troubadour.

I remember George liked my idea that the concerto was more European than Russian. It has to be played with great nobility and restraint, in the St. Petersburg style. Balanchine appreciated this reasoning, being himself a real Petersburger. Perhaps that's why he loved Tchaikovsky so. Tchaikovsky's "folk" themes are not Russian but, rather, Petersburgian. (Just as in Schubert you hear Viennese melodies, not Austrian ones.)

Tchaikovsky himself, with his silvery beard and gentle gaze, was the epitome of a Petersburg gentleman. Compare him with the unkempt and half-mad Mussorgsky in the famous portrait by Repin—

two different worlds! No wonder Balanchine didn't like Mussorgsky. (In this he disagreed with Stravinsky and, unexpectedly, agreed
with Rachmaninoff, who—and he told me this himself—was not a
big fan of Mussorgsky's either, especially of his *Boris Godunov*. Rachmaninoff considered it too exotic and Oriental.)

After Diaghilev's death the ballet began to lose direction and
shattered into tiny pieces. Balanchine managed to glue the pieces
back together. He united ballet and gave it a universal, cosmopolitan character rather than just a Russian one. Balanchine saved ballet
as an art form for the twenty-first century. He achieved this, in
particular, by injecting a strong dose of music, including modern
music, into ballet. This required a rare musical gift.

I've spoken about Balanchine as a pianist, but few people know
that he also conducted. One time I was present at a Balanchine foray
into this area. Thérèse and I had come to City Center, where Balanchine's company was then performing. We were in a box, it was
about ten minutes before curtain. Suddenly Kolya Kopeikin, the
pianist, ran in. "Do you know that George is going to conduct
tonight?!" Kopeikin explained that Balanchine didn't like the way
his permanent conductor presented the Tchaikovsky, it seemed a bit
crude to him.

Kopeikin's announcement came as a total surprise. I couldn't
believe my eyes when George came out into the orchestra pit. In
tails! And he conducted beautifully. But he kept stretching his neck—
I guess the collar was too high on him. You have to get used to
tails.

Arnold Schoenberg, one time when we were sitting in a café in
Vienna, told me, " 'Don't conduct everything!' Always tell that to
conductors!" What he meant was that the conductor shouldn't give
the orchestra every beat of the composition they're performing. He
can take it easy here and there. The orchestra players will understand, and the work will only benefit.

Balanchine didn't know this precept of Schoenberg's, but that's
the way he conducted instinctively. The orchestra followed him and
played inspiredly. Just one more proof that there is no need to make
a special study of conducting.

Balanchine created in an ephemeral medium, he had no illusions about that. Yet his abstract ballets were nevertheless not abstract creations. He created them for particular dancers. Balanchine was inspired always by a given body, a given temperament, a given character. Theoretically those beautiful movements of his could have been learned by other dancers, but then in such cases George always made adjustments, often substantial ones, for specific performers.

Balanchine knew perfectly well that without him these adjustments would have been impossible. And that consequently, with time, his ballets would inevitably become more and more empty, and could eventually die. But this did not upset him in the least. He believed in a higher justice and, although a determined fatalist, he remained optimistic in any circumstances, even in misfortune, which abounded in his life.

This optimism was another thing that distinguished Balanchine from Stravinsky, who drenched everything around him with bitter sarcasm. I didn't like it, but for Stravinsky it was a natural way of confronting the world, and I don't reproach him for it at all.

Yes, it is likely that Balanchine's ballets will die someday, and that will be a great loss. But George left an inheritance that consists of more than his works. He left his moral example, a considerable legacy: the strength and wholeness of his character; his directness, adherence to principle, and lack of greed; his modesty and confidence in his abilities; his devotion to his art; his independence of fashion, fame, and trappings of success. All that is Balanchine. Indifference to ignorant criticism, disdain for greedy managers—that's also Balanchine.

And in Balanchine's art, beyond the beauty of his ballets, there are lessons for us all. This is art with deep national roots, though not confined to them but open to the whole world. Balanchine was a brilliant master, a connoisseur of the classical tradition, yet he never stopped expanding the frontiers, constantly discovering something new. He was a revolutionary who created instead of destroying. Or, if you like, he was a conservative, capable of changing swiftly.

As I have said, culture today resembles a marketplace, like a mall where everything is bought and sold. Artists lose their sense of shame trying to force their wares, often second-rate and rotten, on the buyer. Balanchine was never a cheap vendor, even though he hardly pretended to be a saint. He didn't live up in the clouds. George liked beautiful and talented women, he savored good food, and he knew about wines (more than I did, even though my knowledge in that area is so modest that it isn't hard to surpass it).

And Balanchine did not attribute prophetic significance to his art. He hated snobbery. I recall how, when he spoke of the ballet, he readily used culinary metaphors. "I'm a chef," Balanchine often said, "making dishes for the audience to suit its taste. I only try to keep the menu varied." But it was real, healthful food—for the mind and for the heart.

When I think of Balanchine, I see him again. There he is—a real Russian personality. His face is sharply drawn; his body is lean, trained, flexible. He walks erect, confidently; quickly but without rushing. That impossible Texan string tie dangles from his neck (he has "regular" ties somewhere, but they're so much trouble). He exudes elegance, energy, joy.

That's how I remember him.

INDEX

Index

Index

Index

Index

Koonen, Alisa, 66
Kopeikin, Nikolai, 248, 250, 255
Korngold, Julius, 79
Koshetz, Nina, 117
Koussevitzky, Natalya, 136, 166
Koussevitzky, Serge, 47, 74, 84; ambition of, 165–66; Rachmaninoff and, 113; Stravinsky and, 136–38, 139, 141
Krasin, Leonid, 73
Krasner, Louis, 93, 94, 255
Kreisler, Fritz, 53, 90, 98, 122, 168–78; attitude toward rehearsals, 170–71; as a composer, 174–75; gambling of, 169–70; injury of, 174; NM's admiration for, 168–69; opinion of Piatigorsky, 187–188; personality of, 170; as a pianist, 177; praise for NM, 170; Prelude and Allegro, 174; Rachmaninoff and, 171; Recitativ and Scherzo-Caprice, 172; "Schön Rosmarin,"168; violin collection of, 176–77
Kreisler, Harriet, 171–73, 176–78, 187
Kremer, Gidon, 90, 229
Kschessinska, Mathilda, 30
Kubatsky, Victor, 50, 87, 216–17
Kubelik, Jan, 7, 8
Kutepov, Alexander, 82
Kuznetsov, Stepan, 8
Kuznetsova, Galina, 249

Labinsky, Alexander, 93
La Fenice theater, 132
Lalo, Edouard, 92, 139, 165, 183; Symphonie espagnole, 92, 139, 165
Lamson, Carl, 171–72
Landowska, Wanda, 77, 83
La Scala, 131, 132, 156
Lawrence, Gertrude, 158
Le Clercq, Tanaquil, 264–65
Lecocq, Alexandre, Giroflé-Girofla, 66
Lehmann, Lotte, 19
Lenin, Vladimir, 30, 31, 49–50, 73, 131, 156, 180–81, 206, 230, 235
Lenin Quartet, 46, 180–81
Lermontov, Mikhail, 213
Levi, Hermann, 161, 162
Liberman, Yevsey, 41
Lieberson, Goddard, 260
Lifar, Serge, 242, 244, 261
Lippmann, Walter, 207, 210
Liszt, Franz, 58, 65, 73, 117, 199, 204; B Minor Sonata, 193; E-Flat Major

Concerto, 58; "Funérailles," 65, 73, 172; Horowitz's affinity for, 193–94; Second Concerto, 222
Longo, Alessandro, 122
L'Opéra Russe à Paris, 75
Lourié, Arthur, 74
Luboshits, Lea, 165–66
Luboshits, Petya, 165, 166
Luboshutz, Anna, 165
Lumumba, Patrice, 209
Lunacharsky, Anatoly, 44, 45, 71, 189

Maazel, Lorin, 51
Maeterlinck, Maurice, 67; The Miracle of St. Antonius, 67
Mahler, Gustav, 125
Malinovskaya, Elena, 50, 69
Malipiero, Gian Francesco, 111–12
Maly Theater, 62–63, 64
Manet, Edouard, 199
Mann, Frederick, 203
Marguerite Long-Jacques Thibaud Competition, 224
Markevitch, Igor, 244
Massenet, Jules, 7, 23, 24; "Meditation" (from Thaïs), 23
Maxwell, Elsa, 85, 176
Meck, Nadezhda von, 92, 101, 253
Medtner, Nikolai, 52, 55, 110, 117, 204; Fairy Tales, 117; piano concerto, 117; violin sonata, 117
Mehta, Zubin, 104
Mendelssohn, Felix, 2, 192; violin concerto, 92, 103, 158, 255
Mendès-France, Pierre, 231
Menuhin, Yehudi, 230
Merovitch, Alexander, 72, 74, 180, 189
Messiah (violin), 87–88
Metropolitan Museum, 19, 209
Metropolitan Opera, 256
Meyerhold, Vsevolod, 62, 67
Miaskovsky, Nikolai, 52
Midori, 236
Mikhailovsky Theater, 20
Mikhail (Tsar's brother), 30
Milestone, Lewis, 247–48
Milland, Ray, 258
Miller, Frank, 159
Milstein, David (brother), 5, 9
Milstein, Maria (daughter), 87, 156
Milstein, Maria (mother), 1, 2, 3, 6, 7, 11, 12, 15–16, 17, 18, 27, 29, 30, 31,

Index

Milstein (*cont'd*)
34; appearance of, 5; influence of on NM, 21; Judaism and, 4, 5
Milstein, Miron (brother), 2, 10
Milstein, Miron (father), 3, 4, 5, 13, 31, 32-33
Milstein, Nathan: assessment of violin concertos, 91-94; attitude toward death, 202; attitude toward violins, 87-89; Auer and (*see* Auer, Leopold); Balanchine and (*see* Balanchine, George); birth of, 3; childhood of, 1-12; on conductors, 135, 164-66; cooking and, 263; critical acclaim for, 56-57, 58, 73, 76, 79; dissuaded from returning to Russia, 82; early concert tours of, 37-39; early exposure to music, 1-3; early musical education of, 5-7; early press coverage of, 15-16; education of, 5, 22; family of, 3 (*see also specific family members*); first solo of, 37; gambling of, 108-9; Glazunov and (*see* Glazunov, Alexander); Horowitz and (*see* Horowitz, Vladimir); interest of in art, 19, 81, 86, 197-99; Judaism of, 3-4, 5, 17; Kreisler and (*see* Kreisler, Fritz); leaves Russia, 70-71; literary preferences of, 20, 213; love of theater, 61-68; Oistrakh and (*see* Oistrakh, David); opinion of Communism, 207; opinions on ballet, 243-44; "Paganiniana," 90; Piatigorsky and (*see* Piatigorsky, Gregor); Rachmaninoff and (*see* Rachmaninoff, Sergei); refusal to return to Russia, 228-230; Strauss and (*see* Strauss, Richard); Stravinsky and (*see* Stravinsky, Igor); Toscanini and (*see* Toscanini, Arturo); transcriptions of, 89-91; violin concerto written for, 135-36; White House performance of, 233-34; Ysaÿe and (*see* Ysaÿe, Eugène)
Milstein, Rita (first wife), 144, 158, 244, 250
Milstein, Sara (sister), 2, 5, 37
Milstein, Thérèse (wife), 88, 118, 162, 172, 177, 178, 222, 223, 234, 236, 237, 257, 261, 263, 270
Milyukov, Pavel, 110, 245
Mishakoff, Misha, 159
Mitropoulos, Dmitri, 24, 184-85
Moiseiwitsch, Benno, 124
Monte Carlo, 169, 239-42, 243, 244, 249
Monteux, Pierre, 113, 139-40, 141

Moscow, 48, 49, 50, 51, 73, 89, 93, 129, 268; Horowitz and NM in, 61-68; Rachmaninoff's work in, 119; during revolution, 31; theater in, 61-68
Moscow Art Theater, 50, 61-62, 67
Moscow Conservatory, 46
Moscow First Studio Theater, 64
Mozart, Wolfgang, 19, 77, 83, 101, 153, 156, 253; duet for violin and viola, 236; E Minor Sonata, 78; G Minor Quintet, 253; Horowitz's interpretation of, 195-96; NM's opinion of, 183; Soviet musicians and, 223; violin concertos, 91, 164
Muck, Carl, 79-80, 84, 162, 165
Mukhamedov, Irek, 236-37
Munch, Charles, 24, 184-85
Mussolini, Benito, 148, 156-58
Mussolini, Rachele, 157
Mussorgsky, Modest, 36, 90, 101-2, 119, 120, 269-70; *Boris Godunov*, 16, 17, 120, 221, 270; "The Flea," 119; "The Seamstress," 90

Nabokov, Nicholas, 131-32, 226, 227, 245, 261
Nemirovich-Danchenko, Vladimir, 61, 62, 67-68; *Carmencita and the Soldier*, 67, 68; *Lysistrata*, 68
Neuhaus, Heinrich, 40, 41, 48-49, 192
Neuhaus, Zinaida, 48-49
Neveu, Ginette, 224
New Economic Policy (NEP), 49, 50, 55, 59, 73, 235
New Jersey Symphony, 104
New York Philharmonic, 155
Nezhdanova, Antonina, 51
Nicholas II (Tsar), 16, 29, 30, 31, 114, 206, 269
Nijinsky, Kyra, 244
Nikisch, Arthur, 58, 161-62, 215
Nikisch, Mitya, 224, 225
Nikolais, Alwin, 235, 237
Nikolais Theater, 237
Nikolayev, Leonid, 12
Nureyev, Rudolf, 237, 244

Oborin, Lev, 216
October Revolution, 30
Odessa, 71, 95, 98, 208, 233; childhood of NM in, 1-12, 19, 20, 23; cultural importance of, 7-8; history of, 8-9;

278

Index

Kreisler's appearance in, 168; during revolution, 31–37
Odessa Conservatory, 5
Odessa opera, 7, 9, 10
Odessa Philharmonic, 36–37
Oistrakh, David, 23, 102, 253; as a conductor, 214; first U.S. visit of, 222; as a musician, 224; politics of, 151, 212, 213–14, 215, 216, 217–21, 223, 225, 229–30, 231
Oistrakh, Igor, 217–18
Oistrakh, Tamara, 219
Orchestre de Paris, 184
Orchestre de la Suisse Romande, 197
Ormandy, Eugene, 123, 139, 166
Ormandy, Gretel, 166
Ortega y Gasset, Luis, 185
Ortenberg, Edgar, 7, 23
Ossovsky, Alexander, 56
Ostrovsky, Aleksandr Nikolayevich: *The Dowerless Bride*, 63; *The Forest*, 63
Ozawa, Seiji, 84

Paderewski, Ignacy, 111
Paganini, Niccolo, 166–67; *Caprices*, 90, 96, 97, 99, 163; gimmicks used by, 43–44; "Moses Fantasy," 43; NM's early exposure to, 2; NM's transcriptions of, 90; "Perpetuum mobile," 212
Pakelman, Vassily, 50
Paris, 14, 74–75, 81–87, 93, 120, 126, 131, 133, 135, 155, 224, 242, 245; visit to Ysaÿe and, 95–105
Parsons, Geoffrey and Mrs., 194
Pasternak, Boris, 49, 50, 211
Pasternak, Leonid, 50
Pavlovsky, Valentin, 250
Peck, Gregory, 66
Penkovsky, Oleg, 223
Perestroika, 41, 235
Perlman, Itzhak, 236
Persimfans, 46–48, 49
Petipa, Marius, 246
Petrov, Ivan, 221
Philadelphia Orchestra, 113, 123, 258
Philharmonic Hall, 57, 59
Piatigorsky, Gregor, 46, 113, 116, 124, 125, 131, 151, 155, 162, 179–80, 185, 186–88, 189, 230, 245; appearance of, 180; *Comrade Blok*, 187; as a musician, 187–88; performances with NM and Horowitz, 182–83, 184; personality of,

186–87; Rachmaninoff and, 111–12; stories of, 180–82, 222; Stravinsky and, 142–43, 145
Piatigorsky, Jacqueline. *See* Rothschild, Jacqueline
Picasso, Pablo, 85–86, 128, 191, 198–99, 201, 202, 203, 261
Pickford, Mary, 248
Pittsburgh Orchestra, 51
Plaskin, Glenn, 189
Pludermacher, George, 54
Poliakin, Miron, 15, 22, 25
Pollini, Maurizio, 207–8
Poulenc, Francis, 128
Preobrajenska, Olga, 93–94
Price, Leontyne, 234
Primrose, William, 99, 162
Prokofiev, Sergei, 55–57, 72, 128, 136, 269; criticism of, 56–57, 74–75; First (*Classical*) Symphony, 14; First Violin Concerto, 14, 36, 52, 56–57, 92, 94; opinion of Brahms, 183; Piano Concerto no. 3, 72; politics of, 138, 149; Scythian Suite, 74; Second Violin Concerto, 53, 135; talent of, 14–15, 52–53, 80
Protopopov, Aleksandr, 13
Prunières, Henri, 93, 94
Puccini, Giacomo, 7, 67, 161
Pugnani-Kreisler Prelude and Allegro, 172
Purishkevich, Vladimir, 13, 29
Pushkin, Aleksandr, 20, 181, 213, 259

Rabinovich, Isaac, 68, 233
Rachmaninoff, Irina, 116
Rachmaninoff, Natalia Alexandrovna, 109, 110, 113, 116
Rachmaninoff, Sergei, 52, 53, 74, 106–125, 136, 144–45, 159–60, 164, 168, 172, 182–83, 192, 193, 195, 204, 228, 250, 270; abruptness of, 115; alleged anti-Semitism of, 269; anger at NM, 109–10, 111–12; appearance of, 114; *The Bells*, 107; cello sonata, 125; as a composer, 106–7; Diaghilev's opinion of, 245; *Etudes-tableaux*, 107; interests of, 114–15; Kreisler and, 171; *Moments musicaux*, 107; on music, 119–20; as a musician, 127; opinion of Rubinstein, 201; as a performer, 107–8, 121–23; politics of, 119; praises NM, 113; Rhapsody

Index

Index